Time Did It

A Family Saga

Ute Carson

Plain View Press
1101 W 34th Street, STE 404

www.plainviewpress.com
Austin, TX 78705

Copyright © 2025 Ute Carson. All rights reserved under International and Pan-American Copyright Conventions. No part of this book may be reproduced or distributed in any form or by any means, or stored in a data base or retrieval system, without written permission. All rights, including electronic, are reserved by the author and publicsher.

ISBN: 978-1-63210-109-9
Library of Congress Control Number: 2025946745

Cover art by Jeff Powers
Cover design by Pam Knight

We Find Healing In Existing Reality

Plain View Press is a 50-year-old issue-based literary publishing house. Our books result from artistic collaboration between writers, artists, and editors. Over the years we have become a far-flung community of humane and highly creative activists whose energies bring humanitarian enlightenment and hope to individuals and communities grappling with the major issues of our time—peace, justice, the environment, education and gender.

Time Did It

A Family Saga

Ute Carson

Previous Plain View Press Publications
by Ute Carson

*Gypsy Spirit: and Other Stories
of Childhood, Nature, Life Choices, Loss, and Love*
ISBN 9781632100764, 31-JUL-2020

Reflections: New and Selected Poems
ISBN 9781632100320, 1-MAR-2018

Save the Last Kiss: Letters to a Dying Friend
ISBN 9781632100269, 5-SEP-2016

Just a Few Feathers
ISBN 9781935514008, 1-APR-2011

Contents

1 A Simple Twist of Fate	9
2 Up on the Rocks—Under the Cross	13
3 Faraway Tunes	19
4 African Sun	25
5 Cold Moon	31
6 Under the Sign of the Deer	39
7 A Comet in the Winter Sky	43
8 Careening Toward the Brink	47
9 Tree Branches, a Limb	51
10 Pine Trees	55
11 Tree Branches, a Twig	59
12 Stalingrad	63
13 He's My Brother	65
14 A Yellow Flower	69
15 The Trek	73
16 The Owl	77
17 Rubble	81
18 Diamonds in the Heel of Her Shoe	85
19 Calf-Skin Notebook with Rose-Colored Lines	89
20 Forget-Me-Nots	95
21 Sleigh–Easter–Birthday Bells	101
22 Separate Currents	105
23 The Train	115
24 Coming to America	119
25 The Scent of Lilac Bushes	125
26 Sheep, Classics and Light of Wisdom	129
27 Shadows	133
28 Sun-Kissed Florida	135
29 A Meadow of Wildflowers	139
30 Whirlwind Years	145
31 All This and Heaven Too	157
32 Turn Down the Lights Gently	159

33 Turbulent Skies and Triple Crown	163
34 A Pot of Liquid Gold	167
35 Time Travel	173
36 Graying Dandelions	179
37 Ravishes of Time	185
38 Safari	193
39 End Spurt	197
About the Author	203

*a love letter
to my family*

1 A Simple Twist of Fate

"I feel so alive," Maria inhaled the dry air as she stepped onto the gangplank down from the Deutschland which had just anchored. It had been a splendid crossing, she being the only woman in first class on the vessel's voyage in May 1914. She had relished the elegant dinners with the captain, sharing with him her excitement about her voyage around the world, an inheritance from her family on her 21st birthday. It was unusual for a woman to travel alone but she had long learned how to conduct herself by defying the conventions of her class. The port of Lüderitz in South West Africa was the harbor where she disembarked to visit her friend Margarete. They had met at the international boarding school for girls in Eberswalde, near Berlin.

Maria was unaware of her beauty, her reed-like figure, her confident demeanor. Her flowing dress ruffled in the breeze, and her dark gypsy-like hair resisted any defiant strokes and instead fluttered loosely around her smooth face. Sand blew across the planks. She arched her toes and longed to kick off her traveling shoes, put dreary Germany behind her and escape to the brilliant African sun. The sun promised a new beginning. As she squinted into the blinding rays a little black boy handed her a bouquet of Namaqualand daisies, vibrant colors, orange, yellow, white and pink. Joyfully she buried her nose in the blossoms. Then she stepped light-footed into the arms of her friend who led her to a waiting wagon. A craggy kokerboom tree grew next to the wagon which gave little shade to the horse beneath. A spiderweb dangling from one of its bare branches caught Maria's hair and veiled her face. Impatiently, she brushed away the threads of the web.

Margrete and Maria had much to catch up on. After changing into sun-resistant clothes fit for the tropics, the friends rocked in the bamboo swings on a rambling veranda that encircled the large colonial style house of the Farm Hoffnung and talked and talked. They cooled themselves with fans delicately woven from ostrich feathers. Margaret's father, Mr. Anderson, brought them fruit drinks with crystal drops on the rims of the glasses. "Welcome, Maria. You will need plenty of salt in this dry heat. Enjoy your stay with us."

"I already know," Maria replied a bit too quickly, "I will love this country."

With a flare her host reached into his pocket. "Happy belated birthday, Maria. This precious stone was harvested in our mining fields. They are not for export yet as it was only in 1908 that the first jewel was found. But this gift will be safe in your luggage and not be found as you continue your round-the-world-voyage." Maria held a diamond in the rough the size of a walnut in her palm. After expressing her appreciation, she pulled from her pearly purse the handkerchief her mother had embroidered and wrapped the diamond in it.

For the first time since her departure from Germany, did she think of her weeping mother who had desperately objected to her journey. Her words echoed, "Child, please come back home safe."

Luxurious days followed that eventful welcome with long horseback rides and many games of croquet on the manicured lawns. Evenings were festive with small soirées to which neighbors were invited. Maria, who had brought her cherished violin, was often asked to play. And Margrete could not resist telling the story of how at boarding school Maria had sneaked out on occasion to fill her empty violin case with goodies from a bakery. Maria had enjoyed the rare privilege taking violin lessons outside the school's confines.

Maria was introduced to several young men from nearby farms, among them Peter, his brother Balthazar and their sister Vera. She liked Peter, the quiet one on sight. Margrete told her that Peter was known as an animal whisperer. "He has a healing way with animals, especially horses." Peter was often a guide on their rides.

One day when they gathered in the pasture to halter a young mare, Maria stroked its mane and Peter, on the other side of the horse's neck, reached up to touch her hand.

With a picnic basket on board, they made a Sunday afternoon outing in a horse-drawn wagon to Keetmanshoop, a small provincial town with market stalls and an ornate bandstand in its center. Brass horns trumpeted as Margarete and Maria walked arm-in-arm around the square while a boisterous group of young men stood aside, stealing timid glances at the two young women. They shared the picnic of oranges and crusty oven-baked bread under one of the large umbrellas. As the gas lamps on the bandstand were being lit the wagon was waiting to drive them back to the farm.

It had been a strange night in August. Since her arrival at the Farm Hoffnung Maria had slept with her window wide open. She wanted to hear a lion roar. And that night in the far distance she heard mysterious frightening sounds and then the galloping hooves of springboks. It was intimidating and exhilarating. As morning dawned the rosy fingers of the sun appeared on the horizon. Maria stood in the gaping window frame and breathed in the coolness. Then her eyes fell on one of the kokerbooms. Crimson waves like flaming tongues encircled the trunk's side, setting it ablaze. Maria dressed early and went into the dining room. There too the sun rays poured through the large windows and danced over the white linen tablecloth, the fine china and sparkling silverware. One sunbeam illuminated Maria's dainty hand as she cupped her fingers around the stem of a juice glass. She was alone in the room. It was eerily silent. Why was everyone still asleep, she wondered.

A feathery touch on her shoulder woke Maria from her ruminations. "You are up bright and early," the solemn voice of Mr. Anderson intervened.

"We get our news belated here in the colonies but a telegram confirmed what our local paper, *Der Kriegsbote*, had already printed. Germany has gone to war."

"Over the troubles in the Balkans?"

Maria folded her napkin into a perfect square. "What does this mean for us here?"

Before Mr. Anderson answered he placed a wrinkled newspaper note in front of her. It read: The Crown Prince Ferdinand was assassinated by a Serbian nationalist on June 28th, 1914. Dryly he added. "And the wire this morning informed me that the Deutschland was requisitioned by the Army. It sailed last night. We have lost all contact with Germany."

The room started to spin for Maria from right and left. She leaned heavily on Mr. Anderson's arm as he escorted her back to her quarters.

A welcome houseguest had become a penniless prisoner of circumstances.

2 Up on the Rocks—Under the Cross

Maria had come a long way from her birthplace in Germany to Africa. Her family roots lay deep in a faraway land.

Baron Wasmuth Levin von Wintzingerode was a wealthy landowner and president of a bank in Cologne. His landholdings in Wintzingerode stretched over large grazing meadows and pine forests in Lower Saxony, Germany. The mansion in that small village, overgrown with ivy, remained in the family's possession until after World War II. Pictures show Wasmuth as robust, with twinkling eyes and a bushy full beard. He is remembered by his family and acquaintances as fun-loving. "A real Rheinländer," they called him. Wasmuth joined the army in his youth and fought in the Austro-Prussian War. After the battle of Königgratz he was stationed near the charming residence of the Berger family at Sankt Ivan. The Bergers were renowned jewelers.

During Wasmuth's stay as a soldier he became well acquainted with the family. He also fell in love with one of their daughters, Marie. Following military service Wasmuth returned to Sankt Ivan to marry Marie in 1871. After the wedding the couple divided their time between the family residences in Cologne and Wintzingerode. They vacationed at Sankt Ivan.

Was there ever a more mysterious place than the baroque Benedictine Monastery, built in the 15th century "up on the rocks, under a cross," in Svatý Jan Pod near Prague? Among karst stone mountains and dark forests, numerous caves are carved into the chalk formations and joyful springs gush down the hilly slopes. The Berger family moved into the monastery in the early 18th century and converted it into a fabulous castle. Until the early 20th century Sankt Ivan remained a romantic retreat for the family and an enchanted land for children.

Maria coaxed her brother Walter to explore the environs. "Let's find Saint John the Baptist's cave. He arrived here in the 9th century, right?" Walter considered himself an expert in such matters.

"Yes, he was the first Czech Christian hermit and he lived among the caves." Maria held on to her brother's shirtsleeve and followed him over slippery stones to the entrance. They ducked their heads and carefully made their way into the interior. It got dimmer and dimmer, then dark. Walter lit a candle to brighten the way. As they groped along the moist walls the flickering light illuminated religious drawings painted on the walls. They stopped in amazement. Then they crept forward and came to a niche at the end of the grotto.

"Do you think the hermit slept here?" Maria sounded incredulous.

"Yes, he must have gotten straw and clothing from the village people," Walter answered.

Maria had practical concerns. "Do you think he ever washed his garments? Then strung them out to dry on branches?"

Walter knew more about the legend. "I imagine so. And, Sister Anita says that the monk survived on produce from a vegetable garden and local herbs. He got water from a bubbling spring erupting from the ancient stone reservoir. It's the Fountain of Life that hikers still drink to this day."

"Oh," Maria interrupted, "and he performed miracles throughout the valley. He also erected the large wooden cross like a weathervane atop the cliff's edge. And, that's where we have the view that reaches far and wide over our sun-dappled valley below." When the siblings emerged from the gloomy hide-out, Maria confessed, "I get goosebumps just thinking about the Saint."

The castle was vast. The racket children made and the scuttling of multiple feet, large and small, was echoed by marble staircases and tiled flooring. All the rooms were expensively furnished. On the ceiling of the ample music room were paintings depicting biblical scenes. An upright piano stood in the middle of the arch-domed room from which solemn melodies floated softly into the realms above. In the reception area where floral fabrics adorned the walls an ornately hand-carved baroque-style armoire was displayed. The artist's initials, A and P, chiseled into the cupboards are still visible today. Delicate hand-painted fans for ladies-in-waiting at the Prague Court leaned against a sturdy back wall.

In 1874, under the direction of a famous Munich architect, the Bergers built a chapel with a family crypt beneath. A shaft in the crypt lets sunlight into the darkness, shining on several caskets where shimmering brocades draped over them have resisted changing temperatures and time. Wrought iron angels spread protective wings over the caskets, their eyes turned downward. Several clay turtles stand as symbols of eternal life on shelves above. When one relative committed suicide after losing a fortune gambling, he was not allowed to be laid to rest inside the crypt but only outside where a plaque bearing the image of a guardian angel hovers above his gravesite. Only in the company of an adult were children allowed in the crypt, although sometimes they peeked in from outside.

Shuddering, Maria wondered what Great-grandma looked like in the casket? "Is she still pretty like in the portrait in the parlor?"

On green summer afternoons little Maria walked on mossy footpaths under the shady canopy of ancient fir trees. In the thicket mushrooms and wild berries grew which she stuffed into her watering mouth. The pleasing forest ended at the quiet Berounka River where Gypsies parked their wagons during the warm season and pitched their tents. The hike from the castle to the banks of the river was long and strenuous for a child. But Maria enjoyed the freedom. Nobody paid attention when she visited the encampment, got cabbage rolls and rabbit stew and advice from Gypsy fortune tellers who laid out Tarot cards for her on the richly woven rugs covering their tiny wagon-porches. The melancholy tunes of their tambourines affected her with a strange longing. Maria attributed her later religious beliefs to some of the Gypsy folklore she listened to during her forays. She mused that maybe even her untamable hair, her chestnut-colored eyes, her sunburned complexion and wanderlust were inherited from the Gypsies.

Because Wasmuth often had to be on business in Cologne, the couple bought a large stucco townhouse in the city. Wasmuth and Marie were a perfect match. Elf-like Marie was gentle and quiet but she also enjoyed the social life. Wasmuth was outgoing and a devoted family man. They had taken several heirlooms with them after the wedding, some to Wintzingerode, others to Cologne, among them the armoire, several delicate fans and magnificently decorated cases filled with jewelry crafted in Prague. Life in the city was filled with entertainment, concerts and performances. Adults and children alike were dressed expensively. Tulle evening gowns were studded with glass beads and a white handkerchief stuck out of gentlemen's jacket pockets. Each outfit was worn only once and then donated to the theater or opera.

Maria was born in Cologne in 1889. She became Wasmuth's favorite and was spoiled by him as the youngest of six. She remembered attending a gala Nutcracker performance, spellbound next to her father, "Enjoying yourself, my little Maria?" An air of brilliance pervaded the Opera House. Sitting under blazing stage lights, powerful music and the fragrance of flowers tucked into hair and lapels, she became dizzy. As she fell asleep that night, celestial wingless beings danced in front of her drooping eyes.

On her twelfth birthday her parents informed her that in the fall she would be enrolled at Eberswalde, a boarding school her sisters attended. Until then she remained close to both parents, learning to crochet with her mother and taking late afternoon walks with her father, hand-in-hand.

Maria's fondest memory of her father was her bedtime hour. Under the light of a yellow lampshade Wasmuth sat, legs crossed. Maria uttered the same wish, "Papa, tell the story of The Elves of Cologne."

Wasmuth lowered his deep voice and began, "Once upon a time, the legend has it that long ago the city of Cologne was served by little creatures called Heinzelmännchen. They appeared at night and nobody was allowed to see them as they finished all the work that had been left undone during the day."

At this point Maria interrupted. "Why did the elves stop coming?"

Even though she knew the answer, she always asked her father to repeat it. And he did. "The wife of a shoemaker got curious and wanted to catch the elves. So, she scattered peas on the floor of the workroom. Then she secretly stood behind a curtain and spied. As the elves hopped in, they slipped and fell. After that incident the elves never reappeared."

With a sigh Maria's eyelids began to close. "I would so like to see the Heinzelmännchen."

Maria was ten when her beloved father suffered a fatal heart attack. That day was etched in her mind forever. Sleet fell hard in large pellets as Maria blew her warm breath onto the frost-covered window pane and drew a heart in the icy surface. She heard stomping footsteps down from the first floor and loud huffing sounds from her brothers as they hoisted the oak casket bearing their father down the stairs. Her mother and her three sisters sobbed in the drawing room. Shortly before his death Wasmuth had bought Maria a violin. "You will have to wait a few years for lessons," he told her, "but I wanted to be the one to give you your first instrument." Wasmuth and Maria shared a love of music, even though he often sang out of tune. Once the casket was loaded into a horse-drawn hearse, Maria left her lookout at the window and retreated to her bedroom where she lifted the violin from its case and cradled it like a doll.

After her husband's death Marie was lonely and bereft of purpose. She had enjoyed the role of accompanying her busy husband to parties and celebratory functions. All that was now in the past. She had overseen the weddings of her two oldest daughters and sent her two boys to a military academy. The third daughter had chosen to enter a cloister. Now Maria was the only one left to share her mother's grief. She clung to her. But because Maria was a willful, spirited child, Marie had trouble reining her in. When Maria took up side-saddle horseback riding, Marie accompanied her to the stables. There she stood at the railing, clasping a hand over her mouth, trying to conceal her fear. "Do you really need to ride a horse?" she admonished her daughter. "It's so dangerous. What if you fall?"

After Maria left for boarding school—a more painful separation for the mother than for her daughter—Marie sold the house in Cologne and moved back to Wintzingerode. After Maria's graduation from Eberswalde, Marie tried her best to introduce her daughter to high society, the aristocracy, hoping to find a husband for her as she had successfully done with her other daughters. But Maria had a mind of her own. She took no suitors but instead collected maps and, to her mother's dismay, travel destinations. When the invitation from her classmate Margarete arrived, Maria jumped on the idea of using her inheritance for a trip around the world. Marie was inconsolable. She pleaded with Maria, "Please child, stay here where you belong. We all follow the traditional path, get married, and have a family."

But Maria had made up her mind. "I am going around the world, Mama. Support me in this venture. Don't dash my dreams."

Marie retired to her quarters, not speaking for several days. Finally, she relented. She paid a relative to make arrangements for Maria's voyage and forced herself to be at dockside for the departure of the great ship Deutschland and to bid farewell to her headstrong young daughter. Tears soaked the collar of her black mourning dress which she kept wearing.

Marie remained despondent. Despite well-meaning visits with her married daughters, Marie became increasingly homesick for Sankt Ivan. She spent weeks there overseeing the restoration of her childhood room, and sat for hours at the window gazing into the daunting dark fir trees below. She voiced her desire to die at Sankt Ivan and be buried "Under the Cross." As her health began to fail, her confessor paid more frequent calls, during which he attempted to persuade her that she would be absolved of her earthly sins and gain a seat in heaven if she relinquished her wealth. Marie was a pious woman and easily swayed. Only once did she break the increasing control over her interlocutor, and protested after he had urged her to donate her holdings at Sankt Ivan to the church. Marie began to weep as the priest pressed on. "I have always given to the poor. I was a good wife and mother. What do I need to be forgiven for?"

Her confessor answered shrewdly, "You led an extravagant life with many privileges. That's what you must atone for." Looking down through tears at her folded hands Marie finally gave in to his demands.

As fate would have it, Marie was in residence in Wintzingerode when she died. She was not buried in Sankt Ivan but in Wintzingerode instead. After her death Marie's older sister Maximiliane sued the church over the "donated" properties, but in the end lost the battle.

Maria returned to the site of her idyllic childhood, but by the time she came home from Africa for the last time the castle was a property of the Czech state. She became a guest among others. She confided in a friend, "Sankt Ivan is no longer ours, but only I know the secret cave deep in the crevices of the mountain, where you can retreat with a book and dream."

3 Faraway Tunes

Maria admired the poet Eichendorff, especially for his nature descriptions. Now sitting on the casement of her open window at the farm Hoffnung, she recalled the lines, "*Und meine Seele spannte weit ihre Flügel aus, flog durch die stillen Lande, als flöge sie nach Haus.*" She hummed the melody to the accompaniment of her violin. How homesick she was, how lonely after being cut off from her family and Germany. No telegrams seemed to go though. She was without news from her loved ones and surely her mother was beside herself, not hearing anything from her daughter. Could the lines of that melancholy song reach across the ocean and fly into the weeping heart of her mother? The African sun had plunged Maria into emotional darkness. What would happen to her? As she sat in the apple-scented evening twilight she spotted Peter below, leaning against a kokerboom. The tree had become a favorite nesting place for the sociable weavers. Building their habitat among the bright yellow blossoms the birds made a racket that nearly drowned out Maria's violin. But Peter was clearly trying to hear her play. Maria had visited the small farm Anfang of the brothers, where irrigation ditches were dug across the land in need of water in the recurring aridity and drought. Most farms were dominated by cattle, karakul sheep and goats but the brothers tried their luck planting spring onions and maze. Now Maria's thoughts wandered down to Peter. "What would bring two young brothers and their sister to this faraway land? Were they driven by wanderlust like her? In 1884 Germany had established territories in South West Africa. Had the spirit of colonialism that gripped Europe around that time infected them as well? Where had they first sprouted roots?

The kokerboom, a symbol of survival, has a trunk tough as nails with branches that can be shaped into quivers and arrows, and blossoms tucked protectively into the bottom of the stems. They exude a sweet aroma. The tree needs the desert heat. It cannot survive the cold. In contrast, in the winter wonderland of Silesia, a giant oak tree is laden with snow, the foliage underneath still green, gangly branches reaching toward the sky. Arms cannot encompass the ancient trunk. In spring the white blossoms stand erect like burning candles and in the fall nuts plummet to the ground, food for squirrels and rabbits. Rubbing the fleshy leaves against a cheek gives off the scent of smoldering cinder. Moonlight rather than the sun filters through the thick canopy. Both trees boast longevity and have deep roots in different soils. Now Peter was under the influence of the African kokerboom, but his beginnings had taken place under oak trees.

Beneath the umbrella of a lush oak tree the castle Bielwiese was built in 1727, three stories high with the crown seals of Baron von Lüttwitz carved into the massive facade. Yearly, a stork plants its nest atop the gable. Ivy clings to the brick walls and huge clusters of nettles encircle the base. Here Balthazar, Vera, Peter and the youngest brother, Bogoslav were born to Isa and Nicholaus von Lüttwitz. Nicholaus (1856-1926) was the last owner of Bielwiese. He was adored by his family and servants alike. He was known for his kindness and generosity. Lavish events took place on his estate and in his manor. Weddings were celebrated under lanterns dangling from trees in the spacious gardens. Wakes were held in the large entrance hall and no birthday went by without surprises and sumptuous meals. At Christmas a tall spruce was cut in the nearby forest and carried in, still coated with snow and oozing fresh sap. Decorated with white candles, the tree lit up the Christmas Eve festivities. Peter recalled how all the servants were given their presents first before any family member. "I couldn't wait until it was our turn. I stole glances at my small table laden with colorfully wrapped gifts and tried to discern by their shapes if a particular wish had been fulfilled. My siblings did the same."

"Easter seemed designed for us children," Vera remembered. "We all dressed in our finest clothes. Following obligatory church attendance, the gardens echoed with jubilant squeals and laughter. Children of all ages and backgrounds ran from nest to nest, nests we had made ourselves with moss and grass the day before. Soon our baskets brimmed with painted eggs and freshly baked treats."

The highlight of the season was the harvest festival. A team of horses pulled a wagon carrying the last load of wheat into the courtyard. A crown woven by the fieldhands from grain stalks and held together with colorful ribbons was suspended from the rafters in the cleanly swept barn. Nicholaus, who was affectionately called Opapa by all, blessed the richness of the harvest. Then a band began to play for an evening of dancing and merriment. The entire community sat down at long tables stacked with food. Korn schnapps was poured in bountiful quantities. Nicholaus was lenient when his workers stumbled from their dwellings the following morning long after the rooster had crowed its wakeup call.

In the course of a carefree, joyful childhood, storms also ripped through the years. The drama about their grandmother, Clara, born 1800, was gossip in every household in the village. It was Vera skipping through the church cemetery who discovered a child's grave with faded lettering on its tombstone. Their family name was still discernible. Vera knelt down to read the inscription underneath: *Died of a Broken Heart*. She ran to show her siblings. Dumbfounded, they looked at each other. What did this mean? Whom should they ask? Balthazar suggested the local priest. "He is old. He will have an answer," he pondered. On a snowy afternoon the four children rang the doorbell at the parsonage. With expectant faces they greeted the pastor. The wind whistled around them but the pastor started to perspire as he listened to their question, "Who was the child who died of a broken heart?" they asked.

In spite of his reluctance, the pastor felt a duty to his flock. He invited them into his study. "Hang up your wet garments and gather around the fire." He wiped his sweaty forehead with the back of his hand. "Every family, children," he started his lengthy introduction, "has its cross to bear and legends are not easily shredded. You know the abandoned guesthouse, now broken down, walls supported by large poles, with the roof caved in and swallows darting from under the eaves, right? In that house a Russian-born piano teacher, Stanislav, instructed your grandmother and her four children."

The pastor had the siblings' attention. "What then?" they implored.

"I have to backtrack," he paused. "Clara, from a neighboring estate, had been married at seventeen to Heinrich Baron von Lüttwitz, a melancholy man many years her senior. She bore four children in quick succession. Their education took place under her auspice. She hired tutors, including a music teacher. Rumor had it that Clara always attended his lessons—to listen. Then they fell in love."

An audible "Oh," gasped the children in unison.

"No divorces were allowed at that time but Clara confessed to her husband and begged him to set her free. Heinrich realized the gulf between them and suggested to his wife a year of reprieve. They agreed to send Stanislav to America and give Clara a period in which to reconsider her decision. Though your grandmother was delicate in stature, she was unbreakable in her resolve. After the interval had lapsed, Clara made plans to join her lover in Philadelphia in America."

Vera sighed, "Oh no, no."

The pastor spun on with his tale. "It was a sad departure. In her crisp green suit, wearing a wide-brimmed tan hat and following a single elegant steamer trunk, Clara was escorted to the border of the estate where a stagecoach was waiting."

"And then?" the children asked. All faces expressed shocked silence.

The pastor continued, "Heinrich had the interior walls of the mansion draped in black and forbade the utterance of his wife's name."

"What happened to Clara," Balthazar spoke up.

"She corresponded with her parents until her death in 1863. She reported the births of two more sons and a happy relationship with her lover. But tragedy struck as well. Stanislav was teaching when he was kidnapped by a marauding gang of outlaws and was never heard from again. To my knowledge Clara expressed no regrets about leaving Germany or to homesickness."

As the children struggled into their warm winter clothes, Vera sighed, "I don't understand how she could leave her family. And, that poor child that died of a broken heart."

It was a personal tragedy that affected Peter the most. Being the third child, he tagged behind his beloved mother they had dearly christened "Mabushka." She listened to Peter's imaginary stories about animals, often referring to wild ones that he would like to tame. A highlight came with the traveling circus once a year. It was his mother, not a tutor, who took Peter to see the show. He ignored the caged lions and the trumpeting elephants, but the elegant horses fascinated him. A ballerina stood astride one of the white horse's rump, and holding the reins light as feathers, she directed the magnificent animal through a saw-dusted arena.

"Mabushka, I want a horse like that." he begged. Even when she tucked him in at night, he murmured. "I would brush and brush my horse until it shines like the one in the circus. I would care for it and always rub its ears." Peter never lost his love of horses.

The siblings were sent to boarding schools and only returned home for holidays or the long summer months. Peter noticed a change in his beloved mother. She seemed more and more absentminded. And he heard rumors from servants and people in the village. After Bogoslav's long and difficult birth Isa had taken more and more morphine, a sedative regularly administered during deliveries. Women often retained a liking for it. Morphine was not freely available but midwives and doctors carried it on their visits from village to village and from estate to castles. Longtime family doctor Hebel noticed on occasion that the supply of morphine in his brown leather bag was suddenly low. Maybe he was getting feeble, he admitted, and let the matter rest. But one afternoon a servant reported watching Isa rummaging through the basket of the midwife, Rita, before hurrying away.

Nicholaus had brought his cousin Wanda to the castle. She was strong, efficient and oversaw the household with a firm hand. She was an excellent horsewoman, the first woman to win a local race riding side-saddle. She was written up in the newspaper for going foxhunting with an all-male retinue. She confessed that she relished the smell of leather, dust and horse manure more than nursery odors. She preferred to be in the stables or at the training corral than with the children. Wanda and Nicholaus were seen on many cross-country excursions on horseback.

It was when Peter returned after finishing boarding school that his mother was absent. "Where is Mama?" was his first inquiry.

"She became addicted to morphine, my son. We had to send her to a monastery for treatment."

At that time Nicholaus also acquainted his children with the idea of seeking land in the colonies, Paraguay and Africa. "Good money to be made," he encouraged them and the thought stuck. Soon arrangements were made for the three to depart for Süd-West Africa. Bogoslav would stay behind and help in Bielwiese.

The monastery Lubiaz was a massive structure, surrounded by an enormous park. Strewn across the gardens and between the numerous trees, statues of men and animals were erected. To enter the monastery, a portal high enough for a carriage to pass through had been built. Inside, high elongated windows let in spare light illuminating paintings of Rübezahl on nearly every wall. Rübezahl, the legendary giant who helped lost wanderers over the snowy Silesian mountains. A long hall was laid out in geometric patterns of polished wood.

Peter opened the door to his mother's room quietly, fearing to trespass. The interior was furnished with a canopy bed, a rocking chair and a rosewood desk on which sheets of blank paper lay next to an inkwell and several quill pens. His mother rocked and rocked. Everything looked spidery to Peter, her frayed shawl, her white unbound hair, even the bruised lace curtains and her hands, spider-veined blue. Her once sparkling eyes were latticed by blood vessels. Isa smiled and recognized her son.

He dashed forward and kneeled down in front of her, putting his head on her lap. "How are you?" Peter's lips trembled.

"I am fine, sweet son. I went out for a stroll with sister Ursula this morning. Such fine gardens."

"Are you well-treated?"

"Oh, yes, so well." Peter noticed her veiled looks and the slow drawl in her speech. Her words came out ever so softly, ever so slowly. But her bony fingers crawled gently over his hair. "I am," Peter stuttered, "here to tell you that Balthazar, Vera and I are going to the colonies."

"How nice," Isa coughed, "Have a good journey. Will I see you again?" Her words fizzed in his ears.

"Oh yes, you will." He rose and ran wordlessly from the room, never glancing back.

On his way out the monastery Peter stormed into the refectory. A stout nun wearing a fluttering black habit resembling a falcon was bent over a text. "Yes?" she glanced up at Peter.

"You are sedating my mother," he shouted.

Without moving a muscle in her stern face, the nun replied. "Just a little bit, son. Only for her own good." Then she looked down again and continued to study her scriptures.

Fate spun its mysterious ways and Peter would see his mother again after numerous moons had passed the eerie Silesian sky. Maria wondered if Peter ever longed for his Silesian home.

4 African Sun

Cupping her eyes to block out memories from home, Maria felt happiness for a wondrous, enchanted moment. A gust of wind woke her from her ruminations. She made her way downstairs where Peter leaned against the kokerboom. His prolonged glance fell on her like a touch. "Not only has your world capsized during the last weeks," he murmured, "mine has too. Margrete and her mother have already escaped toward Angola and the South African Colonial Forces are on their way. Vera is here to be your companion. Our farm has been confiscated. In a few hours Balthazar and I will be taken into custody." Without another word Peter stepped forward and kissed Maria, pressing her to his chest. "Let's try to stay in touch."

Pinned together for a second, Maria was immobilized, then she extracted herself from his embrace. Peter hurried away.

Dawn came with the smudge of a bright fiery sun and a group of soldiers. They had Balthazar and Peter handcuffed, their faces were blank, expressionless. As Peter climbed into an oxcart, he yelled back "Aus is the name of the prison."

Vera and Maria stood with their arms slung around each other. They would need each other in the coming weeks and months. To the chagrin of many white settlers Vera had befriended some black servants. She was even accused of fraternizing with them when she invited the overseer onto her porch for tea. She was ostracized by most in the white community. Now her connection to the workers paid off. They stood by her and kept the farm running.

Balthazar and Peter had been condescending in their attitudes toward the Hereros and Namas people. Arrogantly they believed themselves more intelligent. Now they paid no heed to the tribal conflicts. The might of the South African Forces and the British had become the danger to watch out for.

Aus was a lightly guarded camp about a hundred miles south of Lüderitz. Each day the prisoners were taken out to clear sand off the narrow-gauge rail line that ran from Lüderitz to Keetmanshoop, which the Otavi Mining & Railway Company had built in 1903. The sun scorched the prisoners' necks as they bent and brushed the glittering steel lines with bamboo brooms.

The rail line passed near the farm Hoffnung and Peter became familiar with the tracks. He was soon able to send word to Maria and Vera that he and Balthazar were decently treated. There was free time daily when the prisoners could stroll in their prison courtyard or sit in front of their cell doors. Peter had always enjoyed working with his hands. He persuaded a friendly guard to bring in some kokerboom wood and started to carve tiny figures for the guards. Eventually he began a project he loved, carving his own footstools. The wood was hard and his designs required dexterity and strength. Two of his footstools have survived to this day.

Maria managed to smuggle a message to Peter saying that she would meet him on the railroad tracks at night with food and other necessary supplies. It worked. Peter sneaked out of camp, and Maria joined him midway along the line.

No lights, only stars on the horizon. The Southern Cross blessed their brief reunions. Peter's firm hands reached around Maria's waist carefully as if gently trying to tame a lion cub. "Will you marry me when all this is over?"

Maria felt as if on stage. The events since her arrival in Africa seemed unreal, like in a play. But she had already experienced some of Africa's hypnotic draw, the sun, the heat, the vastness. "Maybe I'm falling in love with Africa and with you, Peter. Yes, I will marry you."

In response, Peter recited an ode to this new country. "Oh yes, the African sun did it to me. The sun is the spirit of this place, of its limitless expanses. It is as if this country knows no introspection or regret. We follow the light. One day, when you are my wife, I'll take you up north to the Etosha Pan. When I camped there after my arrival, I woke up one morning to shuffling sounds. I peeked out of my tent to discover that I was surrounded by a herd of elephants. They had walked up on us as silently as cats on their big, cushioned feet. Here you still feel the presence of the wild. Humans have not completely taken over. I want to show you that Africa." Peter's voice faded. He had not spoken that many words for a long time.

As war raged in Europe, Peter and Balthazar were freed from Aus. Their farm Anfang lay in British hands but the farm Hoffnung was returned to Mr. Anderson. He offered Balthazar a position but could not extend an offer to the betrothed couple. Peter accepted a job as overseer on the diamond fields of Kolmanskop where the first diamond had been found. There remained a few weeks of hectic planning, for a wedding and housing in Keetmanshoop. Peter proposed to Maria, "There is no time for me to show you the north country but we have a week to see the landmarks here in the south." Peter had his treasured places mapped out: The Namib Desert where towering mounds of sand dunes shift aimlessly for millennia. The two climbed a steep hill and slid down a powdery slope hand-in-hand, squealing with delight. Next, Peter stopped on the jarring dirt thoroughfare so that Maria could touch the rubbery leaves of the strange Welwitschia plant, unique to the desert, the oldest plant in the world. An oryx sprinted across their path. At the Sinclair mine Maria got a short break to collect a few pieces of semi-precious stones, shattuckite and chrysocolla. But Peter had a goal in mind, the staggering Fish Canyon. On the way he pointed to the so-called "Mukurob, Finger of God." Its stone sculpture rises high into the air.

"Is this finger pointing at us? Our destiny?" Maria asked.

"Yes, the future may be rocky but manageable. We will master it together," was Peter's reassuring reply. For a moment Maria's face turned stony gray. But soon they were standing at the spectacular Fish River Canyon and Maria's moody expression melted into awe. Enormous sluggish masses of water meandered below the rim where they were standing.

"Doesn't it look like a majestic beast?" Peter mused. He had brought his box camera along and asked a passerby to take a picture of them, their first among the few they ever took. The couple spent the last night of their trip at Hardap Camp. Sitting in front of their cottage, they were swathed in a blanket of glittering stars, the sound of the wind whistling through the dunes remarkably reminiscent of the ocean.

"Our happiness feels stolen," Maria sighed.

"No," Peter responded, "It is ours to build on."

When a rare opportunity for a bed in a cabin on a postal freighter became available, Vera agreed to return to Germany armed with bags of letters for Maria's family and other relatives. Vera had taught Maria many tasks like household work and gardening when they were stranded on the farm. The first time Maria peeled potatoes she cut her middle finger, bleeding onto her apron. After both brothers were freed, Vera turned her back on Maria. She had always been extremely protective of her two brothers and now was not pleased with the engagement. She looked with envy on their happiness and snapped at Maria, "You had better take good care of Peter." They did not part as loving in-laws.

In September 1916, a bountiful African spring, Peter and Maria recorded their marriage in the registry of the German Lutheran Church at Gibeon, a sturdy brick building with a blue neon cross on the roof. They promised themselves to each other under the German inscription over the altar: *Ehre Sei Gott In Der Höhe* (God Be Praised).

Maria had not forgotten how to dress well. She still lived mostly out of her steamer trunk, but she had learned to mend. For this day she chose an orange-colored dress, with pinned white orange blossoms around the collar. It was the dress she had shown off at the captain's table two years ago. A silver comb tamed the lush hair crowning Maria's head. An emerald-beaded choker from her mother hung elegantly around her neck. The church had no organ but the local congregation boasted a small band which pounded their drums for the ceremony.

As the newlyweds stepped back out into the bright sunlight a chorus of cicadas pitched their tymbals with clicking sounds. "Oh, how lovely," Maria commented, "music similar to the chirping of grasshoppers from my Wintzingerode." There was resolve in both their faces.

The couple found a small bungalow in Keetmanshoop where Maria set up house. The first time Maria visited the diamond mine at Kolmanskop with Peter, the sun burned mercilessly. The heat warped their vision. A hissing wind blew Maria sideways as sand swept at them from all sides. The fine grains crept into her eyes and under her fingernails. She gritted her teeth. As thoroughly as Peter would shake his clothes after returning home from work each evening, the sand still clung in the smallest crevices. "This country is getting under my skin," Maria protested half annoyed, half laughingly.

The German Diamond Corporation owned the mining rights and had fortified the entire area with high wires and large signs, "Restricted Area" (Sperrgebiet). There were houses on the hills, solidly built of rock and wood but looked like they were tipping, as if at any moment they could be washed away by the moving sand. Maria squinted over the fields that looked like thousands of salt crystals shimmering across a dazzling sea. It was fascinating to watch the mining operation as gravel was transported to plants where it was washed and screened for other minerals. White and black workers handled huge sieves for sorting and grading. Entrance and departure from the field was thorough and strictly enforced. Everybody was searched from top to bottom. Some workers were pulled out of line when leaving and sent to a makeshift clinic to make sure they had not swallowed a precious stone. Maria was glad that they lived away from this glittering wasteland. She had not even mentioned her birthday diamond to Peter but kept it safely hidden.

The cross of the Order of Maltese nurses adorned the hospital portal in Keetmanshoop. It was there that in the winter of July 1917, the flag was hoisted at half-mast. It would have been drawn to the top if a boy had been born. But instead, Maria and Peter had a girl, Gerda-Maria. Peter leaned against a post in the hospital room.

Maria, propped against a feather pillow, had tied back her flowing hair. "I am cold. Hold me tight, Peter."

"Was it bad?" came Peter's concerned inquiry. "Like being quartered."

Maria raised her eyebrows into a perfect arch. "But the nurses tell me that I will have plenty of milk to nourish our frail youngster." Next to her, the blonde-haired newborn sprawled on a cushion stitched in old German script,

"Beautiful, simply beautiful." Peter could not let go of the sight.

Keetmanshoop was only a waystation. Because Peter was well paid as an overseer, they could afford to move to Swakopmund, a romantic harbor and resort where the high surf breaks on the rocky shore. "A jewel," Maria marveled when they moved into a yellow pastel-colored colonial house with a straw roof and a flower garden. "I don't want to leave ever again." Swakopmund was quaint, with a large German population. They prided themselves on bringing European culture to this far-away dry land. There was a symphony orchestra, and artists exhibited their drawings and paintings along the boulevard. Maria was invited to play her violin at ladies' luncheons and once at a soirée at the ambassador's mansion. She felt at home in this adopted Germanized town. And Gerda-Maria grew fond of an elderly black servant who rocked her on his knees.

But they had no choice. In 1919 World War I ended and the British victors expelled many of the German settlers, Peter, Maria and their small daughter among them. A British public servant brought the eviction notice. Maria pressed her palm to her mouth, stifling a sob. Her tears were relentless.

Maria was pregnant again. In the rush of packing, she left her beloved violin behind. Instead, she spent precious time taking off one of the heels of her sturdy brown walking shoes, and stuffed the birthday diamond into a hole she dug between sole and heel. She used tiny brass tacks to shut the opening.

The small family stood for the last time on their veranda, looking at the sky. The sun always begins to relent by late afternoon but refuses to slip away gradually. That day the sun put on an electrifying show of fiery sunbursts. "Just for us," Maria wept and pulled Gerda-Maria close to her. From Swakopmund they were driven by cart back to Lüderitz where five years before, the lighthouse fog horn had welcomed Maria. Now its blinking light signaled their farewell.

5 Cold Moon

In the bowels of the vessel "Triumph," Maria navigated around suitcases, squeezed past bodies, looking for a berth. The dampness and foul smell of illness sickened her. She rushed back up on deck and vomited over the railing, letting the sea spray wet her hair. Water lapped against the flanks of the freighter. Seagulls flew along with the wind, then rested on the foam of the swells and drifted back toward shore. Maria swayed with the ship and feared for Gerda-Maria's safety. She took off her scarf and tied it around her child's waist, then held on to the fluttering edges. Gerda-Maria whimpered incessantly, hungry and tired, clinging desperately to her mother. "Oh, my sweet child," Maria murmured, "life will have to toughen you." At night they slept curled up together in a swaying hammock.

Peter was isolated in the men's quarters. Nobody changed their clothes on the weeks-long arduous journey. Sometimes underwear and socks were washed in puddles of rainwater on deck. They had drinking water on board but the daily soup contained little substance. Gerda-Maria used her fingers to fish out a piece of carrot or fish. Maria kept her shoes on at all times. A fellow passenger remarked, "In your condition, you should take your shoes off and put your feet up." Maria's legs were swollen like boa constrictors.

They docked in Hamburg where Peter, Maria and Gerda-Maria lumbered off the boat like cattle. Somehow their telegram sent from Swakopmund had reached Baron Nicholaus in Bielwiese. A loyal servant from the pre-war days met the family at disembarkation. Their clothes hung like rags on their bony bodies, dark shadows circled their eyes, all sun had been pulled from them. The servant wrapped them in heavy horse blankets and bundled them into the carriage. Peter was given a few gulps of schnapps and for the women he had brought bread and two raw eggs which they eagerly slurped. Then they bumped toward Silesia, a long taxing day drive.

A soft golden glow hung over the castle as the carriage rumbled in. The entire building was lit up to welcome them, with servants standing on the front steps ready to assist the new arrivals. A milky creamy light like frosted glass shifted over the family crown on the portal above and the wind gently swung the branches of the old chestnut tree laden with snow. Maria shivered as she was helped from the carriage. She suddenly felt small and insignificant in front of the impressive castle and bewildered as she stared at the lustrous full moon. "We are walking in a dream," she whispered. Then she collapsed in Peter's arms.

Nicholaus welcomed Maria, his daughter-in-law, with open arms. She was given the best suite where a large fireplace had two outlets, one into her room, the other into the corridor. Each morning fires were ignited from outside and Maria could wash in a marble basin, enveloped by warmth. Often she luxuriated until noon in her wide Empire bed of polished mahogany. As soon as the Baron heard of the missing violin, he had one ordered from an antique dealer in Berlin. He was overjoyed when Hubertus was born and when Maria gave him another grandson, Heio, two years later.

Already on the first morning after their arrival he swung Gerda-Maria up in the air, "You are the prettiest little princess in all the land." He was happy to have Peter back. Nobody knew at that point what happened to Balthazar. Vera had married in the interim and lived in one of the castle's wings. She joyfully hugged her brother but avoided Maria and little Gerda-Maria as well.

One of the first outings after their arrival was a visit to Mabushka. Maria stayed behind, not feeling up for a sleigh ride. Peter and his little daughter whisked over rutted roads where the snow swirled up into their faces. They glanced in wonder at dark fir trees glazed with powder. Gerda-Maria buried her hands securely in a fur muff. The encounter between Isa and her granddaughter could have been foreseen. Both delicate and overly emotional, they felt an immediate, intense affinity. Gerda-Maria slung her slender arms around Isa's neck before even addressing her. From their first encounter, they bonded. Whenever Gerda-Maria visited Mabuska she would crouch at Isa's feet and follow the slow movements of her fingers which were still able to crochet and knit. Isa would hum softly during their handiwork. The love of knitting and crocheting stayed with Gerda-Maria all her life and was later passed on to her daughter Ute.

For several years Bielwiese was a paradise for Maria and the children. Maria's mother traveled from Wintzingerode for the baptism of every grandchild and spent weeks at the castle where her daughter was the hostess at candlelit soirées and musical evenings to which they invited guests from all the neighboring estates. Maria read poetry and recommended books. She was an avid reader. Peter cringed when hearing about books. Reading was not his forte. But Nicholaus brimmed with contentment at the vibrant life that Maria's presence brought to Bielwiese. Because he liked to hear his own voice, he let it boom through gatherings, introducing his daughter-in-law as "the artist in our midst." As the lady of the mansion, Maria outshone Wanda who had become Nicholaus' companion, a substitute for Isa.

But Wanda triumphed when it came to horses. She remained a champion. Because she was passionate about riding, she had horses saddled each morning and brought to the circular driveway at the front of the castle. Anybody could join a ride across fields, meadows and into the mysterious woodlands.

The children had a happy, secure childhood. Gerda-Maria later remembered it in a letter: "Carefree, time to myself to roam through meadows and forests, my younger brothers often in tow. We picked blue cornflowers and red poppies which I braided into wreaths to crown our heads. We stripped and splashed on the muddy banks of a stream. We climbed apple trees and heaved ourselves over a rusty fence. We cornered an old mare and rode her bareback. We nestled into the crowns of trees with our books, out of reach of our English nanny and our French tutor. We returned obediently to the music parlor for piano instruction, but during violin lessons our teacher usually snored at the open window or in an easy chair near the fireplace. In spite of our tutors, our formal education was meager. But the manor hummed like a beehive. Because we had little supervision we crouched on stairs after dark and listened to the clacking and clattering of the adult world. Or we would spy on our nanny disappearing into the servants' quarters after our bedtime."

Nicholaus was fond of his grandkids. For each christening he ordered a gold ring with a bloodstone on which the Lüttwitz family seal was engraved. The family rings have been passed down through the generations and are still admired today. Nicholaus enjoyed spending much of his leisure time with the children. He instructed them about planting a variety of crops and bragged about magnificent harvest times. On strolls through the woods, he taught them to distinguish edible mushrooms from poisonous ones.

But he could lose his temper when they played pranks on him. The castle had fancy bathrooms. Opapa had his own private one. It was Heio who giggled as he let his siblings in on his plan. Excited about the idea, they wrapped garlands of ivy around Opapa's toilet bowl and strung fresh branches across the seat, making the toilet inaccessible. When Opapa rushed from an elegant dinner party into his bathroom and stared at the green obstruction, he instructed a servant to bring him a switch. All three of his beloved grandkids earned red welts across their bottoms.

The siblings were close. It was Gerda-Maria who mothered the younger ones. She kept track of them when playing unsupervised outside, and she made sure they never explored the castle after bedtime unless she gave them permission. Day and night, she was in charge. She and Hubertus were inseparable and it was he who played house with her, helping dress her dolls and spoon feeding them porridge which they sneaked from the kitchen. Hubertus was a gentle, slender boy. When everyone seemed asleep his steps could be heard on the floor of an icy corridor until he safely reached his mother's bedroom. Sometimes he just crawled into bed with Gerda-Maria, slinging his cold legs across her hips. In his dreams he protected her from water moccasins and snakes and fought monsters off that were after him. Maria attributed Hubertus's anxieties to the choppy crossing of the "Triumph" where the loud rumblings of the ship must have crept into his bones and frightened his mind.

Heio was robust, round and a mischief-maker. He could not stop his legs from moving. He loved to run barefoot over the forest floor, pine needles pricking his soles. From Peter he inherited a passion for horses and a wondrous regard for all living creatures. When he was three years old, he would accompany Peter on rides, sitting in front of a flat English saddle. He also climbed with his father onto the high deer blinds at the edge of the forest. Once Peter brought his shotgun and although he never killed an animal in front of Heio, he let him hear the roaring blast of the weapon. Heio later recalled that he felt oddly exhilarated by the sound and that his heart began to race. Thereafter, when he noticed blood dripping from the gamebags his father lugged back to the castle's kitchen, he rightly surmised that the bags contained rabbits and pheasants and shotgun pellets.

One breezy June morning Peter led Heio to a bale of hay in the barn. Peter was six feet tall and Heio had to hold on to his pinky finger. The surprise was a litter of kittens. Heio was told to pick one and he grabbed the darkest, fluffiest one from the bunch. He was allowed to keep the little Panther in their nursery where it was spoiled by the three children. It was allowed to take turns snuggling in their beds.

Gerda-Maria was adored by both Peter and Nicholaus. She was learned like her mother but had a soothing, conciliatory disposition. Her beauty set her apart from all her agemates, mostly girls on adjacent estates. She alone was the one who sensed that something was amiss between her parents. Peter spent many lonely hours watching wildlife from one of the high hunting seats. He was seldom seen at Maria's entertainments. Instead, he made frequent visits to ailing Isa. Maria was consumed by her social functions and rarely registered Peter's absences.

Only once did Opapa sense tension between the couple. He immediately took action and sent them on a mission to Rio de Janeiro to inspect a farm there that was for sale. The towering Sugarloaf with Christ the Redeemer standing on the highest point above the city impressed Maria and reminded her of the wooden cross above Sankt Ivan. But when they rode a tram through the notorious favelas, violent and crime-ridden, with no basic services for the poor, she recoiled. She pleaded with Peter to return to Silesia which they did, their task unfinished.

One evening as the children were spying on household activities, the hours slipped by. They should have long been tucked in bed but curiously nobody was paying attention. The door to the living room stood ajar and arguments drifted out. It was Peter's voice, sharply edged. "I must have been born with feet that itch to walk in far places. I feel confined here with nothing purposeful to do. Ever since we heard that Balthazar is alive, avoided deportation and remained on the farm Hoffnung, I wanted to join him."

"But we have made a home here for us and the children," Maria was heard sobbing. "I said once in Swakopmund that I would never leave again. I am saying this now about Bielwiese. I will stay here."

"I am like the kokerboom," Peter sounded determined but calm now, "a tree difficult to keep outside its natural habitat. I cannot survive in the cold. I need the African sun. Like a lion behind bars, I feel imprisoned on our estate." Thereafter, the living room door quietly closed.

Days later Peter asked his daughter to join him on the bench under the ancient oak tree where the siblings had carved their names into the backboard. Gerda-Maria moved timidly next to her father who put his arm around her shoulder. "Men will adore you for your beauty and admire your sweet personality as I have done over the years. You are also wise beyond your age. You will understand that I am not abandoning you or your brothers. But I intend to leave and go back to Africa. Your mother and I are estranged and there is nothing here to hold me back."

"How, father, can people ever get estranged when they once loved each other?"

There ensued an awkward silence as Peter repeatedly stroked his chin. Finally he said, "Maybe circumstances? People stop sharing. I am not sure but the warmth disappears in a biting wind."

The cold had shriveled the branches of the old oak tree, now leafless. In the foggy dawn with only a frosty sliver of the moon on the awakening sky, Gerda-Maria watched from her upstairs window as a servant pulled a steamer trunk to the waiting carriage. Then her father jumped in, wearing his drab olive-colored hunting attire, with a gray canvas duffle bag slung over his shoulder, a large monogrammed P visible on the fabric. No one waved as the coach drove off. Maria did not appear for breakfast. When the boys asked about their father, they were briskly told, "he has gone back to Africa."

As years sped by, Peter eventually reconnected with his family. In Africa, christened Namibia, he had found a woman he loved. She bore him two sons. Peter pleaded with Gerda-Maria never to view him as an outsider, nor her two stepbrothers. "I have often thought of my beautiful girl," he wrote, "and only wished her a happy life. Maybe you have it in your heart to welcome your two new brothers into our extended family. It would give me peace and long-needed forgiveness. Be gentle in your judgment with your old father."

Only after Peter began to age did he find the courage to confess to Maria in a letter, "I was a young fool with wanderlust. How I regret my transgressions, leaving you and the children behind in Bielwiese. I know you will never pardon me and I am not pleading for absolution. All I ask for is a bit of understanding." Maria never fully understood but she had stripped any animosity from her feelings for Peter. She had moved on in life.

After Peter left, Maria curtailed her social engagements. She dreaded being asked about her husband's departure. She played her violin daily. As in Africa she sat at an open window, often shivering as the wind tousled her hair. She also lost herself in books, spending hours absorbed in the mansion's library. Books gave her a way out, into different lives.

For an interim the siblings continued to live in the sanctuary of childhood.

Gambling was practiced in aristocratic circles. It infiltrated the Bielwiese family, especially since Walter, Vera's husband, had taken trips to Berlin for gambling tournaments. Poker was the chosen game at the castle where neighbors were also in attendance. Both Maria and Vera adamantly opposed gambling of any kind. The saloon was off limits to the children. It was smoke-filled, with men puffing on expensive cigars. Schnapps was consumed in small but nightly quantities. And there was shouting when a game was won or lost.

When Heio discovered a way into the saloon, he pulled his sister and reluctant brother with him. Under a table, draped by a heavy velveteen tablecloth, they hunkered down, squeezed tightly next to each other. It was a secret sacred hiding place. No giggling or coughing was allowed but it was the best place to watch. They poked peepholes into the fabric and, with eyes wide open, took in the affairs across the saloon. It was Opapa who shuffled the cards and dealt them clockwise. Then the person to his left started the betting. The children knew nothing of the rules but they observed that fingers were always moving as cards fluttered onto the tabletop. They heard hands slapping its surface and loudly spreading out the cards. Once in a while a player would bang an angry fist. It was always Walter who hid his hands under the table, extremely careful not to show his cards. There was infectious laughter among the men but mostly their facial expressions were tense and looked strangely forbidding. Not a muscle moved. When a new wager was called the children in their squatting positions had barely room to jump an inch, sharing the excitement. They had no idea how much money was at stake at each round of the game.

Walter stayed away for weeks in the city. After a lengthy absence he admitted that he had gambled away Vera's inheritance. He vowed to win it back. Vera was not a patient woman. In short order, she divorced him, and took her leave of Bielwiese. She convinced her father to give her a few heirlooms which she sent to a friend for storage in Germany. We own her a black hunting armoire, still a possession in the family. A skilled multi-linguist, she moved to Denmark where she took a position as translator.

Only in her old age did she return to Germany. But she made several trips back to Namibia to visit her brothers.

Nicholaus discontinued the poker sessions at the castle. He seemed diminished after Peter and Vera had left. He and Wanda still rode out daily and he returned invigorated from those rides. But on mild afternoons he was seen snoozing in a lawn chair.

Country doctors with their ominous black bags were no strangers to Bielwiese. They encouraged home remedies such as a steam bath for head colds and grated apples for an upset stomach. They also prescribed morphine for pain, mainly after a finger was injured by a sharp blade or a fallen tree trunk had mangled a leg. As with Isa, the discomfort of giving birth was soothed by morphine. Births and deaths changed places periodically. It was taken for granted that everyone and everything eventually died, even Wanda's favorite mare, Blume, who had borne seven splendid foals. So it came as no surprise when one noon Opapa returned atop of his beloved gelding, hanging limp across the pommel of the saddle. He had suffered a heart attack.

One last time the mansion was filled with hustle and bustle. Nicholaus was admired and loved by his servants and fieldhands, and respected by his neighbors. He was laid out splendidly in the main entrance hall with flowers galore and candles burning day and night. All sorts of mourners streamed by to pay their last respects and shake hands with grieving Maria, Bogoslav and Wanda. Peter, Balthazar and Vera had been notified but were too far away to return for the funeral. The siblings were ignored. They crept past the hall and never ventured in, except that Heio spotted what resembled a long white nightshirt and he whispered. "I saw that Opapa has his shining riding boots with the silver snaps on." For the funeral service their nanny dressed the children in the customary black clothing with dark armbands showing the relation to the deceased. At the graveside the children clung to Maria's long skirt and Hubertus warned, "Stay far away from the hole over there. We don't want to fall in."

Although Nicholaus had been a lenient and providing patron, he had neglected his financial affairs. And now there was no one to take up the reins. Bogoslav had trained as a forester and had no intention of giving up his post. The women had no legal rights and were disqualified from such a demanding position. Because the debt that hung over Bielwiese was great, ultimately the state had to be called in. They inspected the books and regretfully asked the remaining residents to find new domiciles. The castle was used for many purposes but mainly stood empty for long periods of time. The interior had been cleared by kind relatives or stripped by vagrants.

The magnificent castle fell into disrepair and, over time, crumbled into ruins. Nevertheless, the mystery surrounding it remained. When in

2017 two descendants, Zachary and Alexander, stared at the marvelous rubble with an intact facade still crowned by the family seal, they marveled, "Maybe the spirits of our ancestors have guarded the ruins where much drama and happiness reigned."

6 Under the Sign of the Deer

Maria had made her way alone before. Confidently, she moved with her three children to Hirschberg (Jelena Gora), a small vibrant town near the snow-capped Carpathian Mountains, the Riesengebirge. She found a spacious loft apartment. Dark wooden beams protruded from the slanted ceilings and gave the rooms a cozy atmosphere. A view from the windows sailed over the sprightly Bober River where boulders jutted from the rushing waters. Wisps of fog floated above the spray. Watching mornings from an open window, Maria took in the fresh air, pushing some unruly strands of hair from her face. In a flower box mounted on one of the window ledges, she planted geraniums. She would live comfortably in her new abode on a modest monthly income from her holdings in Wintzingerode.

Following the horrors of World War I, Germans adopted "Lebenslust," a kind of "joie de vivre." The Weimar Republic was at its height with a stable peacetime economy. The siblings enrolled in public schools, and Maria found a part-time position at the library, next to the 17th century town hall and a thriving central market. Maria was thrilled to be able to borrow books from the library—Hesse, Mann and Kafka but also French Thyde Monnier and British Charles Morgan. She employed no servants and the children needed no tutors. Maria felt that the deer image of the city embodied her blossoming motherhood. In mythology the deer is often portrayed as a symbol protecting the young. For the first time in her life, she alone had the children in her care and she relished her new responsibilities. At night she read to them and stories spilled off her tongue as easily as the foreign languages she had learned at boarding school.

To celebrate their independence Maria marched with the siblings to a hairdresser. Under the blade of sharp scissors rasping snip... snip... snip, bountiful hair rustled to the floor. Mother and children stared into the mirrors. How could a pageboy cut with bangs across their foreheads change their appearance so much? At first, they laughed when Maria nearly choked on her joke, "Looks like a cooking pot was placed on our heads and turned us into alien beings."

"It's done," Heio pronounced resignedly.

Germany awoke to nature. "Wanderlust" was the slogan. Only later did the Hitler Youth distort that longing. Maria bought a rucksack for each child, decorated with graphic designs of flowers, trees and animals. Each chose a different emblem. Maria wanted a leafy tree, Gerda-Maria a baby bunny, for the boys hunting designs. Maria tried to change the boys' minds but they couldn't be budged. With the sunrise on Saturday mornings, Maria prepared a picnic lunch and whistling ... "valdari, valdara"... they hiked through blooming meadows and splashed in a nearby lake. When the snow made faint clicks on the window panes they laced up their snowshoes and glided over frozen fields. At night they rested in a hut in the mountains, roasted potatoes over an open fire and cracked walnuts. As the light grew low, they listened for cowbells ringing over the dreamy valleys. Bells pealed much louder in the open country than in the city. Here sounds came from a long way off and echoed from the hills. Soon the melodic clinging induced sleep. Maria relished this time with her growing brood.

Years back at boarding school in Eberswalde, Maria had accepted the invitation of her friend Astrid to spend the summer in Norway with her and her family. Maria arrived there with a hefty cold and a delicate chest. Mrs. Trondheim gently instructed her to sit down comfortably, then asked her to close her eyes as she slowly recited some words Maria could not understand. She spoke no Norwegian. "That's it, Maria," Mrs. Trondheim allowed her to open her eyes. "Your cold is gone." And it was. Amazed, Maria mumbled, "How did you do that? It was magic!" Mrs. Trondheim smiled, "Not magic, child, Christian Science." Maria had no idea what Christian Science was but when she returned home, she checked into it. The Trondheims would later answer one of Maria's granddaughter's pressing questions when pummeled by war experiences. "Are all people sad? Is life always full of sorrow and pain?" Maria was able to answer, "No, there is also happiness, like the bond you and I share." And to Ute's probing, "Have you ever met someone who was happy and had an enduring satisfying life?" Maria could reply, "The Trondheims. They lived to a ripe old age, content as a loving couple."

Maria had an inquisitive mind, and was a spiritual seeker. After her return from Norway, she pulled a volume from Mary Baker Eddy's "Science and Health" from a shelf at the library and immersed herself in the founder's teachings. Much of it appealed to her, that the body can heal itself and that the root of sickness may be a mental disorder and not necessarily a physical one. Hesitantly she followed other lines of thought. For example, that true reality is spiritual not material, and that the world is an illusion. She was too deeply grounded in the world of the senses to take to this idea. But she believed in the power of prayer and had faith in healing with mind over matter. She took to warnings from the scriptures to be patient and not grasp for explanations and solutions. The idea that there is a divine plan for everyone took hold in her. She became convinced that there was a reason for every low or high tumble of fate and that we only can see its meaning in retrospect. She would later write to her granddaughter, Ute, "So often I have been distraught, not comprehending why something was happening to me. Only after much disappointment was I given wisdom and insight."

In Hirschberg Maria practiced her newfound beliefs. She reminded her children of the God-given beauty all around them. She had some success with healing. One of her early sessions was later recalled by her granddaughter, Ute. "I was maybe three years old, tossing with fever when my Omi Maria picked me up. The room was dark except for shafts of light from the moon creeping over the beams and along the walls. I saw figures of fluorescent snakes sneak along the wood. I also spotted a potbelly stove and heard the whistling of a red teakettle. Omi walked back and forth with me, humming softly and swaying. Maybe I was whimpering as my fingers clung to her shoulders. Uncle Heio was in the room, ready to leave for the front the next day. A button gleamed on his uniform. Omi reprimanded him, "Hush. You need to be quiet." I awoke to the brightest object in the sky, the sun. Omi Maria kissed me good morning."

Maria started to write notes relating to the teachings of Christian Science which she secretly stuck into the backpacks of her children. When her boys were older and had been deployed to war, her messages arrived at the battle front. Gerda-Maria found snippets of paper rolled up and pinned to her pockets. One of Maria's favorite bible quotations was Isaiah 58:14. There it is written that we will be fed from the heritage of God, the Father, if we follow his demands and live a Christian life. Later Maria was teased that she could be considered a forerunner of hypnosis. But early in her religious journey she had no idea how her beliefs would be tested. In spite of doubts, she held fast to its basic concepts. When she was diagnosed with old-age diabetes, she changed her diet but never took medicines.

Gerda-Maria entered Eberswalde when she turned twelve as her mother had done and then attended nursing school in Potsdam, near Berlin. Following graduation, she stayed on and became a licensed neonatal nurse. Hubertus entered the private boarding school of Spikerook and Heio was admitted at Salem. Both were later drafted.

In 1929 Marie died and two of Maria's sisters moved into their parents' old villa. After Maria had left Bielweise, she and the children made frequent visits to Wintzingerode where the siblings were confirmed in the village chapel of St. Katharina. Above the baptismal fountain hangs a wooden angel carved and painted in luminous blue hues in 1701. During Heio's baptism the minister observed that the name "Maria," recurred often in their family. "Yes," Maria responded. "Maria, the mother of Jesus, is our guiding light. We turn to her with our troubles and motherly needs."

Images of angels seem to glide over much of the lives of the Lüttwitz family but even these benign figures could not prevent the tragedies to come.

7 A Comet in the Winter Sky

Love stories are shrouded in hearsay and legend, veiling intimacies and struggles. But sunrays and moonbeams can penetrate the web.

September was wrapped in a warm, delicious haze. Threads from busy spiders enveloped summer roses and colorful asters. Fumes of smoke rose from heaps where raked leaves smoldered. Dogs barked. Flies hummed, unfolded their wings and flew away. Maria walked from her apartment past plowed fields. Her shoes rustled through knee-deep leaves. She could not resist and grabbed an armful, scattering them ahead of her. She arrived in town with the brief amber evening light. She was on her way to pick up Hubertus and Heio who had entered "Die Bündische Jugend" under the leadership of young Wolfgang Zampis, only a few years their senior. The group was associated with the "Wandervögel" (migrating birds) and shared ideas and goals with the Boy Scouts. Hubertus and Heio had told their mother how they enjoyed the folk songs they were learning, and listening to Nordic ballads that were both frightening and ennobling. Maria was enthusiastic about absorbing old German traditions. Similar groups were springing up all over Germany. They were critical of industrialization, and celebrated the freedom of the individual, the cultivation of conscience. The boys had gone on hikes with their new guide and had returned eager to pronounce the names of new plants and wildflowers they had discovered. "We commune with nature," Heio triumphantly pronounced.

Wolfgang greeted Maria with disarming naturalness. He had a strongly marked face, sharp chin and a high bridged nose but rather tired eyes. His hair was dark, thick and lustrous. He stood back as the boys ran into Maria's open arms. Wolfgang was known in the small community of Hirschberg. He was the only child of strict parents, a sickly overprotective mother and a remote lawyerly father. He attended the one public high school like his charges. After graduation he enrolled in law school at Berlin University. Maria encountered Wolfgang at pickups or at departures for outings into the wilderness. She watched as Wolfgang talked to every participant to make sure each had the needed supplies and was prepared for the day. When he brought back his little flock of boys at night he seemed as full of details about their adventures as they were.

Wolfgang regularly visited the library. He smiled as he greeted Maria but never conversed with her. He would sit in an alcove at the back of the reading room, totally absorbed in his writing. She watched him crumple up one sheet of scribbled paper after another, throwing it into the wastebasket. A few times Maria had to remind him that closing time was approaching.

He would always say, "Oh, sorry, time flies." Often in the afternoon his mother would call the front desk, and if Maria was on duty, she would anxiously whisper, "Please remind my son to be home on time for dinner. His father doesn't tolerate tardiness."

When the boys organized a singing event, Maria and Gerda-Maria attended. During the song "Guter Mond…" Maria felt a surging melancholy and was transported back to the gypsy camp in the forest at Sankt Ivan.

Days sped by and weeks followed weeks. In 1936 Maria was joined by Hubertus and Heio in Berlin. Gerda-Maria was in nursing school but free for the evening to accompany them to a performance of "Drums at Night." An impromptu parade was scheduled for the afternoon and Gerda-Maria's class was summoned to attend. The nurses assembled in the front row of the parade route as they were instructed. Gerda-Maria was the epitome of a German girl with a long blonde braid which she had wound around her head. She also had blue eyes, was tiny and red-cheeked. Her dark blue nurse's uniform was neatly pressed and its white collar starched. As Hitler strutted by, he stopped in front of her, reached for her hand with his gloved fingers and shook them, "A real German working Girl," he bellowed. Gerda-Maria had overheard her mother call Hitler a "Hampelmann" as she predicted that the Nazi Regime would fall like a house of cards. Now Maria was in the crowd a row behind her beaming daughter. Arms flew up into the air for the Hitler salute. Maria kept her arm tightly pressed to her side. "Mother," Hubertus poked her. "Not here and not now. This is dangerous. You are being watched." But Maria stood her ground and remained unmoved. Her defiant posture had been noted.

Following the euphoria of the short-lived Weimar Republic, dark clouds gathered on the horizon. The early sprouting economy floundered and the defeat at Versaille still galled many. Speculations about a war circulated and fear began to spread. Maria returned from her Berlin visit in dejected spirits. As she walked up to her house, Wolfgang was sitting on the front steps. "May I come in? I have something to tell you." It was not prudent to talk in the open, so Wolfgang followed Maria up to her loft. Ill at ease and nervous, he settled on Maria's decorative green and yellow striped couch while she brewed tea in the red kettle. As Wolfgang slowly sipped his drink, she encouraged him to tell her the reason for his unannounced visit. Haltingly, he began, "Die Bündische Jugend" (The Young People's League) has been outlawed by the Nazis. They accuse us of high-mindedness and arrogance. But mainly they believe that we foster homosexual behavior." Both waited for the other to respond. But there was no more to say. "I am afraid we are approaching difficult times," Maria finally replied. "They are already there," answered Wolfgang. Forgetting to thank her for the tea, he left, running down the stairs.

At the library Maria got acquainted with people who shared warnings. Rumors mushroomed. Through Wolfgang she heard of Albrecht Haushofer, a history professor at Berlin University and leader of a small resistance circle. Soon other small protest groups formed. Maria knew the von Molkte family and was invited to attend their Kreisauer Kreis meetings. Communication between groups was sparse. There was the radio but it was dominated by the propaganda of the Reich. Isolated from one another, gatherings were necessarily clandestine. It was customary among the aristocracy to sign a guestbook when calling on a family member, a practice that would become the downfall of many.

Two years later, as fall turned into winter, a soft snowfall with downy puffs sprinkled from the sky, catching Maria's hair. She let the flakes settle, not bothering to cover her head with her furry hood. The snow crunched under her winter boots. She glanced at a few candlelit windows as she passed the parsonage. As the weather worsened and her lips turned blue, she decided to enter the sheltering arches of the colonnade around the marketplace. She had been attending Mass. The church was heated and incense had wafted in the air. The organ music had been sweet but with a sad undertone. She realized that she had been lonely for many years. She made no effort to check the rush of salty tears. The church bells rang out in solemn strokes, muffled by wintery gusts. She felt no desire to hurry home. The children had been with her for Christmas and were spending New Year's Eve with friends. Before leaving for church Maria had lit a fresh fire in the potbelly stove and the apartment would be welcoming on her return. She heard footsteps and a shadow lengthened across the white path. Then the dark reflection was beside her. "Did I frighten you?" Wolfgang's voice sounded apologetic. "You nearly did," Maria chuckled as her throat pulsed with tiny throbs. "Where are you off to?" It did not surprise Maria when he simply said, "To you."

Wolfgang confessed that he had long admired Maria but had not been able to express his feelings. Tonight he had stopped by a pub, a first for him since he did not usually drink. The liquor had invigorated him and encouraged him to speak. Maria had long been without a male companion and there remained no hesitation.

"I have never been with a woman," Wolfgang mumbled as they undressed in front of the glowing coals shimmering through the iron grate of the stove. "It's wonderful to make love to an innocent man," Maria kissed his silky-smooth hair. The burgundy satin curtains had been drawn and in the dim lamplight his young face took on an astonished expression. Maria had developed into a voluptuous woman, no longer the elf-like figure of yore. She showed Wolfgang how to enter her waiting warm body.

They were granted a blooming spring and a spectacular fall. Gerda-Maria was engaged, Hubertus was drafted and Heio was in Switzerland.

Taking advantage of their time together, Maria and Wolfgang traveled through Austria and Tirol. In photographs their faces are as radiant as the landscape. "The entire Alps became our altar," Wolfgang wrote and Maria recalled, "We never felt so close to heaven. It seemed to us that we were the only people in the world." On their sojourn Maria regained her ability to laugh. Hiking one day through the "Riesengebirge," they couldn't find a hotel that had been recommended. Locals seemed perplexed when they asked for directions. Barely able to suppress giggling, Maria replied, "Paradise." Can you please tell us the way to paradise?"

In his high school years, Wolfgang had started a collection of poems, serenading the wonders of nature. Now he added poems dedicated to Maria. They spill over with gratitude for her devotion and love. "You are the only one who ever cared so much…the only one who waits at the end of day…the only one in whose eyes our happiness is mirrored." His praise is boundless as he compares Maria to "a vessel brimming with glorious abundance." Sitting one evening on a mossy rock overlooking a lush meadow, they asked each other, "Will this last?"

They arrived at the Bodensee, the end of their fortnight journey. They lodged at a chalet with a narrow wooden balcony. It was mid-afternoon and the sunlight glittered on the calm surface of the lake. They went down to the dining room and after a country supper of sausage and sauerkraut, they watched a couple dance the polka, weaving with effortless grace in and out around the guests. Maria and Wolfgang were filled with joy. "These days will always be ours, ours alone," Maria whispered. Later that evening they stopped for a last look. They stood rooted to the spot. The lake had changed beyond recognition. Waves swept and slammed on shore with white fury. They clutched each other. What disasters did this portend?

8 Careening Toward the Brink

The following year began with good news. In 1939 Gerda-Maria married Gert Köhler. But blows followed on the heels of rejoicing. Gert was killed only twelve months later in France, a month before Maria's first grandchild, Ute, was born. Wolfgang was drafted in spite of his parents' efforts to keep him at an office at the home front. Hubertus was sent into battle and Heio returned from his safe school in Switzerland against all pleading. He too was drafted. Forebodings permeated every facet of life.

Wolfgang published his novella "Erzählung" in which the question of conscience is raised. Must an individual follow his convictions or subjugate his beliefs to State and Country? Whom should one obey? He told Maria, "I am a poet. I have the word and therefore the duty to express my convictions. The word still has power." Long before Alfred Haushofer's powerful poem "Guilt" came to light, people struggled with fear of being imprisoned when speaking out or living with regrets for not having opposed an evil regime. In this poem, which Haushofer clutched in his hand as he was executed at Moabite Prison, he told about his own realization that had come too late.

Guilt
I am guilty,
But not in the way you think.
I should have more sharply called evil evil,
I reined in my judgment too long.
I did warn.
But not enough, not clearly enough.
And today I knew what I was guilty of.

As Germany plunged into darkness, most people were caught in a trap. Should they stay silent and remain safe or should they speak out, thereby endangering their lives. Personal everyday concerns were considered. Maria worried day and night. She tried to envelop all her loved ones in a circle of protection that Christian Science taught. She sent her prayers out, far and wide. With a heaving chest she had taken leave of Wolfgang before he returned to the front. He had just told her about meeting a woman named Nichole on his short furlough in Paris. He had vehemently assured Maria that nothing could ever come between them. Maria was not so sure. She felt that one day she would have to relinquish her role and let a younger woman take her place. Would she be lonely again? In that mood between dissolution and fears, she immersed herself more deeply in the weekly lessons from Science and Health.

Jackboots echoed on the stairs, clomping their way up. Instinctively, Maria buttoned up her blouse. The pencil point with which she had underlined lines in her lesson broke under the pressure of her fingers. She forced herself to sit calmly as her door was kicked down. Two young Nazi gendarmes, legs apart with outstretched arms, positioned themselves in front of her. "What is this about? It would be polite of you to knock first." The young men seemed unable to speak, then one stammered, "You must come with us to headquarters." "May I ask what for?" Maria was now nearly amused by their awkwardness. "Can't say," the other one blushed. "Just come." They would not let her reach for her shawl that hung at the back of the chair, instead roughly grabbing her by the elbow.

The Nazi headquarters in Hirschberg had been set up in a narrow bungalow next to the school's gymnasium. Maria was led into a sparsely furnished room, dark and silent as an underground cave. The lock of the door snapped shut behind her. The furniture, draped in plastic, looked on loan. An officer, whom Maria thought she recognized from a nature hike, sat ramrod straight behind an elongated table. His face had a greenish pallor in the dim lamplight. With scornful shoulders and nervous intensity his long colorless hands shuffled through a stack of papers. He only glanced up as Maria's footsteps squeaked on the planks of the wooden floor. With her sweeping gate, she crossed in view of him. He focused on her, still standing. Sweat broke out around Maria's neck but she remained alert, on her guard. She knew herself in a dangerous whirlpool of intrigues and false accusations. The officer's voice matched her composure. He spoke softly, buzzing into her ear. With a sweep of his hands, he finally motioned her to sit down on a round swivel stool. An unsettling dread crawled over Maria's skin. It took all the willpower she could muster to steady herself on that rickety seat. She focused on the pelting rain against a window.

The officer was ready with his questions.

"Your name."

"Baroness Maria von Lüttwitz."

He checked off her name on a list.

"A Baroness. Must be nice to be so privileged while a war is going on." Maria's nostrils quivered but she remained quiet.

"We know about your association with aristocratic families. True?" Maria simply nodded, "Yes."

"Names." The officer glowered at her with his naked eyes, hard little seeds about to burst behind his wire-rimmed glasses.

"I have many friends and acquaintances. Any particular names?" Maria clasped and unclasped her hands.

The officer shifted his interrogation and intensified his stare. His eyes were now torches.

"You have not signed the oath to the Führer! And it was reported to us that at a rally in Berlin you refused the honor salute." The officer thought he had her trapped.

"My arm had been injured before the rally where my daughter was greeted by the Führer. And as for an oath. I am a Christian Scientist. My only oath is given to God alone."

"Your loyalty must first be to the Führer, father of our Fatherland."

A gray stillness settled between them. Maria took her time.

"My two sons are fighting for the Fatherland. My son-law died for the Fatherland in France."

The officer started to rub his temples in a circular motion. He searched in his papers. "I was not aware of this," his voice barely audible. Against Maria's tranquil statement, his accusations, so orderly laid out in his mind, crumbled. With the back of one hand, he wiped across his eyes as if to clear away cobwebs. "You may go," was all he muttered.

The rain had turned into drizzle when Maria stepped outside. Her head throbbed and her old vitality had weakened. The street started to swim in a haze. Confused, she asked herself, "What has happened to my beloved country? What am I seeing? A desert fox? Iridescent onyx eyes, horizontal whiskers, taut sinews under russet fur, the tail a flag?" Maria blinked twice. Then she thought she spotted a hawk with dusty feathers clawing the top of a telephone pole. The bird smoothed its ruffled plumage. There appeared more, a tabby dodged shadows, dashing under a bush. She heard an owl screech. Maria was astute enough to realize that she was hallucinating. But what did those images mean?

Maria walked the long way home. She was cold and drenched when she arrived at her apartment. There Gerda-Maria and Ute were waiting. Ever since Maria had cradled Ute as a newborn in her arms, she had called her "beloved." And later she confessed, "That child kept me from sinking into despair when her plump little fingers reached for my cheeks, whispering,

"How are you, Omi?" Now Gerda-Maria took her mother's stiff hands and rubbed them between her palms.

9 Tree Branches, a Limb

How do you graft a kokerboom with an oak tree? A merciless sun burns your skin as you search for the delicious yellow fruit nestling deep in the bark of the kokerboom. Then you inhale its intoxicating strange aroma. Balmy moonbeams caper through sun-dappled leaves as you stand barefoot under an oak tree. It scatters its white blossoms like confetti over your hair, down your body. Steadied by a sturdy trunk, growing branches, lush leaves and swelling buds renew the lives of both trees.

It was wartime. Maria could not get permission to travel to Brünn (Brno) in the southern region of Czechoslovakia for Gerda-Maria's wedding. In the morning of that special day, she rose early. Next to the rushing Bober River, in a meadow still damp with dew, she searched and found a four-leaf clover. It was a symbol of herself with the siblings, all so different in personality, yet bound by family inheritance and loyalty to each other. She smoothed out each leaf with her forefingers and hummed the summer incantation they all cherished… Geh aus mein Herz und suche Freud…" How much joy lay in store for her oldest?

Gerda-Maria had met Gert at a ball for new recruits and they seemed destined to fall in love. She called the stiff high collar of her nursing uniform her "Kuss Abwehrgeschütz" (kiss defense gear). Gert teased that his first kiss had landed on Gerda-Maria's cheek.

They were married in a civil service in Brünn where Gert was stationed. They had their wedding picture taken on the steps of the 13th century town hall, she slender as a fawn, in dark blue organza with a wide-brimmed black hat, clutching a profusion of her favorite flowers, roses and irises, an arm linked with Gert in his newly acquired pressed uniform. A handsome couple who vowed that the turmoil around them would not upset their happiness.

A finely bound leather album, its pages well thumbed through, has survived. A yellowed photo taken the morning after their wedding can barely be made out. In Gerda-Maria's legible handwriting she wrote: "That's how it began." She underlined BEGAN. They snapped pictures of each other with Gert's box camera. Their unmade bed in a sun-flooded room is in plain view. Gerda-Maria is fixing a bra strap and smiling coyly. Gert is grinning from ear to ear, glancing in amusement at his bride. He is wearing boxer shorts and is swinging a white t-shirt through the air like a triumphant flag.

A few friends organized a small dinner party for the newlyweds. Toasting the couple, one remarked, "Gerda-Maria you are the most beautiful woman I have ever laid eyes on. You are even more stunning than the young English Queen." Gerda-Maria indeed resembled the queen. She looked regal and held her head high as if in stern reproach. Her eyes were dazzling like the sun she worshiped and blue like the cornflowers she adored. She could have been given a medal for grooming. She never appeared unkempt. Even later in the air-raid shelter she would wear her pearls. She extended the cigarette she always had lit in an ebony holder between fine-boned fingers, showing off her emerald ring, set high in spikes of white gold, rounded by diamonds. She carried starched monogrammed linen handkerchiefs. "Rituals endure like a hardy kokerboom," she once said, "able to survive in the most inhospitable desert terrain." She possessed a natural beauty and in spite of all the admiration men paid her, she met their approaches with shyness and reserve.

Prague was Gerda-Maria's favorite city, located in close proximity to Sankt Ivan. Their honeymoon took the couple to this mystical city on the melancholy Volga River. Gerda-Maria felt at home in Prague and believed that in another incarnation she had lived there. They walked across the Charles Bridge arm-in-arm. Maria stopped at the Statue of St. John of Nepomuk and touched the icon, dark from soot and smoke, a moody color. "Please bring us good luck," she murmured.

On their return to Brünn, they had a few days to visit Naumburg where Gert wanted Gerda-Maria to see the cathedral with the 13th century statue of Uta, the Duchess of Naumburg. They had already discussed names for their children but Gert was convinced that their firstborn would be a girl. He decided on the spot. "We'll name our daughter Ute, only change the spelling slightly to give her name a softer sound. Gert marveled at the beautiful and self-contained expression of the Duchess. Gerda-Maria shyly interjected, "We don't even have a baby yet."

Soon thereafter, Gert's regiment was ordered to France. Morning sickness told Gerda-Maria that she was pregnant. She left for Köslin on the Baltic Sea, Gert's hometown where he wanted his first child to be born.

Karl and Aenne Köhler welcomed Gerda-Maria with open arms. Karl was the town judge, an intelligent man with a roaring temper. He had been orphaned as a young boy and was handed from one family to another. He struggled to become a lawyer and paid for university studies with his own earnings, doing odd jobs. Frugal, he owned only one pair of shoes and wore his hair long to avoid the barber. By middle age he was bald. He exhibited a stringent work ethic and demanded morally upright behavior from himself and others. As a student he lost one eye in a duel which left him with a lifelong nervous tick. He refused to talk about the incident.

Aenne was a learned woman who could recite Schiller's ballads by heart and confessed that she would have liked to have gone to the university. At that time women could enter service professions like nursing or teaching but seldom embarked on university studies. Their assigned place was in the home as mothers and wives. Aenne remarked regretfully, "If only I had been born a man." She went to a teachers' college and became an athletic instructor. She grew up in a large circle of brothers and sisters. Her family, the Eigenbrodts, were renowned in Köslin for their love of the arts. Aenne and her sister Else wrote a play that was performed by the community theater. Their talent for drawing and painting was valued and they were called a family with "Lust zum Fabulieren," (a penchant for story-telling). Aenne remembered the portraits of her great-grandparents who had proudly pasted love poems on the back of the frames and written, "A show of our love, a testimony to coming generations."

Aenne dedicated herself to her four sons and grieved deeply when their three-year old daughter, Rothtraud, was killed by a motorcyclist while riding her tricycle on their sidewalk. Aenne was not told that the child might have survived if a student doctor had not given her a mistaken injection. When Karl was later questioned why he did not investigate the accident, he ruefully shrugged his shoulders. "The young doctor will carry his guilt for the rest of his life."

Aenne stayed in bed during Rothtraud's funeral. When she was able to leave her bedroom again, she implored Gert and his brother, Eberhard, to dig up the grave at the local cemetery and bring her daughter home. In the depth of one night the men fulfilled their mother's wish. Rothtraud was reburied in the rose garden of their mansion where Aenne knelt and submerged her face in the damp soil.

After Rothtraud's tragic death, Gerda-Maria's pregnancy was greeted with much warmth and a lot of fuss. She was spoiled, served meals in bed or on their wide veranda. Both Aenne and Karl went on elaborate shopping sprees, buying a hand-painted cradle furnished with white linen and decorated with lace ruffles. Aenne began knitting in colorful wool, and Maria sent crocheted baby clothes in neutral shades. Between bouts of nausea, Gerda-Maria also took up knitting a loopy multicolored blanket. Karl surprised the household by coming home one evening with a dollhouse he had commissioned, a replica of rooms and furnishings like an adult dwelling. Their talk was all about the coming baby.

A package from Gert arrived. Once in Paris, Gert found an antique jewelry store where he purchased a ring, wrapped it in cotton and had it delivered to the Köhler residence. In an enthusiastic note Gert wrote, "This ring is for our daughter. I know it will be a girl. Should I be wrong (which I doubt) I will build a glider with our son." Gert guessed right and soon Ute was the proof. In anticipation of the birth the Köhler house echoed with laughter and predictions as to whom the newborn would most closely resemble.

Leaning against the wooden balustrade of the porch that wound around the house, Gerda-Maria awaited the daily mail. Her due date was only a few weeks away. Gert had requested a leave of absence so that he could be at his wife's side for the arrival of their firstborn.

Gerda-Maria opened the telegram, her knees buckled and she sank to the stone floor. Gert had been killed in an ambush after France had surrendered.

Gerda-Maria's grief robbed her of her will to live. Ute was also reluctant to take the dive. She had to be coaxed into this world with forceps. Did she already sense pain and sorrow in utero?

News of Gert's death and Ute's birth arrived simultaneously in Hirschberg. Maria departed on the next train north. Now both grandmothers hovered over the newborn, seldom leaving her side. One splendid, bright morning some weeks later, Maria pushed Ute's pram through a park adjacent to the Köhler residence. Out of nowhere a gypsy appeared and leaned over the pram before Maria could shoo her away. A crooked finger traced a sign in the air above Ute's forehead. "A special child," she crooned, with brows upswept, "a gem," and was gone. Maria later swore that she recognized the gypsy from the Sankt Ivan clan.

10 Pine Trees

Pine trees, evergreen conifers with needle-like foliage, guard the perimeter of the dunes along the Baltic Coast. Tough trees, with roots digging into sandy soil. The sky is a luminous green, spreading over fields of potatoes. In Schlawe (Stawno), not far from Köslin, Gert was born and spent his youth with the arid winds sweeping over rows of earthy furrows.

"If only Gert had lived. What he could have given the next generation," Aenne wiped her eyes. "Oh, this war. This terrible war." Any recollection of her oldest son overwhelmed her. They had been especially close, a bond with Aenne from the tough umbilical cord that had connected them at his birth. "My heart is heavy," she said, "when I think of the terrible waste of a young life. He was endowed with so many talents." Gert seemed to have inherited qualities from both parents. Like his father, he struggled with a volatile temper. Already as a toddler he was throwing toys across the room like missiles. And, from his father he got a sense of fairness in all judgments. He tried to be truthful. He also had a deeply caring side, shared luncheons with impoverished comrades at school and befriended two Russian prisoners whom he quietly brought food. After overhearing an adult conversation about his beloved Aunt Minnie who had fallen on hard times, he secreted part of his weekly allowance onto her nightstand. A romantic fascination with poets like Joseph Eichendorff, sharing his mother's yearnings, slumbered in him. He also confided in his mother when he dated Gerda-Maria. He wrote, "I have got her… I think she is mine," followed by numerous exclamation marks all across the page.

The Köhler house was open to friends and strangers alike. Gert led the school debating team and discussions often continued into the late hours of the night. They argued incessantly about politics, lamented the Versailles Treaty and hoped for a revival of German national pride. They joined a youth movement with its credo of return to nature.

Gert's journal survived the war. For a week he had wandered along the Baltic Coast as a youngster, noting down his impressions:

"I know the Baltic Coast like my own room. I have listened to the sea's boisterous roars and calm murmurs, inhaled the seaweed-scented air, felt the warm sun rippling over my shoulders. I have climbed up and down sand dunes and waded through many inlets and rivulets around little islands, abloom in spring, butterflies everywhere. Sometimes I catch a whiff of the acidic odor from the iodine in the water as the waves wash gently against the beach and the ocean looks like rippled fabric reflecting a blue sky."

Gert recorded two discoveries from his sojourn, a jewel and a dead bird.

Tired, as the sun was beginning to dip along a rose-shaded horizon, he stumbled upon a rare find, an aquamarine-colored shard of amber in the shape of a teardrop. Holding the fossilized jewel up to the waning light, the transparent color turned deep blue and displayed the outline of a petrified leaf in its center. "History is enshrined in this gift from the Sea," Gert wrote, "and my personal life as well. It's a once in a lifetime discovery."

That night Gert slept in a barn, after the kind farmer brought him a jug of warm milk and slices of fresh baked bread. Next morning, in the cool breeze, Gert smoothed his thick brown hair back into shape, rinsed his mouth and splashed his face under a garden pump. He whistled as he left. His notes continued, "I watched several seagulls looping over the dunes in a love dance, wings meeting over their backs. They squealed loudly as I stumbled upon a fallen comrade, gray with black markings on head and wings. When I picked up the lifeless body I noticed a red spot on its beak. It was the sign of a mother bird. I took it with me to be preserved by a taxidermist." Years later the stuffed seagull hung over Ute's crib, its bony claws clutching a leafless branch that was festooned to the wall. Sometimes a piece of chocolate would dangle from its beak.

Like the seagulls Gert loved, he lived in both kingdoms, the air and the sea. He was skilled at sailing the family sailboat. But his proudest accomplishment was building his own glider. He received his glider pilot license when he was eighteen. "Now I can swim and fly," he triumphantly recorded in his journal.

Franz, Gert's best friend, was drafted with Gert. Together they were deployed to France. Maybe Gert had a premonition. He scribbled a note to Gerda-Maria a few days before his death, "Don't cry, my love, if days turn dark. Just know that they have been. That memory will sustain us."

It was Franz who brought the news of Gert's death to the Köhlers.

"We were bivouacked in an abandoned farmhouse. After hearing of France's surrender, we let our guard down and decided to celebrate. Our entire platoon was in a festive mood. There was food stocked in the kitchen of the old farmhouse but not as much liquor in the cupboards as we had hoped. So, Gert and I decided to venture down the lane to a house that looked unoccupied. Maybe some lovely French wine would be waiting for us there. As we traipsed through tall weeds and grass not mowed in many moons, we laughed at everything and nothing, so great was our relief that the capitulation had been swift in coming. Everything was eerily quiet as we entered the dwelling. As we expected, there was no one in sight. Happening upon the cellar steps, we thought that's where the wine would be. Gert descended first, I stumbled after him on the rickety wooden staircase. It was pitch dark. Suddenly I heard a shot. A soldier scrambled out of hiding and up the stairs in my direction. I shot him point blank with my revolver. Gert was sprawled on the foot of the stairs, bleeding profusely. As his breathing ebbed, he said calmly and clearly, 'I was so very happy.' He died in my arms."

Franz buried Gert among the high grasses of a meadow near a bountiful apple orchard. He hastily erected a wooden cross to mark Gert's resting place so far from his beloved homeland.

Aenne wailed and swore, "Death... Death, I can't endure another one." A few weeks later her second son, Eberhard, was killed. Only Klaus, the third son, was still serving at the front and their youngest, Jost-Henrich was in high school.

The situation on the Eastern Front worsened and the Regime announced plans to conscript school-age youngsters. Huddled together around roaring flames in the big brick fireplace of their villa, Aenne and Karl's conversations grew heated and lengthy. Unable to sleep, Aenne wandered the corridor between their upstairs bedrooms. Only the wind rattling the icicles on the eves of the roof picked up her laments, "I have lost a daughter and two sons. I can't lose another child."

They decided to send Jost-Henrich to visit relatives in Sweden for the Christmas break. Jost-Henrich was not thrilled at the thought of spending the holidays away from his friends who were organizing a campout. Besides, he was ready to volunteer in the youth organization which was chosen to serve the Fatherland. Only the prospect that his relatives would be going on an expedition near Uppsala to gather ice samples from frozen springs thawed his reluctance. His parents assured Jost-Henrich that he would be back before the start of his final school semester. On the evening before his departure Karl handed him a fancy camera, "Take pictures. We will be interested in seeing them when you return." Jost-Henrich was momentarily unnerved when at bedtime his mother rumpled his hair a bit longer than usual. He wondered why she dabbed her eyes.

When Jost-Henrich boarded the ship to Stockholm and stood at the railing waving a red-and-white checkered handkerchief, Aenne clutched Karl's arm so forcefully that he winced.

Jost-Henrich was furious when he found out that his parents had sent him off with a one-way ticket. He vowed to find his way home but he spoke no Swedish and had no money. Only years later, after his Swedish relatives had adopted him and he became a citizen, did he thank his parents for saving his life.

In the spring of 1945, prosperous with flowers and budding trees, Aenne and Karl decided to remain in Köslin and not join the swarm of refugees trekking through town. They spoke Polish and believed themselves woven into the local community. But the Russian army made no distinction between ethnic groups. They surrounded the city, set houses on fire, plundered and raped. From their upstairs window the old people watched as marauding troops encircled their neighborhood. But they avoided the mansion, instead attacking their neighbor's house whose residents had long fled. Aenne whispered to Karl, "We are next. To the train station," and slipped out the back door. She made her way along well-known paths, ducking behind bushes when she spotted soldiers. Having arrived at a familiar lake, she felt trapped, being pursued by two men. Aenne was an excellent swimmer. Like a water turtle she dove deep beneath the surface. As she came up for air a sniper bullet grazed her hair but she remained unharmed. Scrambling up the bank on the other side of the lake, she ran until she was lost to the sight of her pursuers. She rested in a thicket until nightfall, then crept toward the train station. The station was empty. In the last months trains seldom rumbled through and escapees had long avoided the dust-covered building.

Karl stood inside the terminal with blankets. Then they saw, hovering in a far corner, their old servant with the ferocious red beard, Jake. He was barefooted, without a jacket. As a coal train was heard whistling in the distance, Karl quickly took off his boots and handed them to Jake. As the train slowed at the station all three jumped aboard.

Aenne and Karl made it to West Germany. At the Mansion Lauterbach in Hessen, home of the brother of Aenne's father, they found shelter.

11 Tree Branches, a Twig

Gerda-Maria's face turned tender whenever she saw her brothers. The trio had remained close. An idyllic childhood had woven a treasured bond around them. Gerda-Maria had moved to Märzdorf, a village not far from Hirschberg. She had found a spacious ground floor apartment in a mansion overlooking the Bober River. There they celebrated festivities and furloughs together. Maria spent as much time there as she did in her own town.

There was a special connection between Gerda-Maria and Hubertus. As children they had played house together, and when Ute was born and Gerda-Maria widowed, Hubertus visited often. He would carry Ute on his shoulders, push her on the swing set under the apple tree and at night sat silently when his sister read bedtime stories. "When this war is over, I want to marry and have children," he told Gerda-Maria.

Hubertus had a classical profile, elongated face with a Romanesque nose. He teased Heio about his stubby nose. Hubertus also had blue eyes, Heio's were brown. But Heio boasted a shock of dark unruly locks while Hubertus's hair was wispy and straight. Hubertus preferred the sea, and Heio was partial to the mountains. Heio was a free spirit, Hubertus formal but on occasion a bemused smile wrinkled his lips. Both brothers were attached to Bielwiese and had made a pact to get the castle back into the Lüttwitz' possession. They wrote to Aunt Vera for assistance and even to their father in Namibia. But Bielwiese remained a future dream.

In 1937 Hubertus stepped on the island of Siekeroog, part of the East Frisian Islands. There he enrolled in the "Insel Schule," guided by the philosophy of Herman Lietz. They were disinclined toward traditional learning and emphasized character development. The holistic educational program suited Hubertus. He was an average student in the classroom but excelled when they explored the outdoors. Hubertus absorbed the essence of the island, salt-laden, whispering sea and rustling grass. He would look out at the North Sea and say, "There are secrets on the horizon with ships, storms and distant islands."

Hubertus was shy but not aloof. He quickly formed friendships. He wrote to Maria that he was excited about the Northern Lights project they were studying. At night a group of boys would be out with their flashlights gazing at the constellation. And then once a year they were fortunate to witness the Northern Lights, the Aurora Borealis which creates vibrant streaks of blue, green, pinks, and violet that dance across the dark expanse above.

At the far end of the island stood a shimmering lighthouse, plastered in white, a beacon for ships. It was Hubertus's favorite destination. He often wandered there by himself and observed the blinking signals, "like a million stars, a brilliant cornucopia." He imagined himself on a vessel far out at sea, beckoned by the lamps of the lighthouse to safe harbor.

When Hubertus was drafted, he requested a secretarial job and was lucky to get assigned to an older officer in Hirschberg. He confessed to Gerda-Maria, "I have no desire to be a soldier, or to defend the Fatherland. I don't want a weapon, and I could not shoot anyone."

Until 1942 he was spared. Then he was sent to the Eastern Front. By sheer luck Hubertus and Heio met at a briefing in Kiev after having been out of touch for weeks. Heio could be recognized by a white lock at the neckline of his dark hair. Hubertus instantly spotted him sitting in the front row of the briefing room. They embraced with a bone-breaking hug. "Stay strong, brother," Heio encouraged, "We HAVE to survive this."

"God must have left before the massacre at Stalingrad," a fellow soldier mumbled as he climbed up the steps to Hubertus's field office. "I knew from the slowness of the boots that something was wrong," Hubertus wrote his mother. With polite deliberation the soldier pushed the door open and blurted out, "Herr Leutnant, we just got a wire, your brother has been shot." Hubertus's hands shook so badly he could hardly steady himself on the desk. "No, No," he wailed, "Not Heio. Heio can't be killed." Hubertus swallowed, "I am not Heio, could never be Heio. But I could live if he had lived."

Overnight wild grief gripped Hubertus. His usual optimism changed to grim depression. There is one picture of him during his last days at the battlefield. He is sitting in front of a tent, hands resting on his knees, staring blankly at the ground. This man, who prided himself on perfect grooming, appears indifferent and disheveled. He used to fold his clothes with orderly precision. Now his uniform jacket is unbuttoned, his shirt hangs out and flutters in the air. His dog tags dangle crooked on his bare chest. A picture of utter dejection.

Swallows fluttered like cupids over the quivering warm May landscape. The earth was melodious with birdsong and blanketed in wildflowers. Bluebells swayed dolefully in the morning breeze when Huberutus emerged from his tent, stretched his arms toward the rising sun, and was instantly felled by a sniper.

Hubertus was buried in a small cemetery in Romny and his remains later moved to memorial burial grounds on the outskirts of Kharkov.

When Maria received the news, her chest heaved with guttural outcries, "Oh my faith! Where was my God when he should have protected my sons?" Another sob shook her.

"If at least one would come back. At least one! Is there a reason to keep living when what I love most is taken from me? They were my sunshine."

Friends and acquaintances came by to comfort Maria but nothing helped, nothing made any sense. She was plunged into the darkness of grief.

From then on, she never participated in New Year's Eve festivities. When asked why, she replied, "It was the last time that I heard from Heio."

12 Stalingrad

The city of Stalingrad was destroyed during World War II and rebuilt as Volgograd in the gray cement-block style of the Stalinist era. On a high hill above the city a statue of Mother Russia, a massive woman with outstretched arms, one hand menacingly wielding a sword, towers over town and country beyond. Martial music booms out over loudspeakers from behind rocks and concrete battle scenes, as haunting as Wagnerian Valkyries. Up steep steps, next to numerous fountains, stands another female figure carved in stone, cradling a wounded soldier in her arms. Both images, might and fight as well as caring and comfort, are embodied in these enormous figures.

Rossoschka, a military cemetery, lies just outside the city. Eleven and a half million Germans and Russians from World War II are buried there. "Bones from both sides mingle," a guard tells visitors. A nine-foot-high wall encircles the resting place. Huge granite blocks with names and dates in black lettering stand all around in a circle and in an adjacent open field. To find a name one has to stand on tiptoes.

With an index finger Heio's name can be traced along a deep dark groove on a burning hot stone in summer and on an ice-caked stone in winter.

Hitler had been under the illusion that General Paulus's Sixth Army, in which Heio served, could prevail over the Russian Army. The German troops had entered the city of Stalingrad without much resistance. They had no knowledge of the Soviet commander Marshal Zhukov's tactical brilliance and determination to defeat the Germans. The Marshall shrewdly planned to wait out the Germans. The Sixth battalion set up camp at Baburkin about an hour away from the city. A deep riverbed was the demarcation line. Beyond a ragged gorge the two sides faced each other during the final confrontation. In the late summer of 1942, the Germans encountered a dry season on the steppe and were confident to win. By the time the Russian winter arrived with subzero temperatures, the troops were surrounded by Russian tank divisions with no escapes. The encirclement became known as the "Kessel von Stalingrad." The Germans lacked warm clothing, food was running out, and their supply lines were cut. Even then Hitler bellowed to his high command that Paulus had to hold the position under all circumstances and at all costs. Paulus was secure in his cemented bunker. Who knows if he ever reflected on the number of young men that would be killed and the sorrow he caused at home. Only after the total defeat of the Sixth Army in February 1943, did Paulus finally surrender.

Heio's last letter to Maria was from Baburkin, dated New Year's Eve 1942. *"Nobody will come out of this hellhole alive. Only the memory of my idyllic childhood keeps me sane."* Then through the freezing fog of nightmares past, Heio's voice echoed: *"I am snuggly dug into a foxhole but I can no longer feel my feet. I wrapped my boots in burlap before leaving the tent. My fingers are pressed around the gun barrel. They too are numb. I wonder if I can even pull the trigger. Gerda-Maria sent knitted woolen mittens. She must have patterned them after her own hands because they barely fit over mine. I like them though. They are sky blue, not the usual mouse gray color. It's snowing softly. The flakes seem to multiply as I stare into the powdery veil. Am I in a trance? The night stretches on and I whistle to Helmut who is in the hole nearest to mine. No answer. He must have fallen asleep. I need to wake him. I whistle again and then swallow several times. My mouth is dry but I can almost taste the snow soup we had on New Year's Eve, which was seasoned with the last of our horse flesh. The snowflakes look like froth on the broth.'*

'There! The first sunrays. They glide over the glaring surface and light up the nebulous haze. I have no sensation in my legs or arms. I don't want to freeze. It's quiet at Helmut's hideout and I can only just spot his helmet sticking up. No movement. Without the cover of darkness, I am not allowed to whistle. My eyelashes are stuck together. I can hardly make out the shapes creeping toward us. Huge turtles with feelers. Suddenly I hear crunching. These monsters are driving over our foxholes. I want to scream at them. Stop! Could this be Russian tanks? Why am I suddenly afraid? There must be a way to escape this moving menace. Why do I feel like laughing? I see Gerda-Maria and Hubertus and Opapa. We decorated his toilet with garlands of ivy! We got a spanking! Now we are holding our painful behinds. I can't stop laughing. I must drop my weapon and raise my arms to greet the glorious morning."

Baburkin was burned down and never rebuilt. In the spring of 1945, the snow thawed and left a field of bodies. Bones were strewn across blooming meadows. The area is forbidden to travelers without a special permit.

The thick grass blades swayed and the wind blew in from all directions. Dry bones began to jostle and rattle with Ezekiel's prophecy. The prophet saw before his inner eyes, bones growing layers of sinew, and flesh connecting to bones and skin again covering muscles. Then an army of men rose with shrill moans and loud howls like the lone wolves who patrol the tundra on bitter cold nights.

Skulls, fingers, feet, all weathered but not gone. Over a lifetime the sands have swept through the looming grass, covering and uncovering the remains as once the snow had carpeted the footprints left by terror.

13 He's My Brother

That was only prologue.
When books are burned,
eventually people will be
burned as well.
    Heinrich Heine 1820

The autumn air had deepened and thick mist was drifting through the Swiss valley near Lausanne. Biting winds whipped over the mountains. Madame Cécile, a slender woman, wearing tan slacks and a blue mohair sweater, her gray hair pulled back into a chignon, sat on a flower-patterned sofa in her oak-paneled study. A sturdy cardboard box stood next to her. It was crammed with loose photos, family pictures, landscape shots and vacation mementoes. A fire crackled in the large stone fireplace.

Cécile's former teacher, Dr. Bondy, was visiting from America. With bushy white hair and a mustache, he bore a certain likeness to Mark Twain, but he had shrunk in stature since they last met years ago. He rocked calmly in his chair, his eyes sharply focused on Cécile. Under his steady gaze she felt like the shy student who had been dazzled by his lectures and intimidated by his kind but demanding demeanor. Dr. Bondy had come to assemble a collection of stories and articles about his former school at Marienau and Gland and its pupils.

As they talked, Cécile's small hands rifled through a pile of photographs. With squirrel-like dexterity she picked up one picture, then another, discarding them until her face twitched with recognition. "Here," she whispered.

Dr. Bondy reached for the photo and studied it at arm's length. Then, uncharacteristically emotional, he said, "Oh, I remember Heio well. It seems like only yesterday. But it happened so long ago."

Dr. Bondy began to reminisce. "Following the 1933 book burning on the Bebelplatz at Humboldt University my worries about the National Socialist regime mounted. I considered accepting an offer to found a new school here near Lausanne, but I could not bring myself to leave my beloved school at Marienau."

"What made you change your mind?" Cécile interjected.

"It was not that I changed my mind. I waited too long and the Nazis closed me down." Dr. Bondy then recalled an incident from Marienau where Heio was a student. "It was a few days before the Kristallnacht in 1938. My school was already under strict surveillance and controlled by

Nazi officers who patrolled the grounds at all times, inspecting dorms and classrooms without warning. I was standing at the window of my study watching students cross the lawn from the refectory to the classrooms. I saw an SS officer approach Jacob Bernstein who had a fearful shuffling gait since his father had been roughed up by a gang shouting antisemitic slurs. The SS officer grabbed Jacob by the sleeve and shoved him to the side where he stumbled and fell. Heio was a few steps behind him and ran to the boy's side. He lifted him up, brushed off his jacket and straightened his cap before escorting him to the front door of the school. But before Heio himself could enter, the SS officer barred his way and turned on him menacingly, "*Judenfreund, eh?*"

With his disarming smile Heio replied, "I am Baron von Lüttwitz, officer, and this is my brother." The SS officer hesitated a few moments and then walked away.

"It's curious, don't you think that the officer let the matter lie?" Cécile asked.

"Yes and no," Dr. Bondy explained. "The officer had been around for weeks, observing the students. He knew who Heio was. The Nazis both loathed and admired aristocrats and still handled them with kid gloves in those days."

In the wake of this incident Dr. Bondy contacted Maria and asked permission for Heio to join him in establishing a new school in Switzerland. "I recognized Heio as a born leader with a sunny disposition and compassion for others. He was always eager to help but never ingratiating. And so it happened that Heio came to Switzerland to attend the same school as you, Cécile, and your brother, Louis."

Cécile's cheeks flushed as she broke in, "Heio was in Louis's class and he became a frequent guest in our house. My parents sometimes interrupted our adolescent conversations with their worries about what was happening in Germany. But we were young and optimistic about life. My parents opened their mountain chalet to us and our friends. That hide-out in the Alps became one of Heio's favorite places. There he was always full of vitality and good humor."

Dr. Bondy had been listening attentively. "Were there ever signs of change in his mood?"

"Not at first when he made regular visits back to Germany. But then his brother-in-law was killed in France and he seemed distracted and gloomy. It was when his older brother, Hubertus, who was not cut out to be a soldier, was drafted that Heio began to question his remote stay with us."

Dr. Bondy wrung his hands. "I remember a conversation with Heio. I knew how he wrestled with qualms of conscience. I too was struggling at the time. Switzerland was no longer safe for me and my family and offers from America had arrived. I implored Heio to emigrate with me to America, but he would not hear of it. He sank deeper into mulling over his own conflicts. One day he appeared in my office, plopped into a chair and leaned forward so I could not see his face. Finally, he spoke. 'Hubertus is my brother. I need to be with him. Staying in Switzerland or going to America would mean abandoning him.' I usually kept my distance from students but at that moment I rose and hugged him. We knew it was a forever farewell."

Cécile was in tears. "We all tried. My parents even tempted Heio by holding out the possibility that he could join the Nestlé firm. We reminded him that he would be drafted as soon as he crossed the border but he only shook his head. 'I must go, Cécile. I simply must.' We had only a single weekend together before his departure."

"Tell me your story, Cécile. How did you relate to Heio? I know this is a personal request and I usually don't pry but under the circumstances I would like to hear it.

Cécile let the moment pass, then took a long breath in and out and began. "Heio and I were comfortable around each other, and silences were a natural part of our relationship. But sadness hovered between us as we hiked up to my parents' chalet without uttering a single word. In late summer our forest teems with delicious blueberries, and bluebells sway in the clear balmy breeze in the meadows. The days are pleasant and the nights refreshingly cool, often crisp enough for a fire in the cast-iron stove. Heio was splitting wood for the evening fire when I snapped this last picture of him, shirtless, his blond hair tousled, an ax swinging high above an upturned block of wood. In retrospect an awful omen, but at the time I could only admire the well-sculpted body of my first love. After a simple supper with milk from the fat meadow cows, bowls filled to the brim with blueberries we had picked in the afternoon, and crusty brown bread with Swiss cheese, Heio brought a bottle of red wine to the steps of the chalet. As we sipped the wine, bells from the village below began to peal. Like wedding bells, I remember thinking. We listened and held each other tight until the sounds no longer echoed through the mountains and night enveloped us."

The story ended with the fateful return to Germany. As predicted, Heio was captured at the border. Shortly thereafter he was dispatched to Stalingrad. Heio never lost his sense of humor. He was put in charge of a small group of fellow soldiers who were commanded to march to national military songs. Heio instructed his men only to sing love songs, starting with "Lili Marleen."

Evening dimmed the study. Cécile meandered over to the fireplace. Dr. Bondy too stood up and stepped to her side, gently placing a hand on her shoulder.

"Thank you, my dear, for this painful, beautiful look back. May I borrow this photo? I promise to return it to you with a copy of the book."

And with that the old teacher took his leave.

14 A Yellow Flower

In the spring of 1944, the fresh grass in the meadows around Märzdorf was interspersed with cornflowers and poppies. Bright yellow, the joyful faces of the dandelions mirrored the sun.

The dandelion, queen among flowers, has special healing powers. It is a companion flower, which attracts pollination, brings up multiple nutrients and vitamins, but can also produce without pollination, resulting in offspring identical to the parent plant.

Ute, lifting the hem of her blue Dirndl skirt, leaped through the high grass, dew brushing her bare legs. "Omi, let's see the newborn lambs. Can you hear them calling?" Maria's granddaughter was the answer to her lament, "what is there to live for?"

"Another child has been given to me," she mused, and "I am learning to live again. She is a buoyant child, a delight to my weary eyes and aching heart."

Most dandelions were in early bloom and Ute picked them out from among all the bountiful flowers. Maria braided them into a wreath crowning the little girl's head. "Look Omi," Ute held on to a dandelion with a swaying head. A few seeds, fine as threads had already loosened from their stems. They flew through the air. "This one already has gray hair like you." Ute began to blow and tiny kites were carried away by the breeze. "What do you wish for?" Maria asked.

Ute's face wrinkled into a frown, "That you and Mama never cry again."

Maria pulled Ute close. "My Seelchen, if only your wish can be granted."

The horrors of war arrived at Märzdorf as faraway stories, like hearing of a shipwreck at sea. Atrocities seemed remote. Everyday lives in the village were consumed by other worries. Most able-bodied men were drafted. Cars owned by civilians were requisitioned. Even horses were taken away from fieldwork and transported to the troops in the East. Food was in short supply. The widowed Gerda-Maria was a much sought after guest, and men came courting her. During Gerda-Maria's absences Maria took care of Ute and their bond tightened.

Maria placed the dandelions Ute had gathered into a bowl filled with water and turned the bowl so that the sun through the window could light up the blossoms, glittering like gold. "Do you know," Maria asked Ute, "that dandelion in French 'dent-de-lion' means lion's tooth?" Ute shook her head. "Let's visit a real lion at the Breslau (Wroclaw) zoo," Maria suggested. Ute jumped up and down in response, clapping her hands.

Maria believed that animals attacked when hungry or threatened or smelling fear. She told Ute the story of "Daniel in the Lion's Den," and that he was not devoured because he faced great danger without fear.

On a warm June Sunday morning Maria took Ute to the zoo. There were birds chirping in the bushes and monkeys scampering from tree branch to tree branch. Ute was decked out in a sky-blue chiffon dress, a white bow clipped into her blond braids. Her mood was as chipper as her outfit. Maria hummed for the first time since she had dried her tears. Ute slipped her hand from Omi Maria's and skipped along the pebbled path, eager to meet as many animals as possible. On a secluded slope studded with crabgrass and a few stony cliffs, they spotted a lion. His mane and coat were tattered and dark brown lashes marked his closed eyelids. He was stretched out along a chain-link fence, resting his heavy head on his tawny paws. Few barriers separated visitors from the wild beasts. There was no high fence to climb, nor a ditch to cross. It was easy to reach through the meshes of the fence. Ute did just that and tenderly touched the lion's right ear which flopped across his cheek. "The ear feels so soft, like velvet," Ute cooed to the lion and called him "Liebe grosse Mietze Katze." (Big sweet Pussy Cat) Maria stood behind Ute and watched. Only when a woman passing by screamed, "Child, get your hand out of there," did Maria pull Ute back. The commotion must have roused the lion. He shook his head as if to swat away a fly and yawned. "May I touch him again?" Ute asked. "Another time," Maria answered and they ambled on in buoyant spirits. "We have many more animal friends to greet," Maria suggested.

That night Maria indulged herself with two glasses of wine, dandelion wine, the best for keeping the liver healthy.

Gerda-Maria met Count Fritz von Hardenberg, only son of rich landowners who had adopted him as a baby. The entire county of Seidorf (Sosnowka) in Southern Silesia lay in his domain. He was also a military man and their nuptials had to be fit into his furloughs. If the wedding to Gert had been celebrated in a civil service attended by a few friends, the entire neighboring nobility was present at the church when Gerda-Maria, veiled in a plume of white lace, walked down the aisle. "Stunning," people whispered, and, "how young." From the moment Gerda-Maria had said "Yes" to the Count's marriage proposal, she felt the born Countess. She confessed that Gert was the love of her life "if only he had not been a commoner." Since her childhood in Bielwiese she had been singled out for her beauty and noble bearing. Being a Countess was her signature.

Ute begrudged Fritz the time he spent with Gerda-Maria. There were now fewer snuggling hours for mother and daughter. After the wedding the newlyweds departed for their honeymoon. Ute rebelled. She had resented being a flower girl. Following the ceremony, she could not be found. She crawled into a hiding spot in a thorny thicket next to the church. There she sat, sucking her thumb. Only Maria's gentle coaxing could bring her out. An aunt took the child to her home for the night where Ute refused to eat or speak. When Maria came to pick her up the next morning, Ute would not let herself be hugged. She stiffened and wiggled out of Maria's embrace.

Maria was inventive. She knew of Ute's love for animals, great and small. She suggested that Ute think of something special to strengthen her relationship with her stepfather. Ute believed that all people liked animals. She had an idea. Gerda-Maria had given her a book about snails. She learned that snails close their doors in the fall against the cold with a membrane made of calcium carbonate and protein. They are survivors, knowing when to retreat and when to advance, probing, testing, learning. She now remembered her little companions and sought comfort in their presence. In wet grass under a drooping lilac bush Ute had built snail huts with moss and sticks. Carefully, she lifted one snail from its habitat and let it crawl across her hand, along her arm, leaving its silvery mucus trail. Its raspy tongue cut into a grass blade Ute provided. When Ute touched an antenna with its pinprick eye, the feeler retracted, only to reappear when she pulled away. She counted the whorls on its house. This one was very young, having only five rings. Ute decided to fill a jar with her most remarkable snails and bring them to the house.

Fritz had not intruded into the management of the household. He left it up to Gerda-Maria to redecorate their home. Gerda-Maria could make a room take on unexpected beauty merely by adding another picture. She only cleared the spacious front parlor and bought Fritz a massive oak desk where his maps lay strewn about among stacks of papers. Otherwise, the house had not changed its appearance.

Once when her stepfather was absent, Ute sneaked into his office and opened her jar. She let her creatures march like soldiers over the map of Europe which Fritz had been tracing with red and blue markers. A web of glossy paths soon crisscrossed the entirety of Central Europe.

To his credit Fritz did not scold Ute when he resumed his work but sternly instructed her, "snails are not pets." Dutifully, Ute collected her charges, dropping them back into the jar. She tolerated Fritz but never warmed to his strait-laced persona. She was not aware that he had launched an adoption process.

Nazi Germany required girls to do a year of community service. Frieda, who was sixteen, lived with her family in the village. She helped her parents with chores. They owned a plot of land which they plowed with an ox, and they kept dogs, cats and poultry galore. In 1941 Frieda had been summoned as Ute's nanny. Gerda-Maria had insisted that she was perfectly capable of taking care of her baby and that there was no need for a nanny. They already employed servants, a cleaner, a cook and gardeners. But she was overruled.

Frieda cried when she was ordered to appear at the house, and her eyes remained puffy and red when she arrived in the mornings. She kept several handkerchiefs in her apron pockets and blew into them all the time as if she had a cold. Ute, who could not pronounce her name, called her Deeda.

The two bonded over stuffed animals that filled the nursery. They crouched on the floor pretending to be cats or other fuzzy toy friends.

The Nazis were not fond of churches, but many villagers went to the local Catholic church on Sundays where as soon as Ute could walk, Deeda took her to services. The front pews were reserved for church's patrons. Deeda claimed the seats, with Ute quietly at her side. Deeda's mother was a skilled seamstress. She sewed gorgeous embroidered dresses for Ute, "our adorable little princess," as Deeda soon called her. Parishioners admired them as they walked the long church aisle to their assigned places. Deeda had brushed Ute's curls with care and perseverance and pinned pink or white bows into her hair.

Deeda was extremely bashful and always wore an apron with a flounce of gauze. When Gerda-Maria invited her to the summer cottage at the Baltic Sea, Aenne had to cajole her to momentarily take off her apron for a splash in the ocean. Frieda could not swim. She stood knee deep in the shallow waters and anxiously watched Ute who rolled in the sand and squealed when a wave washed over her.

Ute and Deeda shared a secret. One day after church Deeda took Ute to the fairgrounds. They admired the carved wooden horses on the merry-go-round. Ute mounted a brilliant black stallion with a flowing mane. During the dizzying rounds Ute got sick and threw up all over her new spring-green dress with countless stitched flowers. Deeda grabbed her up and rushed to a nearby brook, stripped off the dress and washed it in the gurgling flow. After the dress had dried in the sun, Deeda put it back on. The pair ambled home singing hymns. Nobody was the wiser.

When the family prepared to flee the Russian army, Deeda wanted to go with them. Instead, she stayed behind with her ailing parents. As she kissed Ute on the cheek and hugged Gerda-Maria goodbye, she sobbed, "The years in your household were the most joyful ones I have ever had. And how I love that sweet little thing."

No one knew that Frieda would one day play a major role in their lives.

15 The Trek

Rustic brown shadows hovered over the fields in the fall of 1944, prophesying a severe winter. Wild geese flew south ahead of schedule, and squirrels hoarded their nuts weeks early. The cats' fur grew thick and the oak tree branches shriveled before their time.

Christmas was celebrated in the parlor with a tall fir tree glowing with dripping wax candles. Jubilantly, Ute exclaimed, "Are the angels bringing us all this light?"

Maria, Gerda-Maria, Frieda and a remaining servant haltingly sang the traditional songs. There was no news from Fritz from the front. Frieda managed to prepare a goose leg with red cabbage and for dessert, berries from the summer harvest. It snowed continuously as wagon after wagon drove by the mansion, loaded with haggard, weary refugees. Gerda-Maria had emptied the floors of the house of rugs and Frieda had pulled curtains from their rods, handing them to strangers for warmth. Seeing all the misery, Gerda-Maria was determined to stay put.

Two months later the local priest arrived under cover of darkness. "Countess, you have to leave. Neighboring villages are going up in flames, countless rapes are reported and tomorrow the bridge over the Bober River will be detonated to slow the advance of Russian troops."

The women had one night to pack. How could they pack their entire lives into a suitcase? Silver cutlery and fine china were ignored, as were spring and summer wear. Albums with photos and letters from loved ones were stacked into a small wooden chest, painted with Silesian wildflowers. Portraits of ancestors were removed from gilded frames and added to the pile. Last, Ute's teddy bear was stuffed under the lid. While Ute slept in her eiderdown bed Gerda-Maria sowed jewelry into the hems of their coats.

In February 1945 they abandoned everything that was dear to them, trekking westward. It was bitterly cold and a full moon shone through the fir tree branches, swaying a ghostly goodbye. Bright moonbeams halted directly over the gable atop the house, promising protection.

After locking the portal to the mansion with a heavy set of brass keys, Gerda-Maria threw the bundle into a snow pile. Maria pressed her forehead against the doorpost, tears streaming down her cheeks. Ute clutched her furry coat sleeve. A horse-drawn wagon drove the three to the Hirschberg railway station where they were hoisted aboard a train carrying wounded soldiers. It was Gerda-Maria's nursing credentials that saved their lives. They would have frozen on the icy platform along with hundreds of others who were desperately waiting for transport.

Inside a cramped compartment a horrific sight confronted them. Death exposed its ugly brutality for the first time, not disguised as in picture books but for real. A sea of bandaged and moaning soldiers lay in bunk beds in the dim light. The air was stuffy and foul smelling. Maria and Ute were shunted into something resembling a lawn chair. "An enormous moving casket filled with death," Maria murmured. Gerda-Maria was whisked away, to dress and clean wounds, give injections and comfort the dying.

"Let's go home," Ute begged, "I don't like it here." She gagged on the watery soup for supper. The open latrine, located next to the buffers between train cars, was a stink hole. Maria held Ute above it, and buried her nose in her crochet shawl. "What if we fall in," Ute whimpered.

Some experiences were etched into their souls. During the second night they were shaken from dozing by an ear-piercing cry, "Mutti! Help me." A wounded soldier started to thrash, tearing his sheets and throwing them off. A nurse hurried to his side and pushed a needle into his arm, quieting him down. The locomotive hooted loudly and the train slowed to a crawl.

From the safe perch on Maria's lap Ute watched as several orderlies moved from bunk to bunk, wrapping motionless bodies into soiled sheets and knotting the ends together. Blinds sprang up and windows were pushed down. Two men grabbed the ends of each sheet, lifted it high and then...one...two...three...the bundle was heaved through the window. They repeated that frightful spectacle along the corridor. Then the windows were closed again, blinds lowered, and darkness descended into the carriage, illuminated only by dangling light bulbs.

Horrified Ute asked, "What are they doing?"

"They are taking the soldiers to a place to sleep."

"Where though?"

"In the soft snow."

Bunks had emptied and an exhausted Maria collapsed on a stripped mattress. She coaxed Ute to lie next to her. But Ute kicked and screamed, "Never... Ever..." and no pleading nor a spanking could persuade her. Ute stayed crouched on the floor beside the bed, reaching for Maria's hand, holding on for dear life.

The following day Maria had a premonition and urged them to get off. Gerda-Maria objected, "I would feel negligent leaving my duties." Her conscience gnawed at her, but when the train stopped to take on coal, she too stepped down.

A desolate icy landscape stared at them. They trudged to a deserted barrack and pushed through the wooden slats into a bare room. A bleak winter sun streamed through the dusty windows. Specks of snow had settled on their faces and the frost penetrated their thick fur coats. Suddenly a man burst through the door. "The train just took a direct hit in the tunnel near our fields. Everything exploded in fire and smoke. I was just checking for survivors. You must be it." He lifted Ute up and marched toward his ox-drawn wagon, Maria and Gerda-Maria stumbling after him. A light from a farmhouse signaled rescue. An ample-bodied woman came to the wagon and helped them into a warm inside.

After a bath in a copper tub next to a wood-burning stove Ute spooned a nourishing soup. There she spied a stuffed black cat on a shelf across the table. Spellbound, she looked and as if in a trance the cat took the shape of her favorite calico at home. Ute believed that the cat must have followed them here. Her eyes sparkled with excitement. She was still ogling the cat when the farmer's wife asked, "Would you like the cat for the night?"

"Oh yes," Ute sighed.

Tucked under the cover of a blue-striped featherbed the cat snuggled in the crook of Ute's left arm. She pressed the soft toy so tight that their faces touched and she kissed its tiny pink nose. Falling into a restful slumber, Ute was the happiest four-year-old in this windblown land.

Morning broke bright and sunny. Ute rushed into the kitchen where Maria and Gerda-Maria were sipping tea, making ready for the trek ahead. Hot chocolate was waiting for Ute. But she had only one thought, "Where is my cat?"

A furtive look passed between the women. "The cat was only yours for the night," the farmer's wife said with an edge in her voice.

"Oh no," Ute protested. "It is mine. It loves me."

The wife was no longer friendly. Sternly she replied, "The cat belongs to my son who is fighting at the front."

Ute broke in, pleading, "I can tell your son. He will understand. The cat wants to be with me. It said so last night."

"I lent you the cat for one night, you ungrateful brat." She turned to Maria and Gerda-Maria. "Get out of my house."

Ute was rigid with disappointment and could not stop crying, even when the farmer swaddled her in her winter wear and carried her to the wagon. Ute refused to shake hands with him. For a moment she regretted having pushed away the hot chocolate. Overwhelmed by hunger and thirst, she nestled next to Maria, "The cat is mine. It slept with me," she sobbed.

Maria stroked her hair and hummed a sweet folk song, "*Es geht alles vorüber, es geht alles vorbei...*" (everything passes, this too will end), as the cart rumbled over frozen ruts toward the promise of the West.

16 The Owl

They traveled through Bavaria to Hessen, to the bombed-out city of Kassel. The estate Mittelhof was their destination. They were taken in by pre-war friends along with countless other refugees. Amazing how so many strangers could exist peaceably under one roof. Maybe the war had left no energy for quarrels.

The lady of the mansion, Frau von Heissen, ran the household and ordered its newcomers about like a sergeant. Tasks were divided, meals eaten in shifts and in the evenings, everyone was required to attend a reading or vocal performance in the former library. Because everything lay in ruins, fieldwork was mandatory, digging up potatoes and harvesting beets and carrots. The children were assigned in groups to gather dandelions, nettles and sorrel for salads. Under trees that had not been felled for firewood they searched for nutritious beechnuts to be shelled. They learned about the edible porcini and chanterelle mushrooms and to avoid the poisonous toadstool, so attractive in its red cap with white dots. They ran along the railroad tracks to find elderberries to be pressed into soup with teaspoon-sized wheat dumplings swimming on top.

Ute's stubbornness broke through. She disliked Herr von Heissen, a stern veteran trained in the Prussian military. It was customary in German households at the time to shake hands. Every morning the host had the children line up and greet him and his wife with a "Guten Morgen" and a handshake. Ute hid her hands behind her back and refused to shake hands with him. Infuriated by the snotty attitude, he ordered Ute to stand aside while all the other children ate breakfast. Later Omi Maria sneaked Ute a piece of bread and an apple.

More refugees arrived with their horror stories. Soldiers returned home, maimed and shellshocked. They brought news from the front and the end of the war. When a death was reported the children were barred from the "mourning room." One adult after another, clutching handkerchiefs, would enter, stay a while, then come out, wet eyes, quietly shutting the door behind them. An older girl whispered, "They are reading a notice that someone has been killed."

Reinhardt, brother of Fritz, brought Gerda-Maria a message that her second husband had been shot down in an air transport. Gerda-Maria left the mourning room, stumbled across the garden path, through a gate into the open field. She returned late that evening, went to her room without looking at or speaking to anyone. Maria had been present when Gerda-Maria was told the tragic news. She hugged her. "My poor girl," she sniffled, then left to find Ute. While most refugees were housed in the big mansion, Maria had been assigned an attic room in a worker's cottage.

It was not long before Gerda-Maria sought comfort in Reinhardt's arms. Weeks later, she began vomiting in the fields where they picked yellow bugs off potato leaves. "Oh no, we don't need this," Maria sighed. Gerda-Maria was shunned by other women for "letting herself go." The situation was so full of animosity that Reinhardt decided to leave with Gerda-Maria and find work in a village called Linden, near the city of Wolfenbüttel where he had distant relatives. Ute would stay with Maria until they were settled.

When in later years Ute recalled the weeks with her Omi Maria, she christened them "Owl Paradise," the happiest times of her childhood. At the end of each day Maria usually drank a cup of tea, brewed with catnip, linden blossoms or fennel. She recommended tea for every ailment, including sadness. "Tea drowns our sorrows, calms the senses," she advised. After the tea ritual Maria urged a walk. Ute asked, "Why do we go on walks just before dark?" "Because during twilight hours we see things we miss in the light of day." So they strolled as the surroundings grew into shadows and the countryside blurred. Their destination led them past a high-steepled church, a broken-down barn, a pasture encircled by a peeling white fence. At the ruins of a former monastery, they sat down on a low stone wall and looked at the hollow windows, the blackened remains of arches above. The moon sent pearls of light down on them and the enfolding darkness stirred Omi Maria's stories. She talked of things which no longer existed, of people no longer around. But she also spun imaginary stories from the present and here the mysterious owl came alive.

A silky, soft-plumaged owl started to fly over their heads when they sat very still. They could distinguish the beat of its wings from the rustling of trees. It's lamenting cry cut through the grayness as it swooped down on a scurrying mouse or a motionless lizard. On rare evenings they could spy an owl with its yellow eyes, perched on a branch, immobile as a statue, only slightly swiveling its head. Omi Maria called its keen sense of hearing and sharp eyesight, "owl wisdom." Ute imitated its sound, "Kiwitt." Together they pronounced it faster and faster, "Kiwit, kiwit," so close to "*Komm mit, komm mit,* come with me."

Ute had heard that the screeching of an owl announces a death. She asked Omi Maria if that was true. "It's superstition, child. Just the opposite is the case. The owl accompanies us, gently imparting knowledge and insight, leading the way, flying in front as our destiny. Owls are symbols with supernatural powers. In our imagination owls can inhabit people."

A featherbed was a comfort and a hideout. Snuggling deep into its thickness, the cold and fears of the night vanished. Ute tucked her feet against Omi Maria's thighs and wiggled into the hollow of an arm. Omi

Maria's body shielded Ute with the softness of age. Like a fledgling, Ute slept undisturbed long after Omi Maria had slipped out of bed. Upon waking Ute heard her bustling about. She would stay motionless and watch with childlike pleasure.

In the cold morning hours, Omi Maria crossed in front of the window panes iced like glazed glass, started a peat moss fire, then poured gooey syrup over watery oatmeal. The evening before Ute had been handed a wooden ladle to help stir boiling sugar beets down to molasses. That had been their dinner, and now it was their breakfast too.

There was no running water. Omi Maria pumped water from a well and carried it up to the room by the bucket full. Power lines were down from the Allied bombings, but they had candles. Ute felt snug in this nest with its unhurried evenings. She begged for tales about owls and wanted them repeated over and over again. The stories lulled Ute to sleep like fantastic falling stars. It was impossible to tell where the stories left off and dreams began.

When Gerda-Maria and Reinhardt found lodging, it was time for Ute to be reunited with them. Omi Maria did not want to let Ute go. She grimaced at the thought and began to grind her teeth. They had found contentment amidst chaos and tragedy. But there was no arguing against Gerda-Maria's wish to have her daughter back. Omi Maria tried to soften the departure for Ute by forecasting a wonderful family life in Linden. But Ute squeezed her little fists into balls and announced, "I won't go. I like it here."

Omi Maria made preparations for a journey south. She packed two backpacks, one small, the other one large enough for necessary provisions and a thermos of water. Few trains were running. They walked a lot and had to rely on helpful farmers to give them a lift in their carts. At the edge of a village a sign pointed to a community shelter. It was getting dark as they spotted a grass-covered mound which resembled an underground icehouse. Foreseeing that there would be no toilets in the shelter, Omi Maria urged them to relieve themselves behind a bush.

As they entered the bowel of this well-constructed bunker, cold damp blasts engulfed them. It smelled of earth. The steps were slippery. They heard a chorus of voices but shapes were barely discernable. Only as their eyes adjusted did they realize how crowded the shelter was. From one end to the other people were squeezed together. A small pot-bellied pipe stove stood in the middle of the floor which gave out little light and even less warmth. The fumes made Omi Maria cough. The candlelight drew circles and swirls on the ceiling. Omi Maria spied an empty corner where they unrolled their brown horse blanket. They did not shed a single piece of clothing but bedded down, curling up, body to body. Their breath mingled and Omi Maria's arms encircled the child. Suddenly Ute began to shiver.

"There are monsters," she pointed to a black shovel and a huge spiky rake leaning against the wall. A spider web swung back and forth, entrapping the tools. "We need to flee right away," Ute whispered but Omi Maria pulled her closer and cooed, "No monsters. You are safe with me."

They had arranged a meeting place between Kassel and Linden. Reinhardt was waiting with a horse-drawn wagon. Ute flung her arms around Omi Maria's neck, "What can we do about our tears, Omi?"

Silence lingered, "Think of our owl when you are sad. It will fly with us and around us." Ute wrinkled up her nose, not knowing how that could work.

17 Rubble

Spring eased in as warm as a lagoon, with trees leafing out and meadows starred with anemones as Ute arrived in Linden. She had no eyes for the budding beauty. She was happy to hug her mother but shuddered at the sight of the drab cottage, one large room with bare walls, two beds, a stove, washbasin and an outdoor toilet. Gerda-Maria had divided the space with flowered fabric for some privacy, and a vase with daffodils decorated the table, surrounded by four straight-back chairs. She had washed the single windowpane and scrubbed the floor planks until her fingers were raw. She had set traps for rats that had the run of the place at night. "I'm doing my best. We'll get some pictures," she consoled Ute.

It took some getting used to Reinhardt. He resembled Fritz in looks, both slight with straight chestnut hair, clear gray eyes and taut skin on freckled faces. But they embodied quite different personalities. Reinhardt was a chameleon. He could be charming, even generous but also had a cruel temperament. He spent his youth in the war and was ready for a new life, not a family. "Come on, little shit," he greeted Ute. "If I'm going to have to put up with you, you have to help me make ends meet."

Ute was no longer a toddler but a girl of five-and-a half. She became a thief, a food thief with Reinhardt as instructor, she the eager pupil.

It started with raids on coal trains. On the outskirts of the village, the loud-squeaking trains had to slow down and were often halted by a red and white signal before moving onto a single track leading into the main station. Whenever a coal train stopped, the word spread like wildfire from house to house. "Coal train...coal train...." Reinhardt would sprint away carrying burlap sacks. He would climb aboard a coal wagon and throw coal down in Ute's direction, using his hands like huge shovels. They gathered the chunks as fast as they could, filling the sacks and dragging them home. They had to wait for nightfall before they could empty the loot down a chute into the cellar. Once in a while a policeman caught them and confiscated the coal. "He'll keep every bit for himself," grumbled Reinhardt. "You can't tell me he hands them over to the authorities."

Fields were forbidden targets but they did their best there. Ute climbed on a fencepost to survey the terrain before giving an "all clear" to Reinhardt. Sometimes they stuffed their own mouths so full of berries that they looked like chipmunks.

Reinhardt kept his prize possession, a rusty, rattling bicycle with crooked handlebars and no lights in a broken-down shed. Bakeries had begun to reopen. As before the war, shopkeepers set out their goods in large baskets. Early mornings, Ute would straddle the handlebars as Reinhardt pedaled to a corner bakery. Ute would slip down, reconnoiter the area, then bolt past the store as quickly as a weasel, grabbing a fresh roll or two without missing a step. She would run to the end of the street where Reinhardt would swing her back onto the handlebars. Because the shopkeepers were quick to shout for the police or chase them with a broom, they pulled this trick only occasionally.

Like the fox in the fairytale, they often raided chicken coops for eggs. When they were extra lucky, they would catch a squawking hen or duck.

Slaughtered pigs were strung up by their hind feet in the open entrance of a barn and sliced down the middle. Blood was gathered in a pail, vital organs were carefully removed and chunks of meat gingerly carved from the body, each worth its weight in gold. Ute hated the sight of a dead pig and usually looked away. But she was with Reinhardt as he sneaked to a butchered pig one evening. With one deft stroke Reinhardt cut two long slivers from its thigh and broke off a large bone. He stuffed the meat into the front of his shirt and carried the bone under his arm like a weapon. They ambled home nonchalantly. Gerda-Maria cooked the meat and boiled the bone, extracting nourishment from the marrow.

At times Reinhardt protected Ute. She had filled her basket with pears. A boy pretended to amble by, reached over and dumped the basket. He started to pick up handfuls of fruit, before Ute yelled, "Don't do this. These are mine."

"Yours?" the boy smirked and reached for more pears, pushing Ute aside. Ute grabbed the boy's shoulder but the boy lunged for her sweater, her only one, the one her mother had knitted with leftover yarn. Seeing her sweater unravel she tore into the boy just as Reinhardt intervened and dragged her off the ground.

"Let's go," he urged, gathering up the rest of the spilled fruit.

"I have something for you," Reinhardt said as he opened his frayed jacket. A tiny creature with black ears nestled against his chest.

"A rabbit," Ute shrieked. "Is it mine?" Reinhardt nodded benevolently and handed her the small, squirming animal. Nothing could please Ute more. She named the rabbit Flopsy. Reinhardt built a wooden hutch with screen wire at the frame for the opening. On long walks Ute carried her rabbit in a basket and then let it hop across a meadow. She picked salad leaves and often denied herself a carrot, and gave it to Flopsy to nibble. Flopsy became quite tame and learned to come when called.

Reinhardt had roving eyes. He frequently made stops on their rounds through the town. There Ute was told to wait in a foyer among umbrellas in metal stands and winter coats reeking of moisture and stale sweat, or in a kitchen where Ute slumped into a chair, dozing after their long outings.

Sometimes a cat or a dog kept her company. Reinhardt always reemerged in a good mood, and many women gave Ute a treat for being well-behaved.

The money from the jewelry sewn into their winter coats had been used up. Maria and Gerda-Maria had bartered them for their lodgings and food on the trek. But Gerda-Maria still owned a pair of earrings set in garnet stones. "Let me see your earrings," Reinhardt casually asked.

"They are in the ashtray on the window sill." Both went to look. Nothing but several cigarette butts.

"You lost them," Reinhardt yelled. "How could you leave them unprotected on a window sill?"

In tears, Gerda-Maria crawled on her knees and searched. Ute joined her. They investigated every nook and cranny, even tracing along the cracks in the floor boarding. Once Ute raised her eyes, peeking through her fingers fanned before her face. Reinhardt wore a new jacket, clean and without a tear. Instantly Ute knew that the earrings had landed on the flourishing Black Market.

What pull did the water in the duck pond exert on Gerda-Maria's fragile psyche? It was rumored that she sleepwalked as a child and that one evening when her parents returned from a dinner party she was balancing on the iron balustrade of the main steps to the Bielwiese castle. She never remembered her escapades the next day.

Ute was already in bed, huddled in a floor length nightgown Gerda-Maria had sewn from salvaged green curtains. Gerda-Maria wore a similar gray nightgown. The creaking of the door and a gust of wind caused Ute to leap up. In the doorframe Gerda-Maria swayed, clutching her pulled up bulging nightgown. She walked into the darkness slowly, step by step as if carrying a heavy burden. Barefooted, Ute rushed out behind her. She never glanced back but walked as if following an urgent call. As she approached the water Ute pleaded, first softly so not to scare her, then more urgently, her voice rising to a screech. She paid Ute no heed.

Gerda-Maria stumbled into the pond. "Stop, Mutti," Ute yelled as loud as she could, grabbing her mother's gown. "We are sinking. Remember the baby." Their feet submerged into slimy muck. Desperately, Ute climbed onto her mother's back and slung her arms around her neck. "Please, Mutti, turn around." As if Ute's outcry had broken the hypnotic spell, Gerda-Maria reversed her steps. She coughed and gulped for air, pulling her feet from the waters of the dangerous pond.

Inside the cottage the embers in the stove were still aglow. Their nightgowns were waterlogged and Ute's braids, two stiff icicles. A puddle of slush swirled around them as they crouched near the stove. Ute threw some kindling into the embers and then they fell asleep curled up together. At first light Reinhardt returned and spread bed covers over them.

When Gerda-Maria woke, she struggled to her feet and still in a daze, began to weep uncontrollably. "You are the only thing left from your father. Never leave me," she sobbed as she clutched Ute in a desperate embrace. Ute was crying too but she felt that her mother's sorrows were beginning to freeze her heart.

18 Diamonds in the Heel of Her Shoe

When Gabriele was born the sun emptied its energy into the autumn leaves. They sparkled in brilliant colors of gold, brown and turquoise. Gabriele was a content baby adjusting to post-war conditions. Gerda-Maria produced plenty of breast milk and Reinhardt sold the extra milk on the black market. Ute was delighted to have a baby sister, a doll to hold and adore.

Another fall and a brutal winter arrived with frost shaking leaves off the branches and loading down the limbs with snow.

Ute came down with a high fever and was diagnosed with diphtheria. The Allies quarantined everyone with infectious diseases. Taken to a former schoolhouse which had been converted into a provisional children's hospital, Ute clung to Gerda-Maria, scared and whimpering. A nurse forcefully removed Ute's grip and disentangled her from Gerda-Maria's arms. "Have a heart," a distraught Gerda-Maria pleaded, "We have never been apart." An orderly took her by the shoulders and summarily ushered her out. Delirious, Ute was taken to a bed where cold wraps were applied to her body every few hours. There were no medicines. Most of the children died. A sheet was simply pulled over their heads and soon the bed rolled out. The names of the deceased children were written on a large blackboard from the pre-war days.

As soon as Ute spiked a fever, word had been sent to Maria. Wasting not a minute, she dragged out her sturdy African walking shoes. She made her way to Ute's side. She knelt and said her prayers. But when Ute's condition worsened, Omi Maria put her Christian Science beliefs aside and undertook a practical rescue mission. She pried the one heel open, took out the African diamond and cloaked herself in a shabby coat. "Your time has come," she whispered to the precious stone, spit-polished it, wrapped it in her handkerchief and tucked it into her undergarments. She relied on finding transportation to the town of Wolfenbüttel where the black market was teeming. A kind wagon driver let her off in the belly of the city. Smugglers approached her immediately, but seeing an old woman who surely had nothing of value to sell, they laughed and moved on. She crept along walls of houses, then onward through an underground tunnel. It was pitch dark. She admitted later that she prickled with unease. She might be followed and feared being attacked. But her fluttering heart urged her on.

A red sign flashed over a shed spelling "Apotheke" and underneath "Pharmacy." Maria knew she had found her destination. Much commotion echoed through the shed, with glass bottles clinking and papers rustling. She was led to a bespeckled man who spoke to her in English. He examined the diamond with a magnifying glass. "It's real," his eyes widened into blazing brown buttons and he gasped, trying out his German, "*Echt. Ja!*" Then he reached up to a shelf behind him and pulled down a box with black lettering: PENICILLIN. He dismissed Maria with a handwave and warned her, "Be quick and careful. You are carrying a much-desired treasure."

Maria arrived at the hospital. It required all her diplomatic skill to stop a doctor on his way to the ward. She explained her errand and to her amazement he just nodded, "Good deed, grandmother. You are just in time."

Although Ute recovered, her recuperation stretched over weeks during which she contracted additional communicable diseases. She also made a friend.

Erich was a straw-blond farm boy. His parents delivered fresh produce, sometimes eggs and milk to the ward. His bed was wheeled next to Ute's, just enough space between for a doctor or nurse to squeeze through. He was so homesick and cried until his nose was permanently crusted. Ute offered him bedtime stories. Books were new to him. He could not read. Ute eagerly grasped the opportunity. She was in her element. She made up stories about flying carpets and journeys to gilded castles and discovering gold hidden in dungeons. Her owl flew in at dusk. After hearing a tale about pigs in a spring meadow, Erich sent a message to his parents to bring him his toy lamb. With uplifting delight in his droopy eyes, he showed off his toy. It had fluffy pink ears and a movable tail. The coat was made from real lambswool, so soft to the touch.

Erich and Ute shared a special seat on the windowsill where below they could spot relatives trudging back and forth along the frosty sidewalks, waving. Gerda-Maria and Omi Maria continued that vigil until Ute's release.

Ute never knew what Erich suffered from except that his skin was blotched. Bluish spots like big freckles covered his face, neck, arms, even the back of his hands. Once he had to wear gloves so he wouldn't scratch. During his most tormenting days Ute redoubled her storytelling. When Erich was not miserable, he could be funny. By pumping his palms together behind a nurse's back or doing an imitation of a doctor's stern voice, "All these cases are severe. Those poor mites."

Sometimes Erich could not keep his food down and fell asleep during Ute's story hour. One night he reached across the short space between them. Their hands found each other, his small and clammy. Shyly, he asked Ute, "Do you want to sleep with my lamb tonight?" and as much as Ute longed for that comfort, she declined.

The moon shone pearly over their beds when Ute slipped out and crept over to Erich. She placed one ear on his chest as she had seen a doctor or nurse do. She heard no breathing and tentatively touched his face. It was cold and sweaty. His lamb lay beside him on the sheet. Ute fled back to her bed, pulled the pillow over her head and cried as if there was no end to grieving. When they rolled Erich's bed out, the lamb had slipped to the floor. Ute grabbed it up and tugged it where she believed her heart was.

Omi Maria had returned to Mittelhof. Reinhardt picked Ute up. The doctor signed the release stating: "She's been here too long."

It snowed as they drove directly to a neighbor who lived in a real stone house. He and his wife had invited others to a feast to celebrate Ute's return. Gerda-Maria was already there when they arrived. Much fuss was made about Ute. "So glad you recovered."

"What a great homecoming!" A steaming vegetable soup was brought in. A large beeswax candle burned in the center of the table covered with a checkered tablecloth. The guests filled their stomachs until they could spoon no more soup, then waited for the main course. "Child, you must eat," the host encouraged Ute. "You are so thin. The winter wind will blow you away."

A neighbor let off satisfying puffing sounds when a roast topped with potatoes and sprinkled with thyme was brought before the astonished assembly. "It's a rare duck we are having in your honor, Ute." But Ute seemed distracted and blurted out, "I can't wait to visit Flopsy." The rabbit's hutch had been moved to the neighbor's stable at the beginning of winter.

"You had better wait a few days, dear. The path down to the stables is icy and slippery."

Then the host began to carve the roast. "I need to take baby Gabriele home," Gerda-Maria interrupted. "Thank you for the delicious soup."

"I'll go with you," offered Reinhardt and pushed his plate aside. Ute was ready to leave. She knew that the roast was not a duck. The next morning snow crunched under Ute's shoes when she made her way to find Flopsy. She was prepared for what awaited her. The hutch was empty, only the straw bedding was still there. That night sleep did not come to dry her wet cheeks. In later years Ute read "The Yearling" by Marjarie Kinnan Rawlings to her children showing the difficult choice between love for a pet and a family's survival.

As soon as winter gave a reprieve and snowbells poked their green tips through the crusty earth, Ute packed up Börle, her teddy bear, the one with brown paws and perky ears. Ute liked his little nose best which had threaded crow's feet encircling its edges, giving it a bemused crinkled look. She blew her warm breath into his stubby snout and planted several kisses on that nose as they set off to a thickly entangled thicket, away from buildings near a lake. She had discovered a small entrance, maybe an animal burrow. They crawled into a hollow where the branches rasped against each other. Sun and shadows mingled through the tangled roof. It was dry and Ute liked the womb-like interior. She fortified the secret hide-out with cardboard and the floor with strips from tattered blankets. Now that murmuring spring rain sponged the leaves, their monotonous drumming lulled her. It felt cozy inside. She surveyed her new place and told Börle, "One day you will be a real bear just like the Velveteen Rabbit." A turnover box served as a table where Ute spread her drawing and writing materials and sometimes snacks. She daydreamed but ghosts would also appear, bitter and sweet. "What are we doing here?" she once asked her teddy companion, "Hide? And seek answers to so many worrisome events."

Bordering the entrance to her secret hide-out, sunflowers, drained of color, had risen after the melting snow. Observing the dying and rebirth of nature, Ute thought about Franz. She came up with the idea of building an animal cemetery. Tender and brittle bracken snapped under her feet as she followed the narrow path through wilted grass down to her animal resting place. Mainly birds, some field mice, lots of lizards, and an assortment of spiders and flies slumbered under small mounds of dirt. Once she found a dead squirrel and it was hard to unearth enough soil for its burial. She used a kitchen spoon as a shovel to dig the individual graves which she decorated with luminous greenery. She tied sticks together into crosses and placed them on top of each tiny elevation. For each animal she buried she recited a verse she remembered from her mother or grandmother. "Sweet dreams," was one of her favorite farewells.

Mossy stones stacked on top of each other encircled her cemetery, a barrier from the world beyond. She tended her memorial place with the loving precision of a gardener. Sitting on a rock she waited for birdsong and the occasional sound of a clicking, ticking grasshopper. In May and June, branches feathered out and buds swelled. Flowers sent their tentacles toward the sun. Ute was sure that the buried creatures would enjoy their blooming carpet.

19 Calf-Skin Notebook with Rose-Colored Lines

Gangly long arms from willow trees swayed over a brook running from elementary school to midtown. Switches could be made from the flexible soft wood and the heart-shaped leaves were pressed into books. On their way home from classes Ute and her friend Wölfi set paper boats afloat on the gurgling waters and kicked stones into the wake. They broke off branches and swished them through the swells and laughingly sprayed each other.

Reinhardt had found work as a supervisor in a bricklaying factory and the family had moved into the southern town of Kirchheim. Their aristocratic title helped them to a spacious flat with a high ceiling living room, dining room, two bedrooms and a longed-for indoor toilet in a villa surrounded by a park. The owner, a widow, lived alone on the second floor.

There were gardeners and two maidservants for the old lady. The floors were expensive hard parquet which had to be polished weekly. The maids were instructed to inspect all windows for fingerprints and smudges. Authorities had ordered refugees to be taken into many large, nearly empty houses. Most of the quarters were cramped, often upstairs in attics. The von Hardenbergs had to share a kitchen and a copper bathtub in the basement with others. All inhabitants were only permitted to use the back entrance. The front door was the sole prerogative of the owner.

Refugees were loathed by the townspeople. Because Gerda-Maria and Reinhardt were Count and Countess they were granted some respect. Ute overheard locals, eyeing them with suspicion, mumbling, these "*Flüchtlinge*" should have stayed where they belong "in the East..."

"Times are hard enough for us here. They take away our jobs."

Ute attended third grade. Wooden desks with scratched and ink-spotted retractable tops were lined up in rows. Children's heads moved from left to right over open books, pigtails bounced off ruddy necks and fingers traced the words. The idle hand had to be placed next to the book, on the side of the desk, into a groove worn hollow by past pupils. Children were scolded if they cupped their chin into a palm.

A teacher, Frau Klink dressed like all middle-aged ladies in the late 1940s, wore a cheerless blue suit with a frilly white blouse buttoned all the way up to her throat. Her shoes were a sensible dark color with square, plump heels. She smelled a bit of leather and shoe polish, with a sprinkle of Kölnisch Wasser mixed in. Her hair was parted in the middle, exposing a line of pale scalp, and gathered in a bun. She wore no make-up other than lipstick, poppy-red, the same Gerda-Maria used to touch up her lips. When she turned around to write on the blackboard the seams of her stockings zigzagged up the back of her calves.

Pencils made tapping sounds on smokey-gray sheets of lined paper like woodpeckers attacking a tree. Writing and adding-subtracting ended with the striking of the school clock at noon. Before lunch break the pupils were rewarded with a story. Frau Klink smoothed the pleats of her skirt, lifted her slender hips onto her desk, facing the class. Both legs dangled off the ground, the ankles crossed like scissors. "Children", she would begin in a lilting voice, "Give me a hint, anything, a frog, a leaf, your papa."

The words poured out of her mouth like ink from a fountain pen and, magically, she wove a story around the promptings. Without ever breaking the flow of her words, she also entrusted something to a soft-skin notebook which she balanced on one thigh. At the end of a week her stories were patched together in a quilt-like pattern and she started a new notebook. The teacher's voice traveled through the air like a current and Ute drank in every word, absorbed every image, followed the storyline and mulled over its meaning. She sat in the front row and one morning she leaned forward and glimpsed rose-colored lines in the mysterious notebook.

That day, after school Ute did not linger at the gurgling brook but hurried home. "Mutti," she panted, barely through the door, "I want to tell stories like Frau Klink." Then she confessed that she had craned her neck during story hour and how she had spied into the notebook. Excitedly she whispered, "The lines of the notebook were pink." Gerda-Maria listened but said nothing.

The next day Ute dawdled after school in her usual way. When she got home, there on the kitchen table lay her very own soft calfskin notebook. She thumbed through the pages. It had rose-colored lines just like her teacher's. Overjoyed, she threw her arms around her mother. Then she took out her fountain pen and wrote on the first line of the notebook: Ute Countess von Hardenberg–Writer.

It was Frau Klink who helped publish Ute's essay about her rabbit in a nature magazine. Ute was convinced that the early encouragement of her writing bolstered her confidence, especially when facing later setbacks.

Ute didn't know that she was intelligent. The children in their villa and around her neighborhood had started various trade schools but Ute, Wölfi and her lifelong friend Uschi were assigned to the local postsecondary school, the Gymnasium. During the early years Ute liked school. Later she resented the prescribed demands the German higher educational system imposed. There were no subject choices. Certain areas bored her; others she had trouble mastering. Now she could no longer walk to school but rode her new lime-green Bismark bike. Each morning Wölfi picked her up and they paddled to the Gymnasium together.

The home situation had deteriorated. Reinhardt was on the make and debts mounted. Gerda-Maria tried desperately to hold the family together and attempted to bribe Reinhardt with kind deeds like extra money or ignoring a new lover. But they always failed to reach him. She clutched more strongly to Ute, who witnessed her mother's many illnesses and sad moods. She crouched next to her bed, holding her hands and whispered comforting words.

"I am here, Mutti, I am right here." Ute felt helpless and at times wanted to flee from her mother's teary outbursts. It came as a relief to be invited by friends and extended family members for short stays. But she learned quickly that these escapes brought with them great loneliness.

When she turned twelve, she traveled alone to Jost-Henrich in Sweden where her godmother forgot to pick her up at the train station. Her uncle's wife gave her a daily allowance for which she had to give an accounting each evening. She then was on her own, riding the tram into the city, wandering Stockholm's cobblestone streets, visiting museums and finally ending up on the outskirts, the rocky shore, the "skerries." Sitting on a warm rock she pulled her scarf over her face to conceal her weeping. In bed at night her pillow was wet with bitter tears. With difficulty she learned to swallow the curse of homesickness. There were other trips to various relatives. Most ended in loneliness. Even when she was invited to the glittering Cote d'Azur, where she was surrounded by small children, she felt alone. But she learned how people live in different cultural surroundings.

As the sun eventually breaks through dark clouds, there were also good times. Repeatedly she traveled to Omi Maria, her respite. They resumed their customary walks and at night the owl stories were revived. She also enjoyed stays with her paternal grandparents who tried to fulfill her every wish. Aenne cooked her favorite dishes and Karl took her to animal parks. She never wanted to leave either of them.

At school Ute was shy. When called upon to read aloud, her throat turned dry, her stomach queasy. Going to the blackboard in front of the whole class terrified her. She was a good speller. But when asked to write on the board her hand would shake and the letters would tumble all over themselves. Ute was happiest when bent over her beloved notebook, earnestly composing stories about rabbits and horses and the antics of puppets. Ute's thick braids were a temptation for many of her classmates and when someone ran by her, a quick yank was inevitable. She pleaded when the tugging was too harsh, "Please don't do that. It hurts."

Classroom seating was arranged so that the tallest pupils sat in the back. Tiny Ute ended up in the front row. Short and chubby Heinz had his chair right behind her. He was smart, and as an only child of wealthy parents, spoiled. He believed that he could get away with any prank, and nobody seemed able to stop his nonstop talking.

Physical punishment was permitted in German schools in the 1950s, though not all teachers used it. Herr Bankwitz, a history teacher and gym coach, followed the old rules. When a girl misbehaved, he had her stand at her desk with outstretched fingers which he smacked with a slender reed. Boys were taken out into the hallway where he gave them a stinging lash or two across the bottom with a leather strap.

Both Gerda-Maria and Reinhardt repeatedly petitioned against corporal punishment in the school. Ute had never been spanked and she winced every time she saw the swollen fingers of a classmate. When a boy received a whipping, the sound of the strap made her recoil. She leaned into her notebook, her nose touching the pages, and covered her ears. She disliked having her hair pulled but knew that if she reported it, she would have to witness the perpetrator's punishment. Being bullied was bad but the whippings were worse.

Heinz got a laugh out of the class every time he pulled Ute's braids. When she let out a plaintive "Ouch" he beamed triumphantly and turned to his approving audience. But he tormented Ute only before the start of class or after the closing bell had rung.

Herr Bankwitz was a canny observer who often arrived early on the school grounds and lingered in the hallways. Several times he watched Heinz from afar. Then one day he stepped into the classroom as the opening bell sounded and witnessed Heinz yanking one of Ute's braids and squealing "snagged you!"

Slowly, he put his briefcase on his desk, then took out the book for the day's lesson and placed it face down. Peering over his glasses, he said firmly, "Heinz, do not do that again!"

About halfway through the lesson while writing on the blackboard, he glanced over his shoulder just as Heinz quickly yanked one of Ute's braids. Without a show of emotion, he put the chalk down, walked to the cupboard and retrieved the strap. "Heinz," he said in a stern voice, "step outside."

Heinz, who was unaccustomed to being disciplined, could not believe what he heard. He tried to explain, "I only brushed her hair aside because it was blocking my view of the blackboard."

"Step outside." Herr Bankwitz was clearly irritated. Suddenly, the situation seemed serious. Heinz began to shake, "I will never do it again, I promise."

Herr Bankwitz was not a patient man. "For the last time, Heinz, outside!" Heinz lost his composure and sank to his knees. "Please, please don't!"

Herr Bankwitz got hold of Heinz's shirt and lifted him like a limp kitten, steering him into the hallway. Heinz howled so loudly and pitifully that other teachers emerged to see what was happening. When Heinz returned to the classroom, he hung his head and did not even wipe the snot from his cheeks.

Witnessing Heinz's humiliation, courage surged up in Ute's shy heart. Until now, she had merely been an observer but now she was implicated.

Herr Bankwitz opened his book and was about to pick up where he had left off when Ute's faint voice made him spin around. "I ha-hate spankings," she uttered haltingly.

"What did you say, Ute?" Herr Bankwitz was incredulous.

"I hate spankings," she repeated, her voice quivering.

"How dare you? Apologize," he thundered.

"I can't," Ute said. Her words were clear, her voice steady.

"You can't?" His ears turned red with anger. "Then take your seat and be quiet."

"I can't do that either." Ute was composed now and confident. Herr Bankwitz was about to lose his bearings. That a pupil, especially a girl, would dare to question his authority! He took several steps toward her in an attempt to intimidate her but Ute stood her ground. Suddenly Herr Bankwitz turned, gathered up his belongings and left the room without a word, slamming the door as he left.

A pencil rolled off a desk and clattered to the floor. Ordinarily someone would have picked it up. Instead, the pencil rolled and rolled until it bumped into the wall. Nobody moved a muscle. Ute remained standing, immobile as a statue until the bell rang.

Everyone rushed out except Heinz. He approached Ute. "Wow," he whispered and then touched her hair ever so gently before running outside to spread the word.

Ute was elected class president the following year. She spearheaded the alumni drive for the renovation of the library where her class gathered the most signatures. For that the class won a stay at a vacation retreat where her friend Uli presented Ute with her first rose. Life gifted other opportunities. She, Uschi and Wölfi were confirmed together. Ute's confirmation inscription read: Psalm 56 3-4, "When I am afraid, I put my trust in thee. In God, whose word I praise, in God I trust without a fear. I will not fear what flesh can do to me." She was never afraid for herself but always for her loved ones. Uschi and Ute often discussed religious ideas but came up with more questions than answers.

Ute also started to volunteer reading to elderly nursing home residents. "You sent us an angel," one woman told the pastor. Ute tried to imitate that image. She asked Gerda-Maria to make a dress from a lace curtain.

She wanted to combine caring for others with being pretty. Wölfi often accompanied her to the nursing home where he lounged in the lobby and annoyed the staff by contrasting Ute's elegant appearance with his sloppy pants and long unruly hair.

Gerda-Maria was hospitalized several times. The causes she kept private. During those weeks Ute stayed with another family where in the evenings they read different roles from Shakespeare's plays aloud. It became an introduction into classical literature that Ute valued.

Ute grew and learned among much confusion but also good times.

20 Forget-Me-Nots

Horses galloped through blooming meadows in Ute's daydreams. She was horse crazy. Gerda-Maria, who didn't have the means for a horse or riding lessons, made her a hobby horse from brown sackcloth with black buttons as eyes. Bridle and reins were braided, the nostrils stitched so the toy horse looked like it was neighing.

Ute got a job after school in a stable in exchange for lessons. She relished the scent of leather, manure and steaming hides. She buried her nose in the windblown mane of Sport, a spirited gelding that belonged to the wealthy sheepherding Hausch family. He was ridden occasionally by them but she believed that he was most responsive to her.

Ute wondered about Sport's family and started to pedal her bike through the neighborhood where they lived. The Tudor mansion on a manicured lawn confirmed what Ute had imagined, a life of leisure without worries. Two friendly shepherd dogs greeted her at the wrought iron fence and she watched an old woman rocking under a canopy. She reminded Ute of Omi Maria. She also glimpsed Frau Hausch leaving the house in a fine knitted jacket.

Ute had never run away from home. She knew herself loved and cared for but Reinhardt's behavior poisoned their domestic life. What would it be like to live with the owners of Sport? Ute packed her rucksack with clothes and school supplies and rode to Hausch's villa one late afternoon. She rang the doorbell. Frau Hausch opened, inspecting Ute curiously. Without a lengthy introduction Ute asked, "May I live with you?" If Frau Hausch was surprised, she did not show it. "I know who you are," she said kindly. "I have watched you ride Sport. You have the touch." Ute was invited in, joined the family of five for dinner and later was escorted to an upstairs guest room with a view over their lush garden. Frau Hausch asked no questions but made her promise to go to school the next morning.

They had no telephone, so someone in the Hausch's family must have driven over to inform Gerda-Maria. After school the next day Ute fell into the arms of her sobbing mother. "I feared you lost." "I just wanted to be in a home where they own a horse," Ute apologized timidly.

Ute became a frequent guest at the Hausch's. At the annual jumping and riding competition she was allowed to ride Sport and won a silver medal. Sport was Ute's first love and she remained his friend until he died at the old equine age of 32.

Many years later Ute discovered a papier-mâché horse in a boutique in Guadalajara, Mexico which reminded her of Sport. She wanted to buy the small statue but the store would not send it to America. "It breaks easily." Ute's husband warned that she would not be able to fly with that artwork. At first, Ute relented but the next day she went back to the store and acquired the papier-mâché horse. That afternoon they checked in at the airport. They were already at the gate when an official declared that Ute could not bring that gift onto the small plane and they had no way to ship it. After lengthy arguments all passengers, including Ron, boarded the aircraft. Ute stood alone on the tarmac, cradling her purchase. Her luggage was already gone. The pilot stepped out of the plane and talked to her. "I am not leaving without this gift," Ute declared stubbornly. What would she have done if circumstances had not turned in her favor? The engine revved and once more the pilot appeared in person. "Get in," he snarled. Triumphantly Ute climbed on and took a seat with her fragile treasure. Passengers broke out in loud applause.

Boyfriends were not as important as horses. Ute enjoyed watching horses mate, even though at times the stallions seemed a bit rough. But afterwards the mare and stallion always nuzzled. She had no knowledge of or interest in human sexual behavior. Even at earlier outings with Reinhardt she never questioned what he and the women were doing.

At a tournament Ute's track team SVL assembled at a clubhouse high in the Swabian Alps. They wore their frog-green training suits and when they were ready to start, Eberhard, one of the referees, pulled Ute back by the arm. "Better give me your watch and your pendant. It's a hindrance. Both will be safe with me." Hastily, Ute took them off and handed them to Eberhard. Not until later did she recall that she had been struck by his piercing Tiger eyes, russet with specks of gold.

Sweaty after the run, Ute rushed to the stony trough behind an ivy-covered wall. She ducked her face into the cool water. When she looked up Eberhard was standing there and handed her the jewelry. She stepped forward, reaching out, but instead landed in his wide-open arms. He kissed her and held her until she struggled loose in utter bewilderment. Eberhard smiled as she fled back to the group. Events spanned the morning and after lunch at an open fire pit, Eberhard approached Ute again. "Let's take a walk. I need to tell you something." The shock of the kiss had not worn off but was replaced by a novel excitement burning in her veins. They set out through wide grassy fields dotted with forget-me-nots. Ute skipped away from Eberhard's side and eagerly picked a bunch and handed them to him. "I hope that you will never forget me," he pulled her to him and kissed her again.

The second kiss felt natural, and Ute relaxed. After climbing a steep slope, they mounted the wooden steps of a ski jump. "Like leaping through the air," Eberhard mused as they reached the top platform. "Are you afraid of heights?"

"No, but I prefer the vistas beyond." They stood arm-in-arm. Eberhard asked.

"Have you known men?"

"My stepfather lives with us."

Eberhard barely contained a laugh. "I mean physical contact?"

"You mean have I been kissed? This was my very first kiss ever. I'm only fifteen."

"I thought so, you little Seelchen. I don't know what came over me, kissing you."

With a lump in her throat, Ute stuttered, "I liked it." She suddenly recalled that her Omi Maria had called her Seelchen. They had to hurry back to the waiting bus.

At the gymnasium the bicycle racks were assigned according to class rank. The seniors had a covered roof over their stands. Ute, being among the young students, had to park her bike in the open. Monday after the tournament she was eager to get to school, looking for Eberhard. She caught sight of him among his friends. When she brushed by him, he turned and avoided her "Hi, how are you?" Ute was quick to notice that his behavior toward her had totally changed. But why? Several days later she still waited and then stuck a piece of paper onto his bicycle seat.

"What's wrong? Can we talk?" No answer followed. Ute had scaled the walls of loneliness but how do you break through silence?

Having watched Ute's increasing desperation, Felix, Eberhard's best friend, stepped in. "You caused an uproar at the tournament, Ute. Eberhard is engaged to be married right after graduation." Ute turned on her heels and walked the long way home, then slumped down under a willow tree and let her tears flow.

How could a single kiss provoke such gripping pain? Maybe Ute's heart had been readied, secretly hunting for affection. Now she struggled to overcome her aching disappointment. Like falling through darkness her love for Eberhard trailed her like a menacing shadow. From then on intimacies were restricted and she let no one get close to her. Occasionally, she allowed a kiss as when Felix dropped the books he carried from the library in an attempt to hug her or when Wölfi stayed at her side when she was sick. Wölfi who shared some of his sexual exploits with her would at times run a hand over her arm or down her legs and let it linger. Ute had goosebumps. But that was all. Clinging to a single love protected her for years from any harmful entanglements. Like her mother who tried to keep the waning contact to Reinhardt by increasing attention, Ute too transformed her hurt into deeds. She wrote poems and sent them to Eberhard. She knitted him a blue scarf. And each season a forget-me-not was pasted onto the frame of his mailbox where he lived with his wife. Years later, when Eberhard was diagnosed with pancreatic cancer, he forfeited treatment by saying, "I had everything I wanted in my life, women, wine, a beautiful house, a companion dog and classical music." A few weeks before he died, he gave a lavish party in his teeming garden. Ute was invited. He took her aside, "I never intended to hurt you. I honestly wanted to tell you about my commitment when we walked to the ski jump. But I couldn't." Ute did not utter a pardon but she kissed him goodbye.

The years in Kirchheim came to an end with Reinhardt's absences and his demands for a divorce. Sickly and depressed, Gerda-Maria finally consented. They would move back to Gensungen near Omi Maria. Before their departure Ute had to confront another hurtful experience—coming to the realization that she was poor.

It was a perfect winter in Sölln, Tirol. It had been snowing for weeks, and now frost glazed the soft ground and sun rays bounced off the slick surface in a myriad of golden ringlets. A dozen students had traveled there in a minibus. Now Angela and Ute waited to be taken to the nearby chairlift for beginners. The advanced skiers had left at sunrise to explore more challenging slopes.

Before their departure from Kirchheim Ute had paid no attention to the skis which a kind old lady had lent her. These worn skis were extra long, made of oak with tips curved upward like sleigh runners. They were probably made for cross-country outings. Because purchasing new skis was out of the question, Ute and her mother had gratefully accepted the offer.

The skis felt heavy and Ute shifted them from shoulder to shoulder. She was in good physical condition but soon lagged behind. The attendant at the lift gave her a funny look, "Big boards, young lady." By the time they reached the meeting point Ute was soaked in sweat. She deeply inhaled the biting air.

The instructor stood wide-legged before them, his hands buried in his jacket. He yawned. He demonstrated how to latch on the skis. Ute finished last. The next task was to turn around on the path where snowdrifts were piled high on both sides. Ute could barely swing her skis around, lost her balance and fell on her back. She looked like a snow beetle.

"Oh ho," the instructor bellowed, nearly choking in his guttural Tyrolean brogue, "*Dem Herrgott sei Skifahrer*" (God's very own skier.) The other participants turned toward Ute and giggled.

"Get up," Angela hissed. While everyone stared at her Ute managed to sit up, flip the latch of one ski so the boot slipped off. She managed to untie the second ski and boot, and pulled herself up onto her knees. Exhausted and humiliated, she finally got to her feet, picked up skis and boots and hobbled in the direction of the lift. Unrestrained laughter followed her.

At night Angela questioned, "Are you going to quit?"

"You bet I'll quit." The rest of the vacation Ute wandered through the gingerbread town with its quaint shops and cafes. The incident was never mentioned again.

It would take years before Ute enrolled in ski lessons with brand new skis. As she glided through dense forests where branches laden with snow thudded handfuls of white powder onto her path, she pronounced with exuberance, "Now I am truly God's very own skier."

21 Sleigh-Easter-Birthday Bells

Holidays can be enchanting. Fairy dust is sprinkled across the dreamy eyes of expectant children and nostalgic adults. A sense of wonder, the seed is planted in childhood.

Rainwater puddles had frozen over and the sidewalks were slick as glass. It was the Advent season. The days were sharp with cold, the atmosphere inside welcoming. A big tiled stove stood in the middle of the living room and the deep red flames of four Advent candles that decorated a wreath added warmth. A sweet pungent fragrance of fir sap emanated from its branches. As the snow descended, piling up in thick layers on the windowsills, the family made Christmas presents in the cozy room. It was a gift-giving lesson Ute was only to fully appreciate much later in life.

Each member had a small wooden chest which hid the treasures out of sight. The chests were decorated with stickers, painted or drawn on with images. Ute, Gabriele, her mother, as well as grandmothers and aunts, crocheted multi-colored potholders. They knitted long scarves that would wind around necks like snake tails. They made calendars using pressed flowers or leaves pasted on each page of a month. They glued tiny stones on cardboard boxes for jewelry. They strung necklaces of beads and painted noodles. Coat hangers were wooden with removable hooks. They crocheted narrow sleeves which they slipped over the hangers, then screwed the hooks back in. There was a child's loom on which miniature wall-hangings were woven. Gerda-Maria sliced, then ironed shafts of straw into long flat pieces and cut them to different lengths. They were bound together with yarn in the shape of stars. Knitting sweaters was the most complicated activity. All finished presents were tagged with names for the receivers.

As they gathered, they nibbled on homemade cookies so delicious that no childhood palate could ever forget. The adults drank spiced wine and the children hot cider. The men smoked pipes whose vapors mingled with the rest of all the other good scents. Voices hummed like whizzing fans. When someone started a carol, everyone joined in. They all sang the old familiar hymns with pleasure, but not everyone celebrated with conviction. Minds wandered, letting fantasies roam. The older generation flew on wings of nostalgia back to their beloved homeland, now no longer in German hands.

Gerda-Maria was the puppeteer behind all the creativity and craftsmanship and the protector of the Advent spirit. She flitted from person to person, her small hands busy at catching a loose stitch here, a missed loop there, her lips wet from threading yet another needle. She smoothed many impatient wrinkled brows.

Omi Maria was often a guest during these festive times. She was the reader. When darkness pressed against the windows, the listeners rose into the air with Nils Holgersson by Swedish author Selma Lagerlöf. Timeless, they journeyed across foreign lands on the buoyant power of the imagination.

Finally, the morning of Christmas Eve arrived. One last time everyone trailed their fingers over each present before wrapping it in glittering paper. Then, bundled up in warm coats, caps and mittens they became caroling elves, walking from house to house ringing doorbells and delivering gifts. As soon as they heard footsteps from indoors, they scampered away. Sometimes they bumped into a couple of friends who were also on secret missions. They pretended not to notice. There was never a sense of quid pro quo in the gift-giving, only the hope that others would feel as they did, finding joy in giving and receiving.

Bong, ding-dong bells sounded, echoing through falling snow across distances from miles away. A summons to church services. After hearing the familiar nativity story, families returned home with enriched hearts, expecting the wonders of candlelit trees and the surprises that lay under them.

Doors to the Christmas room would not open before a tiny triangle chimed and spectators were allowed in. Years later, in more cramped spaces with no doors to hide the Christmas tree, sheets would be hung from the ceiling across the entrance. Impatient children often peeked through the slits to glimpse the glorious sight.

Aunt Vera had rescued the hand-carved creche from Bielwiese. Each Christmas Gerda-Maria carefully unwrapped the figurines, a finely chiseled hand here, a brittle oxtail there, cushioned in cotton. Years later it was Ute who gently bedded down the Holy family, the livestock, and the angels following the celebration.

Each season brought festivities celebrated by the family.

Easter sunrise! Meadows retreated in the golden morning light as bells rang through mountains and valleys. Daffodils carpeted gardens and spring's pollen-dust floated in the air. As each bell tolled, it sang of a moment in time, an awakening of mindfulness, announcing the end of sorrow and death, ringing in rebirth, a new beginning, the resurrection of better futures.

A whiff of enchantment hovered over the dew that covered the Easter nests Ute and Gabriele had made from grass blades and bits of moss. Colorful eggs were like flowers poking through the greenery. One had to be watchful so as not to miss the fertile Easter Bunny hopping from nest to nest, depositing sweets and little gifts. Ute and her sister woke with the first glint of the sun and peeked through window curtains hoping for a glimpse of the bunny. Once Gabriele thought she detected the tip of its white tail. Everyone was dressed in their finery and the mood was hopeful and generous. Thoughts went from individual joyment to including others. At the Easter brunch family merged with friends and the community.

Birthdays were timekeepers of permanence in change. One anniversary would be followed by another. Gratitude for yet another year was celebrated. The accumulation of events was praised. Special cakes were baked and decorated with a number of candles for the age of the recipient. The beauty of garlands was extolled as flowers and leaves were wound into crowns, placed on the heads of celebrants. Bells rang out for continuity. Each present honored the birthday child. Under which position of the sun was a child born with the horoscope of a Leo or a Fish? In which lunar month did the zodiac sign appear, its karma giving direction to life. Saluting the Tiger or the Snake symbol? Each birthday was a jubilation, a breakfast in bed, a massage, a secret wish granted. Gerda-Maria always asked for the singing of her favorite song, "*Geh aus mein Herz und suche Freud.*" (Go out, my heart, and search for joy.) Ute and Gabriele longed for new hats as they knew their friends would be wearing them. Chimes commemorated the passing of time, heralding a recurrence. A child arrived and was celebrated by parents and the heavens alike. As above, so below.

Memories from birthdays, Easter and Christmas were embedded in valued traditions that one generation hoped to embed in the minds of the next. Traditions bound them together. In the midst of a troubled family life these holidays were highlights for receptive hearts, especially the children's. Ute would cherish them her entire life.

Traditions also evoked contradictions. Greedy people might melt with kindness and well-meaning ones could turn selfish.

Besides the official holidays there were the private ones, invitations to friends, spending the night. School related festivals like dances and award ceremonies abounded.

There was a dance at Ute's gymnasium she longed to attend before their move away. Gerda-Maria had no money to buy a dress or make a fancy ballroom one for such an occasion. Reinhardt had left with another woman and not sent child support or notice about his whereabouts for weeks. The day before the dance a package arrived for Ute. When she unwrapped the rustling paper, a floor-length pink gown lay inside. Ute held it up with rapture. It was the perfect fit. Reinhardt had not forgotten the days of thievery they once shared.

22 Separate Currents

The Eder River that divided the villages of Gensungen and Felsberg was dishwater-brown. No splashing in fresh cooling waves. Only after a downpour when the nearby dam opened its sluices did the surf swell. Cattails sprouted along the river's edges and geese nested on its muddy banks. Few fishermen had any luck in the sluggish flow but frogs croaked into the late evening hours.

Omi Maria had moved to Gensungen and located an apartment for Gerda-Maria and the two girls above a sawmill. Droning noises from hammering and sawing allowed for little restfulness during working hours but all activities stopped by late afternoon. The apartment faced the train station from where Ute and Gabriele traveled to schools in Kassel.

Ute had taken a tearful farewell from her friends in Kirchheim with whom she continued to stay in touch. Wölfi kept sending her carved toy airplanes. He had teased her at times about her ignorance of sexual matters. In later years he sent her an angel with a missing wing, and a message. "Maybe by now you too have lost a wing?" Uschi continued to discuss religion and politics over the phone. Miriam, a woman of ill-repute who lived in the attic of their villa with five siblings and a widowed mother became a lifetime friend. She supported her family with her seductive body and paid for it with general disrepute. Ute liked her and ignored the damning reputation. She also invited her to craft Christmas presents with them. Miriam looked on as Ute sprinted with the town's relay team and ultimately became a frequent visitor.

The reunion with Omi Maria was, as expected, a joy. Omi Maria had acquired a little white terrier companion. "I need to get up for my Heide Hündchen. She goes on walks with me."

Ute quickly retorted. "Now I'm here. I will walk with you." The threesome soon enjoyed their outings together.

Omi Maria was the first person to whom Ute confided her sadness over the Eberhard encounter. Wise and gentle Omi Maria advised, "There is no silver lining in each experience but there is usually a lesson." Ute longed for more comfort but Omi Maria counseled, "We must learn to let things go, even love and friendships." Though it was good to have Omi Maria's attentive ear, Ute was not ready to acknowledge that love too could vanish.

Gerda-Maria was not ready to let Reinhardt go. After the divorce she tried to lure him back and engaged Ute in her efforts. She had her write pleading letters for "another try," but Reinhardt did not even bother to answer. Once Gerda-Maria arranged for a meeting between the two where

Reinhardt forcefully told Ute, "It's over between me and your mother. Why can't she understand that?"

Gabriele was too young to be involved so Gerda-Maria clung to Ute. She wanted to share every bit of her daughter's life, especially her friendships. "She is clutching me to her like a purse," Ute once complained to Omi Maria. Ute developed a cool remoteness when her mother wept so frequently, became ill or just hung on. Then Ute brought her ailing mother nourishing soup, tucked her into bed, and left. She took long walks along the Eder River. She felt helpless in her care for her mother. Her heart was narrowing. She shed her own tears of weariness.

Gerda-Maria never lacked suitors. She was still a regal beauty but she kept most men on the periphery of her life. Gerda-Maria craved more and more affection. Sometimes it was difficult to decipher where her neediness stopped and her generosity emerged. Ute marveled at how her mother could be both selfish and giving. She rescued people and took them in like strays. On a class trip to Paris one of the war-orphaned students attempted suicide. Ute called her mother who agreed to have her move in with them. Emma stayed until the end of her years at the Kassel Gymnasium. Much later, when Ute broke up with a boyfriend who could not take her rejection and tried to end his life, Gerda-Maria came to the rescue and gave him shelter.

In waltzed Margot, warm, vibrant, artistic, with flaming red hair. She simply pushed her seat next to Ute's after their literature teacher had cut down Ute's essay in front of the entire class. Ute was spoiled from her Kirchheim days, being singled out as a star pupil, especially in writing essays. She was new to the Heinrich-Schütz Gymnasium. She was criticized for her "arrogant views, wordy word choices and overuse of nature images."

Ute was stunned for being called out in front of the class. A repeat of Herr Bankwitz? "He is a beady-eyed jerk," Margot whispered.

Margot became Ute's best friend. Instead of taking the train home, Ute stayed overnight with her friend in Kassel. Margot was a single child of busy parents who owned a trucking firm. Margot was raised mainly by her grandmother. She was the only student who drove a family car to high school. She had little supervision from anyone at home. Her shepherd dog Harry was her beloved companion. Ute often joined their exercise jaunts. The girls' friendship was easygoing and light-hearted. Laughter had been rare as meat in Ute's family. Now both were in ample supply. Margot's grandmother prepared hearty meals of potatoes and sausages or slices of liver. In the evenings the girls did their homework together, then listened to the radio late into the night and giggled at the jokes they heard.

On their strolls they followed a predictable path through fields and meadows. Harry knew the way and was taken off his leash. He bounded ahead, eagerly yapping and jumping at butterflies. One afternoon he followed the scent of a new trail. Margot whistled. When Harry dutifully returned, she scolded him, "Bad dog. Never that lane."

Ute was puzzled. "Why can't we take another route? There is a beautiful villa up that incline."

Margot rudely turned and shook Ute by the arm, breathing heavily. "I was raped by my boyfriend's father in that villa and had an abortion on their kitchen table."

Ute was so shocked she was speechless. She tried to touch her friend and finally stammered, "Oh, how terrible."

"Never, ever mention that subject again," Margot brushed Ute's hand away and blurted out, "Never again a single word, you hear me?"

Ute swallowed a reply but on the train ride home she could not stop thinking about Margot's confession. She had watched soldiers die and thrown through windows from a transport train, seen villages go up in flames, had experienced hunger and learned thieving. She had witnessed her beloved Omi Maria cry. Her mother had been distraught but this was misery she knew nothing about.

A few weeks later a covey of prattling girls exited the locker room. "Ellen was sent away and her baby was given up for adoption."

"Is that true?" Irene asked, a bit skeptical.

"Of course it's true. Marcia told me."

Ute ambled along on a walk with Omi Maria. All this talk about rape and babies given away affected her deeply. She couldn't stop thinking about Margot. She told Omi Maria about the incident and about what she had overheard in the locker room. Omi Maria heard her out and then spun Ute around by the shoulders. "Don't ever repeat a rumor unless you are a witness. Gossip can ruin a reputation, even a life. Remember, it only takes one spark to ignite a fire which then burns out of control." Omi Maria's eyes narrowed. She looked stern and seemed distracted on their way home. "Oh, child," she said before they parted, "A stone is tossed into clear water and sends a ripple which spreads into circles. The circles grow larger and more numerous until they are out of control. That's the path of gossip. A drop of poison can turn innocent events into something rotten and corrupt. Never be a part of it." She took a breath and continued, "Believe me, my views are painfully acquired."

Ute was taken aback. "What did you mean?"

"Wolfgang. How do you think people regarded my relationship with Wolfgang? Even a doubt as slender as a single hair can be damaging." The answer silenced Ute. But at the moment she was more concerned about Margot. She desperately wanted to ask her about the rape. But Margot's angry rebuttal and furious facial expression warned her from even trying. In spite of unanswered questions, an unusual closeness between the two girls continued to grow.

"Roses are red, violets are blue...I'm not an illusion... I'm here for you..." Jean-Pierre was singing as he painted a Picasso imitation of a bluish couple. He was an art student at the École in Neuchâtel where Ute and Margot spent a summer perfecting their French. Jean-Pierre invited a group of his friends to outings at the lake, the cinema and a dance bar, a first for Ute. Jean-Pierre was an excellent dancer but Margot kept a watchful eye on Ute and insisted that they return to their lodgings before curfew. Madame Vögeli, the proprietor of a guest house for girls, had poor eyesight and often confused one lodger with another. But she stood at the front door at midnight and no one was allowed in after the appointed hour.

Neuchâtel was a marvelous retreat away from domestic problems. It was also the first trip on which Ute did not feel lonely. Both girls enjoyed being mischief-makers. Once they were asked to a party but had no flowers. On their way out they snatched a few stems from Madame Vögeli's vases and doubled over in laughter.

Jean-Pierre treated Ute like a princess, invited her to his home where his sweet mother baked them peach cobbler while the two lounged on the couch in the parlor and kissed. With windows flung open they listened to bells ringing from the cathedral on the hill. At the end of the summer stay Jean-Pierre bought Ute an engraved bracelet and promised to find her in Germany and marry her. They corresponded for years.

After graduating from the Heinrich Schütz Schule, Ute and Margot enrolled at the University of Hamburg. They found a small apartment and their friendship continued to flourish. They had their first adventure when the Advent Season arrived with snow.

Many foreign workers and their families from Yugoslavia had been housed near the university in blocks of bleak low-lying concrete buildings. Ute and Margot enlisted family members and friends in a knitting project, making scarves and sweaters of all sizes. The response was spontaneous and beyond all expectations. Now the girls spent evenings wrapping the hand-made woolen articles. On the third Advent Sunday, a new friend of Ute's, Klaus, a medical student who lived near the block, arrived in a small van. They loaded the packages and a fir tree into the back of his vehicle. They placed the tree in the middle of the block and decorated it with silver tinsel. The packages were distributed around the bottom of the tree. There were metal boxes with names on the walls of the buildings. When they finished, Klaus pressed all the call buttons. Then the three ran back to the van and watched as people descended and inspected the display. In a rush of surprise, they started to grab up packages and disappeared again into their apartments. One bearded old man stood quietly and gazed at the tree, then disentangled a few strings of the tinsel and carried them away.

It was their second semester during September, a month which usually brought dense fog and rain to the port of Hamburg. This year the temperature was uncommonly mild and dry. The girls had the door to their balcony wide open. Noises from the neighbors drifted in. It was the beginning of the fall semester, their second year at the university. They lay stretched out on their stomachs reading when a knock at the door surprised them. They were not expecting visitors and their landlady usually screened callers.

"May I come in?" An elderly man pushed his skinny frame through the door. He looked like a detective, wore a long gray trench coat, was bald, and balanced horn-rimmed glasses on his nose. He carried a battered briefcase with big brass snaps which he pressed to his chest as though it contained something valuable. "May I have a word? It's a matter of importance."

Too startled to say no, Ute gestured him to step in. Margot jumped up and removed the books and papers from a hassock and politely offered, "Please sit down." Ute crouched on the floor and pulled her short skirt over her thighs. The prune-like stranger lifted the tail of his coat as if it were a frock and placed himself squarely on the hassock, facing the girls.

"Dr. Schwarz, Dr. Schwarz," he introduced himself in a slow drawl. All the while his fingers drummed on the top of the briefcase so that the letters of his name seemed to engrave themselves into the brown leather. The girls sat quiet, expectant.

"Which of you is Countess Ute?" His gaze flitted from one to the other. Beneath his smudged glasses his eyes were prying. Ute introduced herself and pointed to her friend Margot. The man hesitated and then solemnly asked, "Please Miss Margot, could you give us some privacy?"

"No," Ute blurted out loudly, "She will stay." Ute had no intention of being alone with this hawk-eyed stranger.

The stranger seemed to be trying to take her measure as a smile lifted his sallow cheeks, "You no doubt honor your father's memory."

Ute still had no idea what this was about but her suspicion was aroused, "Yes, of course, but how do you—?"

"Good, good. I presumed as much. I have been apprised of the circumstances of your childhood. I am aware that your father was killed in action early in the war and thus was robbed of the opportunity of watching his only daughter become a beautiful young lady." He seemed to be pondering Ute's puzzlement. "But you can make it up to him. I will get straight to the point of my visit. I have come to encourage you to take back your birth name."

Ute must have looked dumbfounded but before she could speak, he continued, his voice no longer subdued. "Because your adoption was never finalized, your mother, Gerda-Maria, has lived through the postwar years on fraudulently acquired income... *Lastenausgleich*," he bellowed. "Reimbursement for your lost land." He swallowed, "And you are the bearer of a false name."

"Now, wait a minute," Ute stood up, incredulous.

"Who are you? And who is making these foul accusations?"

"Please, please, I am only a messenger," he said, eagerness creeping into his apologetic voice, "You may not be aware that your mother is under indictment for lying under oath. You and she had reaped the benefits of Count Fritz's inheritance while your sister and her father and that poor aunt."

"Which aunt?"

"Why of course Reinhardt's sister, Beate, who feels you have disgraced her honorable name."

Ute's mouth dropped open. "We always shared our monthly income with my sister and Count Reinhardt. We sent them cash."

Enraged, Ute stood up. Dr. Schwarz too rose quickly and began backing toward the door. "No need to get exasperated. I am only here to introduce myself and to inform you that I am representing them in a lawsuit being brought against you and your mother."

As swiftly as Dr. Schwarz had entered, he was now exiting, leaving the door ajar which drew a gust of wind from the balcony that scattered papers across the floor.

Margot closed the door after him and giggled, "Did you hear his accent? Russian, or maybe Polish? And did you notice his boots, dull and scuffed? They had clearly seen better days."

Ute was in shock and, for a minute, speechless. Then she blurted out, "Who in the world is this man?"

Margot got up and patted her on the shoulder. She retrieved a bottle of red wine they had stashed behind the couch. "You need a drink."

Not long after, Reinhardt paid a visit. He had moved to Hamburg to help his sister, Beate, in her dog-grooming business. He was his charming self as he swept into the apartment in his rumpled clothes, embraced Ute and Margot, and exclaimed, "You two look lovelier every time I see you." He was all sincerity and joviality as he went straight for the wine glasses on the coffee table, still unwashed from the previous visit. Acting as if he were at home, he uncorked a pocket-size bottle of French cognac he had brought with him and poured himself a stiff drink. "Santé! Did Dr. Schwarz unnerve you? He is an old friend from the Silesian days. He is just helping us out." He grinned disarmingly. Ute's face turned beetroot red with fury but, again, she was at a loss for words.

Reinhardt instantly lowered his gaze and turned into the old shapeshifter. "I feel a little bad, Ute dear," he began. "You always have been like my own daughter but things have turned difficult in recent months. My sister has discovered a deception. And you know how she is; she will get to the bottom of any falsehood. She has found out, quite by chance I should add, that your adoption by my brother Fritz was never finalized. Your inheritance robbed her of hers."

"So it's all about money, right?" Ute interrupted.

"Oh no," he protested, "it's about honoring the dead. You see, we never considered your father's feelings. What his wishes might have been. I'm sure he would have liked his surname passed on to his daughter." Reinhardt topped up his drink. "I am not pressuring you, only appealing to your sense of fairness. I have always known you as fair-minded. This is your chance to right an old wrong."

Ute smirked. "And the money would go to whom?"

"I'm not sure, really. We would of course see to it that you and your mother are provided for. Please think about my request and the good deed you would be doing." Then he placed the half-empty bottle on the table and with a generous sweep of his hand announced, "I'll leave this for you two to enjoy. I must be off. I know, Ute dear, you will make a just decision" And with a flourish, he vanished.

Ute had never thought about the adoption. She had lived comfortably with her aristocratic name. She mainly recalled how her mother had struggled to keep them afloat and how the war reparations had eased their hardships. Whom could she now ask about this strange incident? She thought of grandfather Karl who provided the support she needed. He was again practicing as a lawyer after resettling in Eschwege, West Germany. Ute took the train to see him. After she told him about the episode, he launched right in. "I advised your mother to remarry and when she did, and your new father suggested an adoption, your grandmother and I felt that you should be integrated into your new family. Gert would have approved. Of course, nobody could have foreseen how the war would end and that there would be no other children, with you the only heir."

Ute impatiently broke in. "What about the adoption? Did you see any papers?"

"Yes, I even looked them over. There was a clause in which Count Fritz designated you and your mother as primary inheritors."

Ute continued to question her grandfather." Have you ever met Dr. Schwarz?"

Karl roared. "He is no doctor, only a clerk, but as a clerk he did have access to the files."

"Please, grandpa. Were the papers signed?"

"I can't say, child. Count Fritz was an honorable man with firm intentions. He promised to sign the adoption papers on his next furlough."

"But did he?" Ute was near tears.

"I cannot be sure. It was a time of great turmoil, near the end of a terrible war." Karl pulled Ute into an embrace. "My warning right now is to be careful around Schwarz. He is an unscrupulous fellow. And he did have access to the documents."

Ute slept fitfully under her grandparents' comforter. Before she dozed off, a scene bubbled up. She had been in her parents' bedroom with Fritz as her stepfather. As Ute jumped onto their bed, Fritz had swept her up and gently lifted her into the air. Giggling, she broke free and chased a loose ball down the hallway. She overheard her mother say, "I am so pleased that you two get along so well. Let's hurry up with the adoption."

"She is indeed a sweet little girl," Fritz responded, "but these are tough times. There is no rush, right?" Gerda-Maria began to sob, from relief or fears?

When Ute next phoned her mother, Gerda-Maria was not amused. "I would never have married Fritz had he not promised to adopt you. You are and always will be my sole aim in life." When Ute pressed her on what they should do now, her mother took a deep breath and said, "Things will work themselves out somehow."

Days later Ute received a letter from her sister. It was brief and calculating, clearly dictated by Aunt Beate. "Sister, I have always admired you but you have never returned my feelings. Everything in life has gone your way and I had to contend myself with being second-best. I am the real Countess. It's my birthright. I have a father who is a real Count. Yours was not. Please do me this one favor and I will never ask anything of you again. Take back your common birth name and give up pretending that you are a Countess. You are not. I beg you, Gabriele."

Ute crumpled up the letter and threw it into the wastebasket.

Gerda-Maria stayed with Ute and Margot the night prior the court hearing. "Everything will be fine," she assured the girls. But she was up several times during the night, wandering around their apartment.

Gerda-Maria had retained her understated poise and style. Her svelte figure matched the pearls she always wore (even in the air raid shelter). At the courthouse she donned a beige, tailored suit with a white high-collared blouse. Her beautiful appearance elicited a caring protectiveness from most men. Reinhardt, Beate and Gabriele looked like bullfighters, dressed in red. Reinhardt even had a red handkerchief tucked into his shirt pocket. Schwarz in his long trench coat, craning his neck, surveying the crowd and basking in his role as sole witness.

The judge, twirling a fountain pen, had each of them tell the adoption story, which was further embellished with each retelling.

Gerda-Maria swore that the adoption papers had been signed. She had to verify her three marriages and the deaths in her family.

When she finished, Schwarz had his moment of glory. He carried his well-guarded briefcase to the bench, snapped the brass locks open and produced a single document. "There is no signature," he proclaimed, "just a follow-up date for finalizing the adoption. But that date never came.

War intervened. I was able to grab these documents at the last minute, at my own peril, I must add. The country around us had already erupted in flames." He glanced over at Ute and Gerda-Maria, sensing victory.

Gerda-Maria was called back to the stand. "Schwarz is correct," she testified. "The signing was later. My husband flew home with the express purpose of making his promise of adoption official. Because Schwarz was not in the office that afternoon we called another witness." An eerie silence ensued.

Schwarz leaped from his seat. "She is lying. There was no witness. She is making this up."

Gerda-Maria remained unperturbed and only responded, "Yes, there was."

Like an apparition, Frieda walked in. Ute had not seen her in years and wanted to rush toward her but Gerda-Maria held her back. Her Deeda looked old, toothless, her lips curled over her gums. A worn head scarf covered her hair, and she wore a brown dress with a colorful knitted shawl draped around her shoulders. Although she was clearly unaccustomed to speaking in public, she testified calmly and forcefully, answering the judge's questions without hesitation.

"I was there that day," she declared. "I had come up to the castle because we had promised Ute a party with girls from the village when she officially became our Countess. To me she was always a Countess, such an adorable little thing. Schwarz was out of the office and could not be found. So I was called as a witness, and I did sign. Count Fritz flew back to the front the same day. When war overtook our homeland, I trekked westward where I found new employment. Years passed with only the occasional letter between us. Then Ute's mother contacted me when this lawsuit was filed to ask if I could help. And here I am." Deeda took a seat and stared at her lap.

The judge called a recess. When he reentered to announce the verdict, Ute's skin prickled. She tried to catch her mother's eyes but she had turned her face away. The judge began by acknowledging that Schwarz's document was a declaration of intent. He rubbed his glasses and continued speaking softly. "Was there an actual signing? Much remains uncertain to this day. Many facts are undiscoverable. Those were war times and documents got lost. What's certain is that this adoption was an act of love, whether in fact or intention. My ruling is in favor of Countess Ute and her mother, Gerda-Maria." It was as if the judge himself had fallen under the spell of the Countess's aristocratic bearing and motherly love and Frieda's loyal devotion.

True to form, Reinhardt blew a kiss in Ute's direction on his way out. Aunt Beate and Gabriele did not even acknowledge them. Schwarz sank back into an empty bench, clutching his briefcase. When he finally looked up, his cheeks blanched with rage. Gerda-Maria and Ute dashed to Deeda and could finally embrace her.

To celebrate the successful ending of the proceedings, they splurged at Hamburg's exclusive Fürstenhof Hotel. Over dessert Ute asked. "Did I ever have that girls' party?" As Deeda busied herself with her chocolate mousse, Gerda-Maria leaned over and tenderly caressed Ute's hand. "Probably," she sighed, "but my memory fails me. The Russian troops were already burning down the neighboring villages. We had to flee. We were lucky to get out alive." Was there a conspiratorial glance flitting between the two women?

Outside the restaurant the night was balmy and a myriad of stars twinkled in the sky. It was as if they were dancing. A promise had been kept. The truth would remain forever hidden.

Hamburg had one more excitement in store for Ute and Margot, and the tracks of Ute's destiny would be switched by a note on a snow-sprinkled tree trunk. On her way to class the following morning she spotted a piece of cardboard with large black lettering tacked into the bark of a tree. Although globs of moisture had smudged the message, it was still legible. Ute pried the cardboard loose and stuffed it into her backpack. Later that evening she showed it to Margot. It was an announcement of an upcoming trip to the Orient. The girls got excited. The next day they went to the student organization and signed up. The excursion was scheduled over Easter break. The girls sprang into action but told no one. Margot found a job in a factory sorting nuts, some of which she squirreled away and brought home. They decided on a strict budget, needing to save all their money for the journey. Ute became a sitter with the Petersen family and helped with their three girls and light housework after class. During those busy months, Margot and Ute seldom saw each other. When they did, they traced the places they would visit on the world map and read about each of them. They also cut and sewed clothes, especially tight jeans for the impending adventure.

When Margot told her parents about the trip, they just shook their heads but did not object. When Gerda-Maria heard the news her face fell, then her body. She fainted. Ute knew how she hurt and worried her mother but could not help it. She stuck to her decision. When she confided in Omi Maria about her intended travels, her grandmother recalled her own departure for Africa years ago and how her mother had been inconsolable. "Go child, but be careful," she counseled. "I will look after your mother."

23 The Train

The engine of the locomotive hissed with a comforting sound before halting inside the station. Travelers boarded, others departed the train just as people do in everyday life. Some stay together for short stretches, others remain companions the entire ride.

A German student group grabbed up their backpacks, absentmindedly hugged their relatives who had come to see them off. The leaders, two older students, directed the participants to their carriages. Margot and Ute were assigned to the leaders' compartment along with a young American, Ronald, from Indiana. Ute spotted him on the platform as a foreigner. No German would wear tennis shoes or sling a camera case crosswise over his chest. He carried a beige-colored raincoat, everybody else had windbreakers. It did not take long in their cramped compartment for the five to get acquainted. The first night on their journey from Stuttgart to Istanbul the girls got the luggage racks, while the three men bedded beneath them on pullout loungers. After darkness dimmed the ceiling lights, they shared information about their backgrounds. Ronald was a foreign exchange student in Mainz. His curiosity about cultures and people revealed itself with his frequent questions. The windows outside the compartment along the narrow aisles, were an ideal place to stretch one's legs. Soon Ute and Ronald met there, engaging in lengthy conversations.

The first thing Ute learned about Ronald was that his appetite for travel could never be satisfied, would never stop. What she discovered in his face were laugh lines spreading from his eyes along creases to his nose. She liked those unusual laugh lines. She would get to like more about this tall, lanky globetrotter during their six-week journey. They made it a habit to sit together at a table wherever they were housed. More and more, they laid their personal histories out between them.

In retrospect Ute could never say what stops along their adventurous journey were more spectacular than others. Was it the solemn Easter procession through Jerusalem or a ride on horseback through the forbidden canyons of Petra? The Nile River was like a poem. They grew quickly to love its banks where women carried jugs on their heads through villages whose tile roofs were silhouetted against a blue sky. They admired water-wheels driven by oxen and ringed by earthenware and pots. They heard the calls from the minarets and spotted villages embedded in palm groves. They were awed by the temple of Karnak where mimosas, acacias and poinsettias bloomed in abundance. They also got seasick on a boat to Athens.

On each juncture of the excursion Ute and Ronald were thrown together by unexpected circumstances. At a Damascus market Ronald enlisted Ute's advice about selecting a tailored suit while she bargained for a hand-painted mocka set. She had not forgotten her skills from her forays with Reinhardt. In Beirut, on Ronald's 21st birthday, they strolled through olive orchards and lost track of time. When they returned to the monastery where the group was staying, the gates were closed. Without phones, nobody responded from inside. As the temperatures dropped drastically during the evening hours, they had no choice but to creep into the backseat of an unlocked car, shivering.

There was a youthful blindness to danger among the group. They took everything in stride. No complaints about hurdles. Margot worried a bit when Ron and Ute did not appear at mealtime. She climbed up the open-air monastery tower and surveyed the land. Though she couldn't spot them, she was sure they would safely reappear the next morning. And they did.

The very first picture of Ron and Ute together was taken near Luxor when an Army officer and his wife invited them to their estate. Transportation was on the backs of donkeys. They stayed overnight and brushed their teeth with a Slivovitz plum brandy. During that interlude Ute made a spontaneous decision to spend the following semester at Mainz University. She later told Omi Maria that she wanted to share more time with Ronald. "I had a feeling about him that Schiller once described as *fremd jedoch innig vertraut* (foreign yet intimately familiar)." Fate had already shuffled the deck and now it held the cards.

It was difficult for Ute to tell Margot about her move to Mainz but they assured each other that it would only be temporary. Margot had recently met a fellow student whom she would later marry. She would have company during this interlude.

Friends, the Dosches, located a small attic room in Finten, a suburb of Mainz. Over the days and weeks Ron and Ute attended classes together, and Ute caught Ron's travel bug. They took off on weekends in his second-hand VW. As they grew closer, Ute dared to ask Ron to take her to Montmédy in France where her father was buried. His body had been exhumed from his apple-tree gravesite in the country and relocated to a large burial ground for fallen soldiers. It was troubling to encounter the sea of white crosses. Even when they located Gert's grave marker, his spirit seemed lost among so many dead.

Not unsurprisingly, so much togetherness would eventually lead to an embrace. And then another...as the sun went down over the tiled rooftops, a bouquet of lilacs perfumed the air in the Finten room. Ute longed to shed her virginity and imagined Ron's hands caressing her. But Ron hesitated. He had scruples. In the course of the trip, he had shown everyone a picture of his girlfriend, Diane. They were promised to each other before he left for Germany. Diane was writing to him weekly, eagerly anticipating his return. The era of sexual freedom was still awaiting. Ron reminded Ute that in his world sex was permitted only within a marriage. Still, he was ever more torn between the two girls. While Ute pressed for more intimacy, Ron was seized by doubts. "I am not sure," he confessed to Ute, looking at her in bewilderment. "Give me time."

He finally confided his moral dilemma to his parents in a letter. The answer came promptly. His father reminded him, "Keep it in your pants. Should I fly over?" When Ron assured him that he could handle his conflicts, his mother wrote more forcefully, "Come back home, Son, where you belong and your girlfriend is waiting. In your old familiar world, you will realize that Europe was a dream that will fade."

The situation was not resolved when they tearfully parted at the end of the semester. Ute returned to Hamburg, Ron to the U.S. How would it end? Ute was sure in her favor. He was the one for her. But she had been wrong about love before.

America seemed remote. Ute had always envisioned that she might live in France or Neuchâtel. But during the ensuing months an omen surfaced. When Ute was eleven, she was permitted her first adult movie. The film *Mutiny on the Bounty* with Clark Gable was playing in the only cinema in town. Ute stayed for repeat viewings and was so enthralled that she wrote a long letter to the actor she now swooned over and sent it to Paramount Pictures in Hollywood. Months passed. On her twelfth birthday Ute was in bed with mumps when Gerda-Maria entered the sickroom with a smile. "I have a surprise," she coaxed the sick girl to peek out from under her covers. "A letter from America."

It contained a signed copy with the inscription "Gratefully Clark Gable." Mumps or not, that photo made Ute a most happy girl. She later wondered who might have taken the trouble to open a letter from a little girl in a faraway German town, read it and send back a signed photo? "Americans must be nice," Ute confided in her diary. She recorded the arrival of the letter–July 18th, 1952.

Ron struggled after his return to the States and attempted to reunite with Diane. But the pull toward Ute proved stronger. When he called in October with a marriage proposal, Ute accepted without hesitation.

The ensuing months were nothing but hectic. Ute got a job in a hospital, so did Ron, working the nightshift. He also needed to finish his BA college degree. They had to save money for a wedding and Ute's move to America. To Ute's great surprise Gerda-Maria was not unnerved. She sprang into action. Her slender hands were made for arranging beautiful things. So she planned a splendid wedding party in her apartment with family and friends galore. A dress according to Gerda-Maria's design was ordered from a local seamstress. Even a dance was organized after the ceremony and festive dinner. Ute invited her former Pastor Burkhardt who had confirmed her, and his wife. He arrived with Uschi and Wölfi in tow. Ron saw his bride right before the church service and exclaimed, "Beautiful, just beautiful."

After the ceremony in the old Romanesque church in Felsberg, Ute looked over the row of guests forming a lane down the gravel path to greet the newlyweds. Her eyes scanned over many loving faces. Some like Wölfi and Felix had envisioned themselves at her side. Ute stole a long glance at Omi Maria who usually wore ordinary dresses. For the wedding she was adorned in a black satin gown, her fine dark hair coiffed. A brooch dotted with pearls, ruby earrings, fine jewelry from the past. Her clear brown eyes sparkled with joy as she took measure of her beloved granddaughter. Gerda-Maria had reserved her gift for Ute for this occasion. It was a solid gold bracelet, representing their aristocratic tradition which she had engraved with the line "*Gott schütze Dich*." (May God protect you). There were so many gifts which Ute barely noticed. In later years she regretted having not acknowledged the forethought and love with which many items had been selected, some handmade, with special notes attached. How ungrateful she must have seemed. Eberhard, whom Ute had not seen in years, was among the guests with his wife. During the dance, he pressed his signet ring into her palm. "Promise not to forget me." She never would, but this evening her thoughts were here and now.

A light shadow hung over the festivities because Ron's parents could not afford to fly in for the occasion. But they were already planning a rededication of vows at their church.

Ron and Ute spent a three-day honeymoon at the Petersens' country house in the heather near Lüneburg. Then a whirlwind swept them along, packing, goodbyes and the journey on the Cunard Ocean Liner, the Queen Mary, to New York. They sailed with buoyant excitement. On the ship they finally relaxed, even foregoing the breakfasts they had looked forward to.

Before they sailed, Ute sat across from Omi Maria, her wise owl grandmother who said, "We are so close. We will remain connected wherever you go. Our love has no boundaries." Then she offered a gentle warning, "You have the ability to reach deeply into peoples' souls. Be careful. Remember, you can harbor only a few soulmates."

As Ute and Ron departed for their life together, Ute knew for sure that their love would last. But a vast ocean still had to be crossed one stroke at a time.

24 Coming to America

With joyful expectancy and early morning brightness the Queen Mary sailed toward a new shore and anchored in a berth in New York's harbor. The open sea with no heavy squalls and a clear sky had brought calm to the young couple's mood. Ron talked about future plans and as Ute listened, she resolved to sink roots into the unknown soil. They had traveled light. Ute's belongings would be shipped.

The city was hot and muggy. Leaves and garbage drifted on the pavement. A gray cloudy horizon covered up the stars, replacing them with a flood of flashing lights from advertisements on buildings and billboards. A few drooping plants survived on the sidewalks. The first night in a youth hostel, Ute thought of Omi Maria and how she had landed alone in Africa. Ute had her loved one snuggling next to her. But he was feverish and sweating profusely and by morning Ute needed to enlist her old self-reliance, and seek help. By then a cooling rain had washed the air and Ute marched off to find a pharmacy. She spotted a hospital emergency room. Using her English for the first time she described her ailing husband's swollen throat. A sympathetic doctor handed her a small bottle of antibiotics. After a day of rest, the young couple, with Ron confidently behind the wheel of his old VW headed for Indiana. As road signs announced the town of Lebanon, Ute began brushing her hair repeatedly.

Wheat colored farms, red barns, wooden covered bridges and low-lying rooftops stretched along the horizon. Here was the wisdom of generations that had worked the land and knew its value. "Amber Waves of Grain" was engraved on the license plates. This was central Indiana, flat as a pancake. Wind trembled and rose through cornrows, husks lined up with long faces. At sunrise the stalks spoke aloud to each other, rustled and whispered at night. From his youth, Ron had waded through these fields. In spring he had hovered over juicy-green shafts, in summer he had harvested their golden crowns, in fall he had squinted up through yellow-tinged stalks into a blue heaven with white clouds. Pumpkin and squash vines crawled along the ground until everything was plowed under before the first frost. It was in these cornfields that Ron felt the first stirrings of Wanderlust.

There was a rededication of the marriage vows at the First Baptist Church, followed by receptions and dinners. Family members scrambled to have the newlyweds over for a meal. Neighborliness abounded, a cherished custom in small Indiana communities. Ute enjoyed a large family gathering with a cookout and croquet played on a large mowed lawn. Curiosity about Ron's new wife permeated the atmosphere. Ute was sized up and heartily welcomed, her German accent and European mannerisms, and all. At times she felt like an exotic plant blown into the rugged rows of corn fields.

Ron's father, William, known as Bill, born in 1917, exuded kindness and won Ute's heart. He took her on walks around Lebanon, helping her make sense of local ways of life. He gently corrected her English and explained why there seemed to be more church steeples than rooftops. Bill was musical. Ron remembered the barbershop quartet that rehearsed weekly in their basement. Bill also played the clarinet in a bar to earn extra money. Ron imbibed the spirit of music in his parents' house. It was there all around him. Bill was a craftsman and took his son with him from little on, teaching him practical skills like fixing up a house and then refinishing the inside from carpentry to painting. He was a master of sanding and polishing wood. "There is a marvelous smell of sap, dust and varnish working with wood," he commented. He also had an eye for antiques which he collected. He was known at auctions. Ute remembered standing next to him, quietly waiting until he lifted a finger, signifying his interest in an object. He was the one who accompanied Ron on his early paper routes and helped him buy his first car. During icy winter mornings he drove Ron in his own car along the paper routes, secretly impressed by his son's perseverance. In later years he visited Ron and Ute and always helped with repairs. He assisted with their countless moves, never complaining or resenting yet another obligation. He was a tolerant man. When gays first voiced their rights, members of his church groups mumbled, "This is sinful. The bible says so." He replied, "but if they are kind to each other?" He welcomed everybody. At Bill's funeral the pastor eulogized him with a characteristic gesture. Standing at his door, Bill would open his arms wide and say, "Hi. I'm Bill Carson, come on in." He knew no stranger. Bill loved flowers. Peonies were his favorites. His workshop was barely visible, camouflaged under ivy. Hugs were not common in the family, so Ute introduced them and Bill took to being hugged.

Claribel, Ron's mother, born 1918, was the disciplinarian and Ron's guide. She loved him with all that she was capable of, hoping to bring him into the ministry like her beloved father. She was a stern woman, always immaculately dressed. She was intelligent. If she had been born in a different century she would have gone to university. She became a highly respected and sought-after secretary. She did her job with the same meticulous care and devotion she required from others. She incorporated everything that was good about a strict upbringing in a small midwestern town, encouraging hard work and conscientious behavior. She gave piano lessons and was the church organist. There was a tenderness in her fingers as she caressed the keys of her black upright piano. She found no faults with her only son, except that he chose a foreign wife. She never fully accepted Ute, whom she blamed for being the wind behind Ron's professional choices. But Ron was always his own guide as he became a leader of others. He followed his inner calling, not his mother's. Claribel was embedded in the morality of her times. Prudery ruled private behavior. Sex before marriage was a sin, even though there were countless marriages right out of high school. Abortions were kept secret but everyone knew of a home for unwed mothers. There was no room for ambiguity. The body was taken for granted but never openly talked about or displayed. No toddler ever ran naked through the rain. While Bill saw the best in everyone, Claribel tended to blame girls when relationships faltered.

At the wedding of a cousin, whose belly bulged with her pregnancy, Claribel comforted the mother of the girl whose lips were pinched, her eyes swollen. It looked like a funeral, not a celebration. Bill, who was more lenient in moral matters murmured, "How can any girl do this to her mother?"

Claribel and Bill had grown up in the small town of Darlington. Bill carried Claribel's saxophone home from school as he later carried her babies. They had a well-matched marriage, full of mutual respect and joy in communal tasks. Claribel once said, "I had the near perfect mate." But she vehemently rejected the role of nursemaid. When Bill sank into dementia in his early nineties and was confined to a nursing home, she began to distance herself. When he died, she sighed, "I took my leave long ago."

It took a lifetime for Ute to realize that emotions change, hers included. What was once of utter importance can fade into insignificance. Ute once asked her mother-in-law, "Tell me about an event in the past." She would respond, "Oh honey, that was so long ago. How could I possibly remember?"

Both Carilbel and Bill cheered Ron on. Father and son had built multicolored kites with different destinations written on the wings: Germany, the Thames, the Highlands, Taj Mahal. One Sunday they took the kites to the local park. Ron ran between the trees until his kites moved beyond entanglement, feathery comets of his dreams. Balancing between heaven and earth, his imagination had free rein. He untied a bunch of balloons and let them go one by one. They flew like birds over the fence, above the rooftops and away with the breeze. "I wanted winged feet," Ron recalled his longings. "I sailed away with the clouds."

In spite of being moored in their everyday life in Lebanon, summers were for vacations. As a family they traveled across the United States. Claribel, who suffered from allergies, had a pile of Kleenex next to her car seat but never complained. Ron remembers their trip to Niagara Falls for his eighth birthday as extra special because he was allowed to sit on a sturdy draft horse. "From now on I'll ride around the whole wide world," he declared. Ron had a balanced upbringing between obligatory church attendance, dignified work and numerous youth activities like being on the football team and playing the cello. His parents were encouraging and always at his side. Strictness also reigned in their household. When Ron was a kid and misbehaved, he got a bare-handed spanking on his behind from his dad. And when he was "old enough to know better," even his mother would box his ears if he talked back to her.

On this first visit to Indiana, Ute was introduced to relatives nearby in small towns.

Florence, born 1895, was Ron's grandmother, a native of Darlington. She was the organist at the Methodist Church and prided herself on growing roses and a variety of velvety flowers nearly year around. She wore fancy hats and attended Ron's graduation from seminary wearing white gloves. She bemoaned wastefulness. "After a big family meal, we always kept what was not eaten. We spread a tablecloth over the leftovers and then stored everything away for the next day." Proudly, she informed Ute how household chores were done the old-fashioned way. "On cleaning day, the furniture is moved into the yard and rugs are laid out on the lawn. Then rugs are beaten and woodwork is polished. On washday, women pump water and carry it in by the bucketful, then heat it in a copper boiler on the coal stove. White things are boiled and stirred with a broom handle. All clothes are then washed in a washing machine and run through a wringer into a big tub of water. Several little balls of bluing, wrapped and tied off, swish through the cold water until it is blue enough to whiten the clothes. After being wrung out, white things are further bleached on the grass, colored clothes hung on lines in the shade to keep them from fading. Curtains dry on flimsy wooden stretchers. At the end of the day everyone washes their hair in the soft rainwater that is collected in a container under the downspouts. Baths are taken that night in one tub of water, kids first." A special freshness clings to everything after washday. It is the odor of country laurel. It lingers in the sheets, the mattresses and the ironed linen.

Florence's husband, Glen, born 1893, was the town barber. Ron recalled that he was fascinated by him as a youngster. On the glass counter over the wash basin of the barber shop, combs, shaving soap, brushes, straight razors, talcum, a towel and a bottle of lotion were neatly arranged. On his twelfth birthday, Ron climbed onto a board laid across the armrests of the barber's chair, as he did every Saturday. "Tuck in your chin," Glen instructed the boy. Then he moved around the chair in a well-worn rhythm, knees slightly bent, elbows spread like wings. He lathered Ron's chin and the back of his neck. Thump, slap, swish went the gleaming blade on the leather strop that dangled at the side of the chair. The razor scraped with short even strokes, shaving away Ron's childhood with every whisker. The fresh skin had not a single nick. Bits of hair fell to the floor. A minute before they were Ron's, now they awaited the broom. "You are a man now," Glen proudly pronounced when finished. However, Ron was never allowed to look into the poolroom, tucked behind the barbershop. Sometimes the door to the backroom would swing open, letting out a chorus of men's voices, whiffs of thick smoke and the sound of pool balls clacking against each other. Glen died at the young age of 62 from lung cancer. He had been a heavy smoker. Florence lived to 92.

Ron's maternal grandparents, Wilda and William Zenor, both born in 1882, were less known to him. He remembered staying with Wilda after school and that she covered herself with newspapers to stay warm for a nap on the sofa. She was the admired pastor's wife in Darlington, tall and stern but with the door to their parsonage open at all times to friends and strangers alike. William Zenor was a beloved pastor who worked himself to death for his congregation on a meager minister's salary. Claribel blamed the church community for his early death of a heart attack at 56. Claribel adored her father and had high hopes for Ron to follow in his footsteps.

In one of Ute's early letters to home, she remarked on customs she observed; strict behavioral rules were embedded in equally strict church observances. Never miss a Sunday service, no matter how late the evening before had been or how tired you were. The separation between men and women was also new to Ute. In social settings, men stood together in a group while women congregated in another. The talk among women was often homespun, a mixture of current goings-on and gossip. The men talked about politics and the local government. Ute had not experienced such role divisions. Omi Maria wrote back. "When Germany lost its men, women moved into their places. As it turned out, women did well in 'men's roles'."

The couple's stay in Indiana was brief. They moved on to Rochester, New York where Ron started seminary studies at Colgate Rochester Divinity School. It would take Ute longer than she had expected to adjust to the new world. She would straddle two cultures all her life. "We have two feet," she pondered, "one striding forward confidently, the other planted firmly in the home ground."

25 The Scent of Lilac Bushes

Highland Park was within walking distance of the divinity school where the lilac festival was held each year in May. Trees, shrubs and flowers blended in with carpeted floral lawns. There was an iris garden and pansies galore. The sweet-smelling lilac blossoms mixed with the damp odor of earth. In winter it snowed, covering the rolling hills.

Ron and Ute had been assigned to student housing, a room with a kitchen and bath in a cross-timbered house on campus. Most other houses in the neighborhood were of reassuring solidity, stone and brick. Ron began his first year as a seminarian, Ute got a job in the school library. Her duties were shelving books and signing them in and out to readers. She was privileged to sit in on a few of Ron's classes.

Ron came under the influence of a charismatic teacher, the "Death of God" theologian William Hamilton. Hamilton not only encouraged his students to question traditional beliefs, he also preached about the life of Jesus as the man for others. Political and social issues were introduced and Dietrich Bonhoeffer, a young German theologian who was executed for participating in a plot to kill Hitler, was required reading. Bob became Ron's best friend. He thumped into their lives while living with Kris in an apartment above ours. Bob had broken his leg and his cast pounded on their ceiling day and night. He decided to introduce himself to his dwellers below. The two men began to work together and take an interest in the racial unrest in town. On May 3rd, 1963 they, along with a few fellow students, participated in a demonstration against unfair housing practices. They chained themselves across a busy street at traffic time and were arrested. This and the murder of President Kennedy armed Ron with a voice against injustice.

Ute could not get over her repugnance at the sight of their apartment. She got to work on remodeling the first chance she had while Ron was away in class. She had already scrubbed the floors and hung pictures on the walls to hide smudge spots. The green plastic-covered sofa and chairs were badly cracked. She pulled them out to the curb for trash pickup and found instead suitable discarded furniture along the street, a table with a glass top and two wicker chairs. She removed the windscreens and bought material for curtains. Her final project was their Pullman bed which was stored in the closet and had to be pulled out each night. She loosened the screws, unbolted the hinges and with a crash the bed thundered to the floor. She covered the mattress with a white and blue-striped bedspread.

Flowerpots soon decorated the headboard. Between the doors she hung strips of beads she had seen in France.

A crew from Buildings and Grounds inspected all student quarters regularly. They did not utter a single word when entering Ron and Ute's place but reported her to the president of the divinity school.

"What did you have in mind when you dismantled your apartment?" the president asked cautiously.

"Beautification," Ute snapped.

He smirked. "How long have you been in this country?"

"Three months."

"As a guest?"

"No, as my husband's wife."

He stroked his chin. "Still from a foreign country, right? You should not meddle, don't you think?"

"I did not intend to meddle, just rearrange. Make an ugly room pretty."

"Well, we seem to have different ideas of beauty. You have the apartment for the rest of the year but next fall would be a good time to find a residence off campus." The president kept his hands behind his back at all times.

The stay on the divinity school hill would have been happier if Gerda-Maria and Gabriele had waited. But with the greening of spring, they arrived for a visit. Ute and Ron lived on a very meager income. Their old cherished German VW had been sold because they could no longer afford repairs. Christa, a new German friend, lent them a room in their house so that Gerda-Maria and Gabriele could move into the student abode. There Ute's mother decorated with more flowers and cooked. She and Gabriele, who seemed to have forgotten the Hamburg drama, were soon sought-after guests. Their aristocratic title drew much curiosity. The head librarian invited them to dinner.

Over Easter break Ron took a bus home, borrowed his parents' car and drove back to pick up Ute, her mother and sister. Together they visited Ron's family where the German relatives received an open welcome. Before they returned to Kennedy Airport they spent two nights in the city, attending a Broadway play and enjoying a carriage ride through Central Park. Ute was on edge during the entire visit even though it went better than expected.

Each fall, members of Temple B'rith Kodesh invited students and their spouses from the divinity school to dinner. Sitting at a finely laid table with candles and bouquets of autumn sprigs, soup was ladled out. Everyone introduced themselves. Ute stated her name and said, "I am German."

The hostess, well-coiffed and sitting straight, put down her spoon and stood up. "Please leave." An embarrassed silence followed but as Ute rose the host sprung up and pushed her back down into her seat.

"NO, you are our guest." Not much conversation could develop thereafter and Ute left her food largely untouched. On their way out, the host intercepted them. "I would ask that you attend our film series about The Third Reich that's offered at our Temple this week." Ute did not answer but Ron said, "We will."

The film was "Treblinka." Ute barely made it out of the theater onto the finely cropped Jewish lawn. She sank to her knees and vomited. A hand touched her shoulder and the voice of the hostess whispered, "You are German."

"There are many Germans," Ute managed to reply.

Ute passed the exams for teacher certification and was offered a position at Palmyra High School for the fall. Ron had found a part-time job at a travel agency. They had moved to Tracy Street, an eyesore, two stories high, drab from lack of paint, a dirt yard with just one sickly green tree for their cat. The room was weatherbeaten. The floorboards were uneven and peeling. The wallpaper was many-layered and curled away from the baseboard. But the landlord allowed them to paper and paint. They fell in love with the house when they met George who lived in a flat downstairs. It was winter and they pointed to the open back door where snow drifted into the hallway. "That's the cat door," he said, "it has to stay open."

"No problem," they replied. "We have a cat of our own." The other tenants were an old couple who were seldom seen and two ladies of the night who slept all day. One sometimes played loud music when a customer stumbled up to her flat. When Käthe and Ronald Gregor Smith, esteemed professors from Scotland visited Ute and Ron on Tracy Street, Ute bought rugs at a flea market and spread them around the hall. She also donated doormats. George, who was always under the influence, unscrewed light bulbs in the entryway and the porch. When the Scottish guests announced their coming, Ute told George that a famous couple from Scotland was visiting. That night the house was lit up like a night at the circus. Nobody knew that Ute had brought her sterling silver cutlery from Germany. Käthe, to her chagrin, mistook the silver coaster for an ashtray.

Ron's present for Ute as a beginning German teacher was a brown velveteen dress from Montgomery Ward. Ron had never bought a female garment and the dress was the size of a very ample woman. They exchanged it for a smaller size, laughing all the while.

Teaching proved to be a joy. The Palmyra administration and fellow teachers were most helpful and cordial. Ute got teased about her accent when she mentioned "mouse wash" and everyone giggled.

"Mrs. Carson, mice need traps. You mean to say mouthwash." Ute was entrusted with a large study hall where she wrote letters to Omi Maria.

Ute had to rely on transportation from the guidance counselor who picked her up each morning in his ancient MG convertible. With top down, rain or shine, he honked in front of her house. Ute rushed out. Tires squealing, the car horn went hoop...hoop and off they went. Ute wore different-colored headscarves like the Queen of England when riding horses. They flapped and fluttered in the wind over the old MG.

When Ute failed a driver's test for sliding backwards on sloping icy exit ramps while double-clutching their old VW, her students enticed her to take driver's education class with them. Bandanas flew into the air to shouts of "HOORAY" as their German teacher passed the driving test. At Christmas the class presented her with a frilly white long-sleeved blouse. They asked her to hold it up against her chest so they could take a picture.

Ute would have stayed at the Palmyra school for a third year had the beckoning winds not blown from across the other side of the ocean. Ron accepted a three-year scholarship from the Faculty of Divinity at the University of Glasgow, Scotland that Professor Gregor Smith had made possible.

26 Sheep, Classics and Light of Wisdom

Ron and Ute bought rainwear, black and white plastic coats with broad-brimmed hats. Even though the climate proved temperate and oceanic, it could change like a weathervane. Daffodils greeted the couple as they rented a flat on Lorraine Gardens in Glasgow. High bay windows let them watch for the cloppity-clop of the milkman's horse-drawn wagon each morning. Wood and coal carts also traveled along the cobblestone street. They had a spacious room but shared a kitchen and bath with an elderly lady. They fumbled with the shilling meter before learning how to use it and were shocked to find themselves without electricity and heat. Soon the daffodils withered and an autumn wind shook leaves from the maple tree in front of their window. Their fireplace was tiny and drafty. A gift from grandmother Aenne arrived unexpectedly. She had a kerosene stove delivered from Germany to Glasgow. Two sturdy workers huffed and puffed as they lugged the big crate up the flight of stairs. "Good grief," one fumed, "who would ship such a thing?" Ron emptied his pockets for a gratuity. Even pipes were included, which Ron installed. Soon their Scottish abode was cozy and warm.

While friends in America burned their draft cards and Vietnam became a slaughterhouse, Ron began his dissertation on Nietzsche. Ute found a position at the British Educational Institute. Bob and Kris and their young daughter joined them for a year in Scotland. Both Gerda-Maria and Bill and Claribel, became welcomed guests. The Gregor Smiths took the young couple under their tutelage and invited them to their white-washed cottage adorned with bright-red doors, near Rowardennan at Loch Lomond. As they journeyed there, sheep blocked the road and a farmer pulled a stubborn goat by a rope across a thoroughfare. Fog mysteriously covered the Highland moors and by August purple heather dotted the countryside.

In the window of a tobacco shop, a 1950 Wolseley was advertised, a classic with rolled-and-pleated leather upholstery, wooden steering wheel, steel spokes, and outside running boards. The vehicle was for sale at 15 pounds. They bought it and later sold it for 20. It guzzled oil and on steep hills Ute had to walk while Ron motored up. On top she would get back into the car and on they would go. As proud car owners they explored the ruins at Melrose and Dryburg in the Scottish Border Country. Cows were grazing under the arches one night as the moon ghostly blinked through the openings. They stopped to admire Wade Bridges and touched the massive stone work. At The Burn, a student retreat in the country, they made new friends, Elspeth and her parents who introduced them to the "Sherry Hour."

The months in Scotland were devoted to studies, reading and theater productions in the Gorbals district of Glasgow. Chinese restaurants were affordable on their student budget, with banana fritters a special treat.

After the second year in Glasgow an invitation arrived from Weimar offering Ron a six-week study leave at the Nietzsche Archive there. Ron and Ute took the train, stopping briefly in Gensungen to see Gerda-Maria and Omi Maria, then on to the German Democratic Republic in a divided Germany. West Germany held a sense of reassuring certainty for Ute but the feeling of familiar permanence vanished as they crossed the border in darkened train compartments, with lengthy stops at the border. Police searched them thoroughly. Their luggage was strewn across train seats. Ron had all the necessary papers but they were mistrusted as foreigners. Their western clothes were suspicious, as were their stated intentions to do research.

In Weimar they found a room with a local family in an unadorned Soviet-style housing block. The tiny apartment which they shared with the Strassburgs and their two sons was cramped. It was furnished in an appalling taste, beat-up furniture, many pieces salvaged from the rubble of war. The curtains were always drawn, giving the rooms a nocturnal atmosphere, whatever the time of day. One of their sons was physically disabled and because no wheelchairs were available, they pulled him in a small wooden wagon. During Ute and Ron's short stay the Strassburgs shared their only bathroom and kitchen facilities. They became their guides, eyes and ears. They warned them that they would be under surveillance the entire visit. Often police stopped them and they became accustomed to showing their papers and IDs.

Weimar had been the seat of the short-lived Weimar Republic. The town was encased in the past, birthplace of Goethe and Schiller, Herder's hometown and the famous cathedral where several of Bach's works had premiered. Ron received permission to use the archives in the Baroque Residence, a castle where once the Duke of Saxony held his parties.

It was the season of snow and biting cold. The roads were full of fallen leaves and slick. A punishing wind blew through their coats. The room at the castle had radiators, the only place to keep warm. At night a hot water bottle was placed at their feet. The old smoke-filled restaurant "Gasthaus Zum Weissen Schwan," became a regular eating place where they also relished the heat from a colorful tiled stove. They toured the Goethe and Schiller residences and bought tickets to the National Theater where they watched both parts of 'Faust'. One weekend they took a bus out to Schloss Belvedere where they were the only customers in the restaurant. To their great delight they were asked to wait and then served slender pieces of wild boar with dumplings and red cabbage, a culinary delight. Another weekend they left with a bus before dawn to visit the Christmas Market in Erfurt. Traditions were revered and the pre-holiday atmosphere soaked into their freezing bones. Drinking hot cider with a thimble of Schnapps mixed in, they temporarily forgot the cold. They felt transported back to ancient times. On weekdays Ron filled his notebooks with valuable information for his thesis and Ute read German classics.

After their return to the West, Ron and Ute stayed in touch with the Strassburgs and sent regular packages with items that were not available in the East. Years later Gerda-Maria and granddaughter Claudia were able to slip a wheelchair across the border for the Strassburgs' disabled son.

On their way back to Scotland they stopped again in Gensungen. Omi Maria was failing and had moved in with Gerda-Maria. Ute could not accept her beloved grandmother's frailty. She had planned for a long time that her Omi would visit them in Scotland. Ute also knew of Omi Maria's secret wish for a great-grandchild and Ute had only recently stopped taking birth control pills. But gently and firmly, Omi Maria taught Ute as she always had. "Growing old has been difficult but dying is even harder." Ute made oatmeal and encouraged little bites. Omi Maria swallowed only a little from the tip of the spoon. "Tea? I can brew you any kind you would like," Ute offered. Omi Maria sipped a few drops while Ute propped her up with a cushion. Ute tended to things she knew that mattered to Omi Maria. She clipped her fingernails and toenails. She read to her from the Christian Science newsletter. One day Omi Maria timidly asked to have her hair washed. Ute helped her to the tub. She was all lightness. Her hands were riddled with liver spots, loose skin hung over legs and ribs. She looked breakable, like bird bones. Her belly was bloated. It pained Ute to see her beloved grandmother so depleted. But it helped her to perform small acts of kindness. She shampooed Omi Maria's hair and combed the wet strands with her African comb carved from a hard kokerboom branch.

The days passed quickly. It was time for Ron and Ute to return to Glasgow. The day before, Omi Maria asked to be taken to her own apartment. Gerda-Maria fretted. "I'll be alright for one night," Omi Maria assured her.

When Ute climbed the stairs to Omi Maria's apartment the next morning, her childhood climbed with her. She smelled the catnip tea before she opened the door. The table was set for an old-time breakfast for two. A shrunken Omi Maria huddled under a loose knitted shawl. An inner radiance enveloped her. Fresh rolls with butter and marmalade were on the table. Ute could hardly eat but she would not rob her grandmother of her triumph at being able to host. Omi Maria balanced a cup of tea in her shaky hands and spilled drops. "This will be our last meal together, my sweet child, but we will always be united. The spirit knows no boundaries." Her eyes were wet. Ute could not control her own tears. She was three years old again and wanted to suck her thumb.

Ron and Ute had been back in Glasgow for a few weeks. It was early spring and light flowed through the maple tree branches. One night two intelligent eyes surrounded by feathers blinked at Ute in her dreams. Then she heard hooting and knew that a messenger, the owl, was delivering a premonition. By morning Gerda-Maria phoned with the news of Omi Maria's death. Omi Maria had not wanted to die yet, longing for a grandchild, but she had asked for a photograph of Ute to be placed in view of her bed. In the end she died peacefully, saying to Gerda-Maria, "Don't call the doctor, just hold my hand." The window had been wide open and an owl had been watching, perched on the top of a willow tree on the bank of the Eder River.

For years Ute had flown under Omi Maria's wings. She would continue to feel their soft protection and hear their calm beatings all her life.

Omi Maria gifted a volume of Wolfgang's poetry to Ute which she had signed in odd curly letters. Believing that handwriting reveals characteristics of the writer, Ute traced her name again and again, barely letting the pen off the lettering. The handwriting was like a footprint on paper, a mirror of personality. It felt to Ute as if Omi Maria's spirit slipped into her fingers, her palm.

27 Shadows

On a ferry from Denmark to Northern England, Ronald Gregor Smith suffered a fatal heart attack. Ron received his Ph. D. but his dissertation, which had been selected for publication, was indefinitely put on hold. His graduate stipend ran out. With no references or other assistance, Ron accepted a position at an experimental college in Vermont. If Indiana had boasted white picket fences and orderly dutiful lives, Brattleboro was hippy land. In Indiana most people followed predictable paths. Clean living was the rule. The nostalgia felt for the Indiana of the 1950s covered up many ruts, but it felt safe and predictable. In Vermont, communes sprang up where free spirits and different lifestyles abounded. Living was noisy and fraught with unfamiliar pitfalls. New sexual orientations were budding. "It even smells different in Vermont," Ute mused. It was a youth culture and Ron and Ute were young. Ute wore a mini skirt, platform shoes and tops without a bra. They imbibed the music of the Beatles and Bob Dylan. They established their first credit line, buying a teak record player on monthly installments.

Ron performed a marriage ritual for Rolf and Priscilla. As a thank-you, the newlyweds invited the couple to their quarters for a sumptuous meal. Rolf pulled out what looked like a cigarette. "What's that?" Ron wanted to know. The hosts smiled at Ron's innocence. Ron and Ute were behind the times and had never tried any psychedelic drugs. Hesitantly, they accepted the offer and slowly puffed, sucking in the smoke as the joint was passed around. The marijuana struck them forcefully and a marvelous calm enveloped them both. Arm-in-arm Ron and Ute traipsed home that night, steps as light as air. "We are bloody beginners," Ron joked.

Ron had been given the title of Dean of Studies under a grouchy, tyrannical president. Soon conflicts between the two erupted. They aspired to opposing educational approaches. Ron was open-minded and liked by the students. The president held on to antiquated educational principles, and was only tolerated. Because Ron and Ute lived in college housing, the president expected total subservience. But Ron's salary barely covered their living expenses. They had no health insurance. And Ron was not a yes-man. Within a year Ron was fired, jobless.

Ute had struggled against motherhood. She feared a repeat of her relationship to her mother. But Omi Maria's last days had evoked a different desire. "You are the result of the love of thousands," Omi Maria had said. "It is time for the love between Ron and Ute to bind the generations." Gerda-Maria also tried her best to be less demanding and more supportive. Following Omi

Maria's death, she felt called to carry the 'Omi' torch forward. She wanted to be a grandmother and to be called "Mumu."

Though Ute finally overcame her reluctance to conceive, she remained barren. Visits to doctors brought no results. In the waiting rooms Ute observed couples like themselves. Sex had become functional but was no longer a pleasure. Ron and Ute considered an adoption. After several consultations, a gynecologist in Boston discovered a hormone deficiency and prescribed a therapeutic regimen. Ute was joyfully pregnant but not for long. She expelled one fetus, then another. Was this punishment for her initial refusal? Each time a miscarriage began, she bit into her pillow, squeezed her legs together and willed the embryo to stay put. Jolt after jolt hit her body as the corkscrew of pain worked inside her. She felt the blood coursing sluggishly down her thighs, taking her precious cargo with it. Like a naked little bird, it slipped out. She warmed it in her blood-soaked sheets and tried to stuff it back into its nest. Once Ute carried a fetus for three months. They announced the pregnancy to family and friends and selected names. But hope dissolved again in a red wave. Each time her uterine walls were scraped out and readied for another try. Ute's mood was as gray as the sky outside her hospital window. She totally missed the changing of the brilliant maple tree leaves. She glared through tear-filled eyes at mothers carrying babies.

Finally, one single embryo held on. Were her little fingers bloody? She had the willpower to cling to the placenta for dear life. In all her longing for children Ute remained a stout defender of women's choices. Not every woman should desire a child, but she wanted children.

Ute's triumph was slow. Her body was not used to the hormone treatment and she vomited until she was skeletal. A general practitioner cared for her in Brattleboro. As Ute lost weight he began to worry. "You are starving yourself, my dear," he concluded. "You need hospital care."

Ute just shook her head. The couple had no health insurance and had used up their savings and help from their families for medical consultations and trial remedies. Ute knew how Ron worried about their finances. He had sent out query letters but no job was in sight. The president wanted them to vacate student housing. Where could they go?

One day Ute went in for a checkup and was so weak that she had to steady herself along the wall of the clinic. The doctor happened to see her. He wasted no time scooping her up and carrying her to his car and on to the local hospital. Ute murmured to the doctor, "No hospital. We can't afford it."

"But I can," he consoled. They were never charged a penny.

It was only a sprig of lilacs that Ute could bring to the doctor as a thank-you after her release. She hugged him, which made him blush. Ute regained strength enough for the next part of her pregnancy and their journey onward.

28 Sun-Kissed Florida

Bill Hamilton rescued them with an offer of a part-time position in religious studies at New College in Sarasota, Florida, another experimental college of the 1960s but with a welcoming faculty and open-minded administration. With great relief and gratitude Ron and Ute began to pack. Gerda-Maria had traveled to Brattleboro to care for her now pregnant daughter. The threesome piled into their old station wagon with no air conditioning and faulty tires and set off. Their cat snuggled next to Gerda-Maria in the loaded backseat.

On the lawn of New College, Ute, five months pregnant, slid out of the car and fainted on the lush Bermuda grass. As she regained consciousness she looked at the smooth grayish-white trunk all the way up to a bright green crown shaft of a royal palm tree. Evergreen leaves with small white flowers wafted above. "Omi Maria's kokerboom in the tropics," Ute marveled.

Florida had a golden voice of its own. It brought the babies, Caitlin, Claudia and Cecile. The long wait fell away and the pregnancies became easier as the months went on. Ute was patient with Ron always at her side. She stroked her heavy belly. Her babies would know her touch. Ute talked and sang to them. She listened to her babies. Murmurs vibrated through her womb and kicks responded. She carried her babies high on her left side, right under her heart.

Ute focused on the moon over the Gulf of Mexico as her fertility goddess who waved her beams like a lantern over her contractions. She befriended Ute's breathing and in turn Ute imitated her lunar rhythms. The German word for cervix is *Muttermund*. Fully dilated, Ute opened her mouth with jubilation, cascading new life through the opening. For each birth the moon had rounded out and stood in full power, her breasts engorged, her buttocks fleshed out, her thighs damp, her domed belly laboring. All three girls were born during a full moon. And as the moon began to be eclipsed behind a reddish golden curtain in the mornings, they reached for a finger of the gilded sun. They were early birds.

Giving birth was easy, as uncomplicated as a cat littering her kittens. Ute felt a kinship with cat mothers, how they carried their little ones everywhere by the scruff of their necks. Ute nursed her babies, her milk an abundant river. At the beach, lolling waves rolled over the small naked bodies of the girls. They were waterborne like their grandfather Gert.

In Sarasota the sun continued to shine on them. Sometimes the heat baked the ground, the grass and even the flowers. They had to stop their activities to breathe. They did not regard the mosquitoes or the sandflies as their friends but the blue sky bewitched them. Maybe there was a powder-white heaven which kept peeking through?

Ron moved up to a full-time teaching position. The job carrying papers could be given up. They bought their first house on Bayshore Circle where monkeys were swinging on branches over the rooftop. Many hospitable doors were thrown open. With some acquaintances they shared the elixir of life-giving water, with other friends they imbibed robust red wine.

Ron had always been enterprising. A notice on the bulletin board outside his office announced a short-term fellowship in "Health and Human Values" at the University of Florida, a three-hour drive away. For a semester Ron drove to Gainesville weekly to go on hospital rounds and visit rural clinics with physicians. After completing his fellowship, he was offered an associate professorship in a new center for the humanities in the medical school in Gainesville.

Ute was awarded a tuition scholarship for graduate work at the University of Rochester. They rented their Sarasota house to a "dream analyst" who later reported that their black armoire had materialized into a frightening ghost in her dreams. With two babies, Caitlin and Claudia, Ron and Ute drove north and settled back into student housing in Rochester. Ute had one required semester to be in residence at the university. Later she was allowed to complete her M. A. degree in absentia. Her thesis was on "Hermann und Dorothea" by Goethe. Ron was granted a leave of absence from New College to write a book on Jean Paul Sartre.

While registering for entry into the degree program in Comparative Literature and Women's Studies, Ute was made aware that a routine chest x-ray was required. Because she was breastfeeding Claudia and feared possible detrimental effects of radiation, she refused. Following a brief ruckus, the requirement was waived, although professors often frowned disapproval when she slipped out a bit early to attend to her baby.

Following their return from Rochester a move to Gainesville became imminent. Ute hated to leave their house which they had decorated with much devotion but Ron's professional prospects took priority. They relocated and soon the sun/moon pair brought a third baby, Cecile, into their lives.

Ute's first article to appear in the U. S. was published in *The Floridian*, a Sunday supplement of the *St. Petersburg Times*. It recounted an emergency room experience. Claudia had fallen on the edge of their record player, cut her scalp and had to be rushed to the hospital and stitched up while Ute sang lullabies to calm her. Ute was delighted about the publication. She even got paid!

The years in Gainesville advanced Ron's position in a new field. He went on rounds with Whit, director of a clinical residency program and, with other professionals, they developed a program on perspectives in the medical humanities. The couple formed new relationships, with a dear friend, Gail, and her caring husband, Tom, their pediatrician. Whit, Ruthanne and Robbie entered their lives. For the first time the girls glimpsed what it must be like to raise a physically disabled child like Robbie.

Activities abounded from ballet to music to swimming instruction. The girls had horseback riding lessons at "Pinch Penny Acres" and made their own friends at school and in the neighborhood. Ute and Ron hired a contractor to build a small pool in their backyard. With Ute's first down payment check, the contractor skipped town, leaving a gaping hole behind the house. They had no choice but to finish the pool themselves. There were peals of laughter and ribbons of tears when a downpour washed away the tile they had just plastered to the sides of the pool basin.

Animals–rabbits, cats, a squirrel took shelter in their home and the first stream of visitors announced their arrival. Bill and Claribel came and Bill helped Ron remodel the garage into another room for the girls.

"Look at this golden fruit," Gerda-Maria explained as she spread out her apron full of succulent oranges. The Florida sun had ripened the fruit which she gathered from under neighborhood trees. She served freshly squeezed orange juice every day. Gerda-Maria now stayed with them as long as her visitor visa allowed. She poured her whole being into grandmotherhood. She loved the grandkids, and they adored her. She had been a nurse, a daughter, a wife and lover but was a grandmother at the core. When back in Germany the girls took turns staying a summer month with her where she had moved into an upstairs apartment with the Hilgenbergs who became like family to her and the girls.

American holidays which Ute had not known about in Germany were added. She learned to cook festive dishes for Thanksgiving. At Halloween she would slip into a "good witch" costume, all purple from feathery hat to polish on fingernails and toes.

Among the unannounced visitors in Florida was Reinhardt. He was divorced again and traveling with a wealthy new lover. While she stayed with friends in New York Reinhardt surprised Ute and Ron. He was his charming old self, rocked baby Cecile on his knees while drinking vodka and smoking nonstop. On a walk with Ute, she asked him if he had ever loved her mother. "Oh sure," was his casual reply. "But we were young. It was right after the war and we were both needy. I just moved on." Reinhardt parted from Gainesville, leaving Ute with a promised gift. "I have a valuable insect collection. You should have it someday. It might bring a good price." Shortly after his return to Germany, Reinhardt died of a brain hemorrhage. Months later Gabriele informed Ute of his death. The insect collection was never mentioned.

Caitlin, Claudia and Cecile thrived and grew under the nourishing rays of the Florida sun. Ron was busy in his new field. And Ute was filled with happy mothering, a honeycomb full of sweet nectar of children. "When children are small, they are all yours," she said longingly in later years. She also realized that only children are capable of transforming mudpies into delicious cakes.

29 A Meadow of Wildflowers

Denn wir können die Kinder nach unserem Willen nicht formen. So wie Gott sie uns gab, so müssen wir sie haben und lieben. Sie erziehen aufs Beste und ein Jedes lassen gewähren.
(It is not possible for parents to shape their children in their own image. They were given to us to hold and love, to bring them up as best as we can, and then let be what will be.)

The children brought a sense of completeness to Ron and Ute's marriage. Ute had found a solid footing in America. "You belong to this country," she told Ron. "You have shared it with me and I have taken root. Maybe not completely," she joked.

The children left their footprints on the path of family life. Each girl exuded her unique aroma, displayed a color pulled from the rainbow and swayed in the breeze according to different talents. All three girls were capable of deep love, instilled in them by the love of their parents. The parents' love was not perfect but it was the best they could give.

Ute was reading Ray Bradbury's *Dandelion Wine* at the time and was moved by his flattering introduction of his parents and grandparents. He stated unapologetically that he loved them. Ute knew that the same event can be seen in different shades. Curious about what their girls might say about themselves, their lives, their talents and their dreams she proposed to juxtapose her reflections with short life sketches about themselves.

What Ron and Ute recall. "Caitlin was born close to Christmas. As Ron and Ute held their firstborn, they whispered, 'Unto us a child is born.' Grateful, they sprinkled the holy water of joyful tears on her tiny face. Caitlin had been conceived out of desperate longing and maybe hopes were carried on from birth. Caitlin always emphatically made up her own mind. A nurse told her to control herself as she was crying too loudly, waking other newborns. Caitlin was forever hungry even though there was no lack of Ute's milk. Ron and Ute often did not know what Caitlin wanted or what she needed. What they had to give as parents was often not the right formula. Ute blamed herself for being unable to find a smoother path for Caitlin. Caitlin was the animal whisperer in the family, a direct link to great-grandfather Peter. Physical closeness bound mother and daughter. Rubbing rose oil on Caitlin's delicate feet was a ritual, as was cuddling. 'Move over,' Caitlin mumbled, 'I want to snuggle.' As the years went by early struggles subsided and Ron's temper abated. He had often been impatient with Caitlin's 'You can't tell me what to do.' Music was a strong bond between father and daughter."

This is how Caitlin sees herself. "When I was a young girl, I remember a toy consisting of a tube which one would look through containing mirrors and pieces of colored glass whose reflections changed patterns as the tube rotated. This toy represents me and the ever changing and endless possibilities contained in the human experience and it's called the kaleidoscope. My unique patterns and characteristics reveal themselves in different lights, around different people, and different environments. If someone were to read this, I'd have them know I'm a passionate person. My relationship with life is intimate and intricate, always evolving. I have a natural ability to connect with people and they often reveal their deepest and most private sides to me as well as being able to feel non-judged and carefree with me. (Hence my degree in Human Development and Family Studies). I am compassionate and see things in gray rather than black and white. I am not Switzerland and stand my ground but I can also see the other sides to things. I have a love of horses. They allow me to be free and completely myself and I am a skilled rider. I also enjoy travel which makes me feel much the same as the freedom horses do. I am a truth teller and strong minded. I am guarded and private and have few people I feel close enough to let into my inner circle. I am emotional, yet strong and very spirited. I delight in live music of various genres and always end up dancing and singing along. I am most proud of being a mother to the loves of my life, Dylan and Nicholas. My favorite color is green, also due to my children both having green eyes. I am fortunate that later in life I found my soulmate, Tony, whom I adore and love. I look forward to seeing what the rest of my life brings."

This is how Tony, Caitlin's husband, sees himself. "God screwed me and I should have been a rockstar. However, all joking aside, I am very happy and love the life I've been fortunate to lead so far. I have lived a life full of experiences and have accomplished many notable achievements. Being a highly motivated and determined individual, I was able to successfully bring about many desired results in numerous areas of my life. I was the first American selected in the 1980 National Hockey League draft and continued my career in hockey later in the coaching ranks. After my playing career which included a brief stint with the Calgary Flames along with many stops in Triple A, I moved on to coaching. I found coaching to be the most rewarding because I was not only able to develop hockey players, I was also able to touch the lives of many young men with whom I have relationships lasting to the present day. During my coaching career, I modestly say, I won over 4 state championships and 5 US Junior A national championships, spanning over the states of Texas and Illinois. I pride myself in being direct, yet caring, and I am very much a people person. I love a good political debate and enjoy conversing on various topics such as religion and philosophy. I have traveled extensively in the US and Canada. I've been a restaurateur in Colorado and Illinois and am now part of a successful New York stock exchange company. I love to read and learn new things and am most proud of my two children, two stepchildren, seven grandchildren, and the love of my life, Caitlin."

What Ron and Ute recall. "Claudia remained in the intensive care unit after birth because her liver was not fully functioning and her tiny heels had to be pricked like pincushions. As Ute's heart melted with concern she became a tigress, often breaking hospital rules. Night and day she prowled the baby station and nursed her infant every two hours. The nurses baked Ute a cake expressing admiration when Claudia was released. Claudia imbibed the tenacity of a tigress from her mother, defending her young. She was also clinging, finding Ute's back (Huckepack) a perfect seat from which to survey the world but also to hiss at strangers. The closeness between the two never subsided. From her grandmother, Mumu, Claudia inherited a sense of decorum and beauty. From her father, a love for learning. Being a middle child, she often had to be the equalizer. She tempered that role with humor. In kindergarten she asked Ute for baby food jars that her teacher needed for a demonstration. Ute washed out several jars, and next morning a contented little girl set off for school. She returned with a disappointed look and handed the jars back. 'Mama, Mrs. Turner wants you to take all the labels off.' Dutifully, Ute peeled off the labels. The next day a downtrodden Claudia came home and exclaimed in a whiny voice, 'Mrs. Turner wants you to take all the lids off.' Ute ripped the bag from Claudia's hand. 'That's about enough from....' Claudia's face cleared. 'Just kidding.' At night Claudia would slip into her mother's room and put lotion on her forehead. Like an underground stream, Ron and Ute's strengths flowed into Claudia's life. They never clipped her wings."

This is how Claudia sees herself. "Claudia is the middle child who possesses many qualities thereof. Independent yet adaptable, she finds peace among consistency and permanence. Always one to take her studies seriously, she dives into learning a new subject matter or exploring a talent with vigor. A design and fashion aficionado, she adds flair to a room or an outfit, even if it includes simply fasten black and white photography to a wall or putting on a colorful neck scarf. An interior designer by trade, she revels in being family-oriented, and her greatest pride has been raising her boys. Each has inherited some of her signature characteristics, whether it be her sense of punctuality and organization, her love of pranks, or her propensity for overdressing rather than underdressing. Confident, passionate, and meticulous, Claudia feels best when surrounded by loved ones... especially grounded with her feet in the sand along a picturesque coastline."

This is how Tommy, Claudia's husband, sees himself. "Comfortable both on stage and behind the camera, Tommy is a storyteller, filmmaker, and dog lover, whose greatest joy is being a dad to his three beautiful sons. He spent years flat track motorcycle racing, showing cutting horses, and was inducted into the Foosball Hall of Fame before heading to California to pursue his dreams in television. Golf, watching football games, and vintage cars are favorite pastimes. With him, past and present family ties run deep and strongly influence his goals in life. Learning the story behind a fellow person (or animal for that matter) is an important part of how he approaches life. Constant, loyal, and kind, Tommy is never afraid to take life by the horns."

What Ron and Ute recall. "Cecile slid into life as calmly and easily as an underwater swimmer with breath to spare. She carried herself through life as if she might really walk on water. Because there was no room in the hospital following her birth, mother and daughter were sent home and never separated, not even for the routine physical baby checkup. Cecile remained at Ute's breast, unperturbed and sound asleep. After Cecile's birth Ute boasted, 'Now I can have a dozen children.' Cecile received the best qualities from both parents, the dedication to the young from Ute and a concern for the world from Ron. Being the youngest by a span of years she was treated like an only child. She was born with multicolored feathers, one varied like her singing voice, one white like her ballet costume, another brown like her horse's mane and yet another with polka dots like her acting. She was often up front, as when she jumped from the highest diving board on a dare from her sisters. Nearing a slippery dam on a trail ride with her mother, she had her horse take the lead. There is an open horizon to her personality. Grounded within herself, she still remains deeply connected to her parents. She stays devoted to them as she is to her boys, her husband and her chosen profession.

This is how Cecile sees herself. "I love Joe Biden's quote, 'You aren't better than anyone and no one is better than you.' If I were to brag, I would say I am worldly, very smart, and giving, having integrity, and can be lots of fun. I am a family woman: mother, wife, daughter, granddaughter, sister, mother-in-law. I love my family time. And enjoy friends and community too. Especially when we share things we love. Those things that I love to share (and even do independently sometimes) are nature-hiking, horseback riding, swimming, walking, bike riding, canoeing, just breathing in the trees, watching the rain. I love animals; an Animal Seer, I love observing or interacting with them. I also love to sing and dance, and watch shows from time to time or listen to cool things like Stardate on the radio; I love to read and tell stories and write poetry; I love getting massages. I love my husband Jeff and boys Kaius and Lucas making me laugh, dancing with me, playing board and card games together, watching them make amazing art, be strong, kind, creative, smart, joyful and athletic-and engaging in the occasional climb, golf or soccer play with them (don't forget I got the spin move!). I enjoy eating good food, see beauty, and like talking with them and my parents about politics, the world, right and wrong, how to influence toward the side of good versus evil. We do good work individually and together too- paid or volunteer work, home and garden, whatever is needed. At my organization I have been a valued colleague and leader as well as a worker, outspoken, a systems thinker, prioritizing well, a lawyer and a bit of a businesswoman. I can see moving into a political position if called, or working on environmental issues later in life- ideally in the field since I don't like tech, especially to learn new software. I am sensitive in multiple ways and trust my instincts. I am lucky to be safe, strong, pretty and happy (enough) with myself. I am very grateful to have a wonderful family, sweet house and decent jobs and schools. I am anxious and a fighter, and work to use structure to channel those things for peace and good as best as I can. I employ work, routine, meditation and all the joys above. I get frustrated that things like compostable plastic aren't universal (yet!) and that communities don't stay loyal. and rooted and take so much energy, that people don't listen to me when I have a good answer or allow me enough influence-that all tries my patience and confidence. But I give myself and those around me a break, as Mumu and judge Takasugi would say. But not too much of a break."

This is how Jeff, Cecile's husband, sees himself. "Jeffrey Allen Powers was born just about right. Smart, but not too smart. Athletic, but not too athletic. Physically attractive, but not too attractive. When a person hits the sweet spot like that, they have a special power. With just the right amount of focus (not too much, not too little) they can do anything and can enjoy anything. This power is not always available, because the ups and downs of life distract, delight, and exhaust, creating a similar wave of motivation and confidence (or their lack thereof). Certainly, those ups and downs have been a great experience for Jeff. From son and brother, to promising student, to state champion track athlete, to Ivy-league graduate, to professional artist, moving coast to coast across the USA, to husband and father, life is an infinitely interesting adventure. Just yesterday, Jeff was reminded of how lucky he is to have any consciousness at all. That is about the right amount of appreciation to ignite his special power."

The girls mirror the lives of their ancestors. They fold their arms uniquely, yet each carrying a bouquet of bountiful wildflowers, petals overlapping.

The maelstrom of history does not flow straight. It curves around and has many tributaries, countless rivulets, and waterways. From Omi Maria's heart a love cord uncoiled and rolled into Omi Ute and then circuitously from her to her children and grandchildren. Gerda-Maria became an important stream channeling her love to Ute and her granddaughters. As Cecile later thanked her mother, "You gave me a grandmother, Mumu." Now love trickles in all directions from the springs of new mothers and fathers.

Ron and Ute are fortunate that their girls' partners respect them. They admire Ron's professional achievements and are grateful to Ute for her help with child rearing. Hardworking Tony speaks through flowers, Tommy is always an enthusiastic travel companion ("I'm in"), and Jeff creates Ute's book covers and once carried Ron, losing consciousness, slung over his shoulders to a doctor's office.

The individual life sketches bring insights into this marvelously multicolored family.

30 Whirlwind Years

A punishing wind howled, cracked branches and shook leaves off trees. Our rented camper bounced back and forth on its broad tires but steadied itself after each blow. Snug inside, Ron read John Gardner's *In the Suicide Mountains* aloud as his girls stretched out on bunkbeds and listened, wide-eyed. A magical current circulated through the camper.

In a phone booth in Banff National Park in Canada, Ron received an offer from the University of Texas Medical Branch to assume the directorship of the newly established Institute for the Medical Humanities. He accepted on the spot, holding the receiver away from the draft whistling through the unhinged metal phone booth door. The position at the medical school would change their lives. They became solvent and Ron started to put his mark on a brand-new field.

They arrived in Galveston several days before Christmas as Gerda-Maria and their cat arrived at Houston's Hobby Airport. They rushed around to buy the last Christmas tree on the market which Ute and her mother decorated in feverish haste. Neighbors brought over casseroles and Gerda-Maria was the recipient of a "Yellow Rose of Texas." She glowed like the candles on the tree as she was singled out. The family was able to afford a spacious house with a yard in a flourishing area behind the seawall. Their whirlwind years began.

The girls' activities increased and a stream of visitors arrived nonstop. German families sent their children for summer vacations, others dropped by during travels through the U. S. A nephew trained with a local veterinarian, and Gabriele sent one of her daughters for a year. Ron's sister was a frequent guest. One of her sons traveled with them to Europe. The girls were permitted to invite friends along. How Ute managed with housework, yard and all the hosting is unclear. The years swam by in a blur.

Disappointments stood out. Margot's son boasted about his stay with the Carsons. Then his sister wanted a turn. She suffered from sun allergies. Ute wrapped strips of cloth around her arms and legs every time they went to the beach. When the girl returned to Germany she complained to Margot of neglect. In vain, Ute defended herself. No explanation helped and Margot broke off the friendship. Ute could never figure out how she had failed that child.

Horses became a center in their lives. They bought an elderly American quarter horse, Pegasus, joined a riding co-op and entered competitions. Before sunrise their trailer would be loaded with grain, hay and water and their well-groomed mare. The girls would occasionally win trophies. Evening brought more horse chores before the family could eat and rest.

Ever since her encounter with Sport, Ute had dreamed of owning a horse. In her middle years that dream came true. With the birth of Pandora, Pegasus's only foal, their horse odyssey began in earnest.

On the morning of Pandora's birth, Cecile and Ute crawled stiff-legged out of their truck where they had held a nightly vigil. A glitter-winged omen unfolded in front of their sleepy eyes. A great blue heron with a greenish oily sheen on its feathers stood in the marshes near the pond, balancing on one leg, the other one tucked into the downy plumage of its underside. Its neck feathers stuck out like a frayed collar. It released its hidden leg and stepped through the mud. With a slow beat or two it opened its immense wings and lifted off like a kite. It glided toward the herd. In mid-air over Pegasus's back it hovered a moment, spreading protective shade over the mare's body. Shortly thereafter, Pegasus stretched out on the ground. The delivery happened in the blink of an eye. The contractions were fast and when the foal slipped out and struggled to stand, the umbilical cord broke on impact. On wobbly legs the foal found her mother's milk and started sucking, making loud smacking sounds.

That night Cecile wrote in her diary: "It's a girl. Goodness, I had expected a cute foal but this little filly is a beauty. She is mouse gray like Mom had hoped for. She inherited that color from her grandpa, Pegasus's sire. She is also a dun. Everyone was surprised. A gray dun is very rare. She has long straight legs and tiny feet. Otherwise, she doesn't have any markings except for the white blaze down her nose, identical to her mother's."

They handled Pandora daily and trained her in all the equestrian gaits. Ute remembered the thrill of sliding from a fence onto Pandora's back and grabbing the mane with all her might as the young mare bolted away like a bucking bronco. Following that initial mounting, the training was easy and fun.

Caitlin and Claudia were away at college when Ron was offered a one-semester visiting professorship at the University of Montana. Ute would not leave without Pandora. A ranch was found for the mare. On a morning with the sun at their backs, Pandora, Ron, Ute, Cecile and their cairn terrier Princess took to the open road away from storms and floods to fire and dust. They drove west through flatland and oil rigs among cactus shrubs and mesquite trees. The next day by nightfall they arrived in Colorado and traced the line of the first Rocky Mountain peak exactly on the window pane. Snowcaps played peek-a-boo. Then one more day, and they pulled into Missoula where a yellow-painted rental house and wide-open ranchland welcomed them. As during the nightly rest stops on the road at "horse motels," Pandora bolted from the trailer, free at last, her tail flying like a blustery flag, her hooves kicking up tufts of grass.

They trailered Pandora back to Galveston six months later during a blustery, icy winter. They encountered ranchers at each stop who provided generous hospitality and kindness to animal and human travelers alike. Snow-wet blankets were dried overnight and a cup of steaming coffee accompanied them on their way out when leaving a friendly host.

Pegasus died on Galveston Island at a ripe old age of 39 with Ute at her side. Pandora moved to Austin and lived on the Elmridge Ranch, a free-roaming horses' paradise, for fifteen years. Ute commemorated the ranch with lines from a poem...

And I knew bliss
lying in grass as high as our mounts' manes
gently combed by an autumn breeze,
frogs croaking in the shimmering algae of the pond,
and a small boy asking, "Can we stay here all day? And swim?"

Pandora lived to be 34. When she died Ute and Cecile stroked her as she let out her last gentle breath. To comfort themselves they hummed their favorite Natalie Merchant song, "See the girl in pink on the milk-white horse." Only family members had been allowed to ride Pandora. The daily training and grooming always fell to Ute and later Cecile. Pandora recognized Ute by the sound of her boots traipsing through a meadow and she would gallop up to greet her.

The family started to see the world. They traversed America from Florida to the Grand Canyon. Birthdays were celebrated in New York, Paris and China. Invitations came from Scotland, Norway, Romania and New Zealand where Ron was invited to teach and lecture. Each stay revealed its treasures, providing a different gaze. Norway's dark forests and glaciers, New Zealand with the giant Albatross who can fly for years without landing, and where they loaded stones into their rental car to be able to drive down the icy roads to the magnificent fjords at Milford Sound. Paris enchanted them with elegant cafes and the famous Père Lachaise Cemetery, Beijing with its traditional Hutongs. There was Spain's mysterious Alhambra, and wilderness when dog-sledding in Ely, Minnesota. Topping off a visit to Russia at Saint Petersburg's venerable Hermitage Museum, they discovered old masters' paintings at the mercy of the elements. With no air-conditioning, the large windows stood wide open. Ute became a treasure hunter on those trips, scouting out items that would fit her girls' and grandkids' wishes. They named them Mitbringsel. Ute never returned home without them.

Ron often surprised his family with a trip, as when at a school auction he bid on a week's vacation at a house on Little Exuma, a fairyland vacation which Gerda-Maria was able to share. There they baked fresh bread in a clay oven, fished off rocky cliffs and watched drug smugglers' boats flit by on the coast at night.

When Ute traveled with Ron, Gerda-Maria stayed with her granddaughters. They relished the closeness and their grandmother's creativity, making artifacts to welcome the parents back. During their summer visits to Germany the girls were woven into a different way of life, switching imperceptibly from one culture to the other. Gerda-Maria was always deeply saddened when it came time for a grandchild to return to America.

For Gerda-Maria's 70th birthday Ron arranged for her and Ute to return to Namibia, Gerda-Maria's birth country. As they traveled the route Maria and Peter had taken from Windhoek to Keetmanshoop, past the Fish River Canyon to Lüderitz, events from the past came alive. All the sights, sounds, the landscape, the people seemed oddly familiar. A déjà vu feeling enveloped both of them. Gerda- Maria stood silently in front of the hospital in Keetmanshoop where she was born. "Are they still hoisting the flag only half-mast when a girl is born?" she wondered. As never before, mother and daughter connected. In a bus crossing the Namib Desert Gerda-Maria's head sank onto Ute's shoulder and she fell asleep. Ute did not dare move lest she interrupt this precious moment. They observed wildlife, elephants and giraffes. They discovered the welwitschia plant, the oldest surviving organism on dry land. Gerda-Maria ran her hand over the fleshy, rubbery leaves. One tiny drop of water glittered at the top of a glossy leaf. She remembered the first word she had learned in Africa as a child...*Bambo ila o nea kaya, Bambo o Bambo...* (we need water.) Even though she seldom drank water as an adult, she did take pleasure in the sound of lapping water.

In Otjiwarongo, a small farming community, the heat burned their dust-covered arms and faces. The sidewalks buckled. On one side of the railroad tracks lay the cemetery reserved for whites and Peter's grave. His name and dates were still visible on the weathered headstone. They had been chiseled in and then painted black. Gerda-Maria plucked some weeds. Then she removed her threadbare shawl, the one she had used against the blowing sand in the desert, the one in which she had swaddled babies. Long ago she had knitted the shawl, wide and loopy, with flowing colors. She draped the shawl over the head-marker and picked up a stone. She rubbed the stone against her breast and then weighed the shawl down with it. She tucked him in with a simple "Good-bye, Father" and turned to Ute. "I am still reaching for his little finger during our walk. He was so tall and I was so little."

Five years later the family celebrated Gerda-Maria's 75th birthday in Vöhl, a remote village in Hessen. Invited guests came from far away bringing flowers. Gerda-Maria's apartment was filled with bloom and smelled like a garden of a thousand perfumes. Toasts abounded and the event ended with a dance. Gerda-Maria had sponsored a delinquent youngster, found him an apprentice position in a woodworking shop and supported his counseling sessions. He gave a short thank-you at the dinner. Then, in the midst of all the teaming celebrants, he disappeared without a word, leaving no hint. The joyful day ended for Gerda-Maria in a flood of tears. The young man was reported to be living in a cabin with his dog in Canada many years after Gerda-Maria died.

Gerda-Maria continued to travel to America but also decided to move into an elegant senior living complex in Bad Arolsen, a cultured provincial town. There she made friends, had a cat, and rejoiced when Ron and Ute and the girls visited her.

She surprised everyone by revealing an artistic talent. Ute discovered her mother's love for painting by chance when she pointed to green smudges under her fingernails. "Mutti, what's that color?" Her mother laughed, "I started to take art lessons. Today I painted a forest." All her pictures are light in color and most of her creations are of gardening, tools like rakes, shovels, and watering cans. Fountains were a favorite motif. She was delighted when the staff of the residency arranged for an exhibition. She even sold a few of her originals. Her life was overshadowed by dark clouds but her art is filled with sunlight.

The girls moved on to colleges, got married and the first grandkids arrived. Ute, who had started to teach at Galveston College, flew twice weekly to Dallas to be with the first four beloved grandkids. She also hurried up there for every emergency, be it a sickness or providing the parents with a break. Ron was given a suite for his growing staff in Old Red, a red brick and sandstone building constructed in 1891, designed by Nicholas Clayton. Ron was becoming well-known in his field, a sought-after speaker. Students also clamored to get into his classes. To the surprise of many he could also be quite demanding. He met with students outside the classroom to help them refine their thinking, and then expected quality work from them.

Ron wrote about the dilemmas of premature births and the tough decisions at life's end, emphasizing in all of his writings the narrative relationship between doctor and patient. He befriended one of his faculty members, Tom, who stayed at his side through the years.

Ute published stories about her family and created portraits of her friends. Here is one memory. She was obsessively punctual which made for a rushing dash between classes. Her friend Fay brought her soup in a blue-and-white checkered thermos for those evening sessions. Fay invited Ute on a journey into the "Heart of Texas" where she grew up among sharecroppers and tomato farmers during the depression. That story was published by the Texas Bullock State Museum. Another of Ute's stories, "The Fall," about original sin, won first place in a writing competition. Ute also wrote about the troubles midlife brings with menopause and an empty nest.

With her friend, Gail, she tried a bit of rabble rousing but their attempts at pushing the limits had more bark than bite. Once in Atlanta they got dressed up, went to a bar and as soon as two burly men approached them, they fled back to their hotel. They giggled and whispered, "Each woman has a secret. Maybe each man has one too." Ute wrote and published a book about Paul, a creative, intelligent young man whose life had been ruined by childhood sexual abuse. Together they tried to find the culprits but ended up empty-handed. Paul painted Ute once as a woman holding a baby, a portrayal of their closeness. His turbulent lifestyle and his demands on her were finally too much for Ute to carry.

Psychedelics fascinated Ute. Paul offered to share his encounters with her but she declined, fearing it might influence her relationship with Ron. Ron wanted nothing to do with drugs. He proudly guarded his reputation and considered mind-altering drugs dangerous. So, Ute turned to her girls. One of them would sit with her, stargazing on their lawn, hoping that the mushrooms Ute consumed would bring extraordinary effects. Ute saw a few beautiful colors. Another one stood by her as she sampled cocaine. But because Ute enjoyed her sleep and one single sniff robbed her of that comfort, she never tried that again. The girls were relieved that their middle-aged mother would not follow a path into the alternative lifestyles she researched and wrote about.

Hypnosis was the next step leading to different realms of consciousness. It reminded Ute of Omi Maria's Christian Science and the power of mind over matter. Every Saturday for two years she traveled to Houston for a training course for clinical hypnotists. Ute was intrigued by the insights she gained into the unconscious. Her mind often lingered on the main chakra, the sun chakra and she realized that she responded to yellow, of all colors. A summer seminar led her to the Cuyamungue Institute near Santa Fe, New Mexico. She slipped into various transformations during the day in a womb-like underground kiva. At night, on a cot on the veranda of the main building, she listened to the howls of prairie wolves.

A silent retreat in Kaufman, Texas convinced Ute that there was more to life than surface perceptions. Her observations called "Lightning over Kaufman" appeared in the Houston Chronicle. She kept a copy.

"I was not to speak or look directly at any person for 10 days."

The countryside quivers in the July heat and the atmosphere is laden with moisture. Thunder rumbles in the distance. Steel-white streaks zig-zag across the flat Texas horizon. Some of them traverse the entire length of the night sky, others pierce big-bellied clouds with quick golden stabs. A flash encircles a cluster of smoky billows near me like a fire-ring, followed by a loud clap. Lightning has struck here. I stare in awe, faintly trembling. Suddenly the energy is released into a pelting rain, falling in coin-sized drops at my feet, forming swirling, gurgling pools in the dust. Just then frogs start a joyful concert.

This is my fifth day at the Vipassana meditation center, a 15-minute car ride from the small farming town of Kaufman. Of the six centers in the country, this is the only one in Texas. After days of silent introspection, my eyes magnify the outside world into dazzling clarity. Time is no longer predictable, and the day of my arrival seems long ago.

Our daughter, Claudia, had driven me to the retreat site. It took us just over an hour from downtown Dallas to reach the bucolic setting. Nestled among meadows sparkling with wildflowers and dotted with grazing black, brown and white cows, the buildings are surrounded by clumps of dark green live oaks and flat-topped mesquite trees. A still pond lies at the edge of the property. Sparrows flutter to and from nests under the eave of the main building and cats stalk through the high grass in search of mice and lizards.

Men and women are housed separately at the center, and there is a free-standing meditation hall between them. For the women there are three dormitories, furnished with hard bunk beds and thin mattresses. I brought along my sleeping bag. Each bed is surrounded by a canvas curtain for privacy, and ceiling fans whirring softly overhead. We are treated to sumptuous vegetarian meals, cooked and served by volunteers. There are no washing machines or dryers. Towels and underwear and socks galore flutter on a clothesline in the lazy summer breeze. Claudia watched me unpack and store away my few belongings. "I hate to leave you here, Mom." Then she departed and I felt like a kid left at camp. I had a fleeting urge to run after her. What was I doing here at 62? Right away I knew this would not be a vacation.

I had learned about Vipassana in yoga class, an ancient Indian meditation practice whose symbol is the ever-changing wheel. The practice differs from other healing techniques in that it is neither verbal nor visual. Vipassana uses the breath, common to all life, as a tool to observe the sensations of the body as calmly and attentively as possible. Human misery is universal, and Vipassana bases all unhappiness on two principles: craving and aversion. Craving causes clinging, the desire to hold on. Aversion produces frustration, negativity and anger. To reach harmony and enlightenment in life, Vipassana teaches mastery of these two negative reactions. During meditation the breath scans the body, never lingering at pleasant or unpleasant sensations, only observing them.

Respiration also builds a bridge between the conscious and unconscious mind. With the breath, old mental conditions (sankharas), which manifest themselves mentally or physically rise to the surface and then dissolve, eventually replacing strife with harmony. The approach seemed full of contradictions. Would it work for me?

Day 1

It is 4 a.m. when a gong wakes me from a deep slumber. The gong will become my signal to rise and assemble for a meal. I soon come to love the reverberating sound of the gong, linking me to centuries of cloistered, peaceful lives.

I wiggle out of my sleeping bag, yawn and stretch. I slip into my beige jogging suit in total silence. I hear only faint rustlings from my neighbors as they dress. Speech fell away easily last night, like shedding a worn-out coat. Even though I do not look at or talk to my fellow students, currents of life sweep through the dorm. Someone snored. Someone called out in her sleep, and female odors reached my nostrils long before the day's breathing drill began. After the wake-up call, I can go to the meditation hall, but I decide to meditate on the rug next to my bed. At 6:30 a.m. I devour my breakfast of hot oatmeal and fruit and drink green tea. At 8 a.m. we are summoned for an hour of group meditation, followed by private meditation until 11 a.m. Lunch is ready, and the dishes are labeled: Vietnamese Salad, Vegetarian Texas Chili, and Indian Curry. I am well-nourished. The lunch break lasts until 1p. m. It gives me time to shower, take a stroll and rest.

Throughout the course, the teachers remain remote, sitting like immobile statues on their thrones, watching their muted flock. Teachers serve as guardians of the regulations. Though most people are determined to stay the course, a few won't last. Rule-breakers are asked to leave. Teachers are also available for consultation, but only questions relating to the practice are permitted. Because I have so many intellectual "whys," I decide to forgo an interview.

We have an hour of group meditation again at 2 p.m., then private meditation until 5. For the last meal of the day newcomers can eat plenty of fruit and have a choice of hot or cold drinks. Those more experienced in the practice are permitted only tea. At 6, it's more group meditation, and then we listen to a video by S. N. Goenka who rediscovered Vipassana. We are dismissed around 9, with just enough time to amble briefly outdoors before we retire to our quarters. Lights out at 9:30 p.m.

Lying in bed, I am discouraged. My first day was nothing but discomfort and anguish. I'm not used to sitting in an upright meditative position for a total of 12 hours. My body aches, my ankles are sore from crossing them and my legs are dead wood by the time I plop onto my bunk. As hard as I tried to pay close attention to my respiration, banishing gently any distracting thoughts, my mind didn't just wander, it ran wild. Will I last 10 days?

However, in spite of my misgivings my mind caught some sparks. Knowledge here is not imposed but experienced, and this knowledge is not abstract. I heard my breath as it streamed through the nasal cavity and felt it as it touched the wings of my nostrils. This is about my body, my sensations. It is about Me. Breathing in and breathing out places me right in the present moment, no retreats into the past or speculations about the future. In daily life, I often revisit the past or plan for tomorrow. But the present is in the Now, in every precious moment. I curl up in my sleeping bag and practice conscious relaxation. My mercurial mind must have dozed off because I did not stir until the gong roused me before dawn.

Day 2

Much easier! I sink into the daily routine. Yesterday I questioned the strict rule forbidding even the use of my notebook and pencil, but today I see the purpose of the regulations. No longer do I think about household chores or whether my husband fed the cat and took the dog for a walk. No phone calls interrupt, no television diverts me from the one activity: observing my respiration.

On entering the course, all participants took five vows: to abstain from killing or harming any being (even the pesky mosquitoes), from stealing, from sexual activity, from telling lies, and from all intoxications. We are also not allowed to communicate with each other through speech, direct glances or physical contact. But soon I noticed people by their footwear, open-toed sandals, scuffed-up tennis shoes or flowery flip-flops. I distinguish walks, shuffling steps, and light, short strides.

Only sometimes do I catch my thoughts scattering to old concerns, everyday preoccupations. I fidget less in my cross-legged position. Drowsiness, as much an enemy as a wandering mind, is held at bay, and I am able to perceive bodily sensations without reacting to them. Respiration is neutral. I do not crave more breath, nor do I dislike my breath. I try only to observe and to sustain the awareness of the present from moment to moment.

Day 3

The focus of the breath is narrowed to the place under my nostrils, above my upper lip. I am to concentrate on that tiny notch to sharpen my mind, to purify it. Calmness sets in, and more insights are ablaze as my breath enters my right nostril and goes out the left, then jumps and reverses the order. Sometimes I feel my breath in both nostrils. I also sense cold when I inhale, warmth when I exhale. Then I notice a tingling on my upper lip, and tiny beads collect as if I were sprouting a wet mustache. Try to be patient, and words from the evening lecture drum through my mind, "Start again, start again." My little grandson, Nicholas, has his first swimming lesson today. I push away the distraction and begin anew. "Everything rises and passes away. Anica-anica-anica-everything is impermanent, everything is changing." In spite of myself, I think of my recent hot flashes before I can return to my task. "A bird needs two wings to fly. You need awareness and equanimity," I hear the instructor. Balance is like a scale, and I try to weigh both sides equally. I am getting to know my breath.

Day 4

Each time I enter the meditation hall I feel as if I am descending into the darkness of an underground cave. The light is weak, the walls are veiled. Every object is covered with sky-blue cloth from the elevated chairs of the teachers, to the television set, even the speakers. No candles light up my dim vision. No calming incense is burning. We sit on our assigned velveteen blue mats, and I think of the blue hues of air and water, two fluid elements. The hall is air-conditioned, and I wrap my black woolen shawl around me, sitting mummified as in a shroud. I feel protected, at ease. Group meditations lend solidarity in a supportive atmosphere. No one moves. Only an occasional cough, clearing of a throat, and the air-conditioning turning on and interrupts the silence. I start to swallow and reflexively have to swallow again and again.

This is a difficult day because we move from the familiar place of concentration around the nostrils to scanning the entire body. It is as if my breath illuminates me. This is the only time during our stay when we are required to sit in a meditative position for two hours. After an hour the yoga position becomes an endurance test and I lose all concentration. Silently I curse under my breath and for the second time since my arrival I harbor thoughts of flight. But as soon as I get over my frustration, the scanning runs smoothly. I let my breath escape through the fontanel of my head, a thrilling sensation, and I realize how much I want to hold on to that pleasant feeling. But I move on and my breath crawls over my face and then from limb to limb, back and front, over bony bumps, through soft crevices. Energy flows easily through some parts of my body. Other parts hurt, my knees burn and my lower back is numb. I try not to linger, but continue my mental walk, just observing, only observing. My mind becomes lucid, it states dispassionate, no longer flutters about. So simple! So difficult!

Day 5 through 8

I have been shown the rudimentary steps of the Vipassana practice. Now all is repetition and training. The success, I am told, is not how easily I scan my body, but how calm and objective, yet alert, I can make my mind. My task is to learn how to act instead of blindly reacting. I am bursting with this helpful insight. Back in the outside world I will try to cultivate a tranquil, detached attitude in the face of life's vicissitudes, its impermanence. Learning to be calm in all situations should make me more tolerant and patient. I could use a less hectic and rushed lifestyle. I also see how valuable it is to seek answers in myself and not blame others for my troubles.

My body is heavy, my mind buoyant. More light has been cast and I am fulfilled. I sleep without dreams.

Day 9

After meditation this evening the previous silence is lifted. We swarm toward each other and crowd into the hallway. Talk buzzes as if coming from a beehive. We are, after all, social beings. We feel gratitude. And we want to share. We have survived a challenge, and now are full of questions: What did you experience? What was difficult for you? Did you ever consider giving up? Why did you come here in the first place? What will you take back with you to your home, your workplace?

Our conversations spill into the late-night hours. I am surprised at the variety of problems people carried with them. They range from eating disorders, concentration impairments and the effect of childhood traumas, to recent losses. Many now feel less burdened. I am curious, are there others like me who want to deepen conscious awareness?

People come from all walks of life. There is the graduate student from India whose colorful sari I admire, who grew up practicing Vipassana and now devotes 10 days each year to a silent meditation retreat. I find out that my bunk bed neighbor is a Vietnamese-American computer expert in Houston. There are teachers and housewives and hordes of young people, searching. There is even a safari instructor from South Africa.

For Vipassana there are no chance encounters, and I wonder about mine. We are squatting on the floor in a large circle listening to amazing animal stories when suddenly I feel compelled to contribute one about our 18-year-old cairn terrier who postponed death, surviving on just a few drops of water a day, waiting for our youngest daughter, Cecile, to return home for the holidays to say good-bye. Then a young woman wearing a flaming-red bandanna and intricate tattoos of butterflies and flowers on her arms and legs bursts into tears. "My dog died a few weeks ago."

"I'm sorry," I say. I have to get used to talking again and feel a headache coming on. A walk is just what I need. "Want to come along?" I ask the girl.

The sky is loaded with powerful gray clouds as the daylight sinks slowly over the peaceful countryside. I smell a threatening fragrance of rain and hustle along the dusty rutted lane. I hear long clipping strides catch up with me.

"Sorry I cried," a sweet girlish voice says. "Suddenly I had this lump in my throat, and I couldn't stop myself." She glances at me with fawn-brown eyes, now clouded with more tears. Her lips tremble. "I have not cried the entire stay. Why now? I can't fit it in with a calm mind and all that."

I slow my walk and say, "It is perfectly alright for you to cry. I am glad to be here to listen to your story." Then Melinda speaks about her feelings of loss, finally telling me, "It's not just my dog. I also lost my mother three months ago."

It is getting dark, and peals of thunder roll in the distance. Yet, at this moment a full July moon still peeks through the indigo sky. I take Melinda's hand. It is warm, and, as if embarrassed, it responds shyly to my gentle squeeze. "Look," I point to the branch of a live oak. A barn owl is perched there, silhouetted against the creamy yellow disk. "And it's not even Halloween," I chuckle. Then a single bolt of lightning radiates the horizon, and an ear-splitting explosion breaks the silence. We hurry back to the house.

Day 10

The last morning is fair and clear. The retreat is not over. We are supplicants, thankful for what we have received. Now it is our turn to give. Not just a donation to this nonprofit organization, but also something of ourselves. So we sweep, wash and scrub the center until the place is as clean as we found it. Then we change back into our worldly attire and stare at each other. I put on makeup, don dangling silver earrings and slip into my suede suit and high-heeled shoes. The transformation complete, the recluse of 10 days turns into a professional and member of a family again.

What do I take away from my inward journey?

Ingrained habits do not die in 10 days. I crave my pen and paper, a glass of red wine and my husband's embrace. But in a world noisy with activities and distractions, calmness and peace have set in. Fresh insights have dawned, and I see things more clearly. Maybe by controlling my mind I can better master my actions with equanimity.

I pass my first test at the airport by shutting out the intrusive cell-phone conversations that usually annoy me. And when my flight is delayed, I smile at the attendant and sit down without protest. I close my eyes and concentrate on my respiration and words echo through my mind: Observe, observe, only observe. And other lines from the retreat return:

"Feeling the entire body, I shall breathe in," thus she trains herself.
"Feeling the entire body, I shall breathe out," thus she trains herself.

Pali Passages (Maha-Satti pat Sutta, Diga Nikaya,22)

"Ute was endowed with an amazing memory which made her a good listener and astute hypnotist. From girlhood on, people confided in her and she could easily relate to their concerns without passing judgment. Hypnosis gave her the privilege of spying deeply into her own childhood. She also remembered details about family and friends. At times people expected too much from Ute, hoping she could change their lives."

Ron was absent from these experiments with hypnosis or other alternative ways of learning. So Ute had to trick him with an unexpected adventure.

31 All This and Heaven Too

Ron was always finding deals. He discovered a stay on Abaco Island where on New Year's Eve the famous Jankanoo parade is held. They rented a cabin, waking up to the heartbeat of the ocean. In the evenings fog rolled onto the island and clouds scurried past the sun. Lulled by a warm dancing breeze, they carried two chairs onto the porch. A sand dune placed them out of earshot of their neighbors and the roar of the waves muffled everything but the sound of their own voices. They put provisions from the village store onto a small stone table. Ron uncorked the wine. They toasted the end of another marvelous day and settled in to watch a veiled sunset. A golden mist glazed the crimson disk. Slowly the evening air wrapped itself around their bodies, squeezing them into a cozy cocoon.

Ute got up and went inside to spread towels over their bedsheets and set their favorite massage oil on the nightstand, a balsam of rosemary, the love charm herb.

"Making preparations for a special bedtime treat," she called to Ron.

"I'm for that."

Ute joined Ron again and asked for more wine. "Old women should be explorers," she said with a fetching smile.

"Said who?"

"Said I." She unfolded a piece of tinfoil revealing two bluish-white pills. The pill faces were inscribed with butterfly logos.

"What's that?" Ron's voice came from deep within his throat. He was alarmed and obviously dubious.

"Ecstasy."

"Are you crazy? It's illegal. I don't have the money to bail you out."

"Just an idea. Don't get all riled up."

Ron rubbed his eyes and coughed twice. "Where did you get these?"

"My physical therapist. Try one, you'll like it," she said.

"Do you trust her?"

"I did my own research but she also uses X with rape victims."

"Rape victims!"

"Or the old and decrepit."

"The old and decrepit. Have mercy!"

"You don't have to take one."

"We have fun...always have fun ...without shit like this."

"I want to explore ...shit like this. You can just stand guard. I'll go ahead."

"The hell you will. Not without me."

The night woke them to a wondrous world. A feathery, mild rain muffled the air and its wetness deepened the tone of all things. The moonlight, just a splinter like a night candle, submerged the cabin in bronze-colored mystery. The lightbulbs on the nightstands shone like miniature suns.

They placed the pills on their tongues and carefully let them melt. Naked, they sprawled on the bed. It took about twenty minutes before adrenaline shot into their fingertips and fire raced through their veins into their toes. Like honeysuckle wrapped around a tree they slithered in and over each other. Their breaths, sweetened with wine, mingled and their hearts pounded in their ears. They felt weightless, on upward winds. Ute trembled as Ron's hot fingers kneaded her dewy body. Several times Ron reached for the water glass. Endlessly their tongues crawled along familiar territory, dipping into crevices, hollows and indentations, a bent knee, the tender elbow curve, dew on Ute's breasts, legs spread in delight. Desire brimmed in their glassy eyes, dark as blackberries. Their pupils dilated, the whites around their irises glowed. They stared at each other with rapture as if seeing each other for the first time. Their minds opened like window shades and they were attuned to each other's emotions, asking, "Does this feel good? ... And that?" Ron sighed with contentment and Ute purred like a happy cat.

Time was like an accordion. What seemed like five minutes was actually five hours. Ron glanced occasionally at the clock to be sure he could reach it and secure help if needed. He also didn't hallucinate but Ute did. She saw purple birds flying out of the tapestry behind the bed. "Now the birds are juicy grapes...plump to bursting."

Ron shook with laughter and nipped Ute's left earlobe. "It does taste delicious," he chuckled. The open door of the cabin gaped into the night. Morning light nudged them awake and on the ledge of the doorframe a Bahamian yellowthroat warbled its morning song.

Rays from the amber crown of a rising sun drew them from their bed and sent them running to the beach. The wet sand sucked at their feet as they waded into the waves. The water rose above their waists, tickling their navels. Ute squealed with delight like a child and vowed, "Let's always remember that the old can be explorers."

32 Turn Down the Lights Gently

Gerda-Maria died the way she had lived, a Countess. Fate had dealt her painful blows. Defenseless, she endured many losses and much loneliness. But she determined the course of her death. She was not afraid of dying, "Death is not evil or frightening, just the end of a difficult life." She hoped that there would be some use for her knitting in the beyond. She could not imagine that her nimble hands would ever rest.

Before she was weakened by osteoporosis, she traveled to America for her 80th birthday, celebrated with balloons, toasts and a cake. In her arms, Dylan, her first American great-grandchild, slept peacefully as all babies had done before her. Claudia took her grandmother shopping, a shared enjoyment and bought her a cream-colored dress. At her funeral Gerda-Maria would be laid to rest in that dress. She was frail during her last trip to America. Ute began to visit her in Bad Arolsen instead and called her every Sunday morning. It only took only one ring for her mother to pick up.

Because mother and daughter loved the Advent season, Ute had made it a habit to fly over for the annual Christmas market. The year Gerda-Maria became largely bedfast, Ute had come to visit but decided to return for the first Christmas at home with Dylan. She could imagine the delight that a one-year-old would show. Gerda-Maria had broken her elbow but was determined to make the best of the visit. She had tickets to her favorite play, *The Snow Queen*, and they made it to the performance in a new red wheelchair that one of Gerda-Maria's doctors had ordered. Her doctors were all taken in by this regal, beautiful lady. But that night Gerda-Maria was in severe pain. A night nurse arrived to start a morphine drip.

How could Ute not have noticed? An event displaying Gerda-Maria's drawings was scheduled in the lobby of the residence. Ute helped her mother dress but she proved too weak to attend and returned to bed. That morning, she had asked her hairdresser to wash "the dullness" out of her hair. The ordeal left her wrung out. Ute went alone to the exhibition. When she returned, she found her mother in good spirits. Her primary doctor had visited. She asked Ute to make potato pancakes. Ute's mouth watered. She knew the recipe by heart, whip up batter from raw, grated potatoes, then fry them in butter until crisp, sprinkle them with cinnamon and sugar and top them with applesauce. Gerda-Maria ate only a few morsels but had Ute bring out her best bottle of champagne. Ute reported about the exhibition and filled her mother in on surprises she planned for Dylan. "And next spring, we will bring you back to Galveston and you can play with Dylan." Gerda-Maria's hand trembled as she took a sip of the sparkling liquid.

"I'm not staying alone another Christmas." She glared directly into Ute's eyes. "Especially not with Gabriele's evil boyfriend around who makes fun of all that I like about Christmas."

Why did Ute remain silent? She propped her mother up with a pillow and with a voice brittle as glass, Gerda-Maria whispered, "NO diapers. Do you hear me? No diapers. And turn down the lights gently."

Insults, being treated like a baby, always worried her mother. "I'll try my best," Ute mumbled, still not comprehending what was being said. She slipped some socks on her mother's cold and bluish feet.

The next morning Gerda-Maria had a shopping list ready for Ute. Ute knew where to find most of the items in town. She read the instructions with unseeing eyes. "Take your time. It's a lovely snowy day," her mother winked as Ute closed the apartment door.

Like a snow angel Ute arrived back at the apartment loaded with wrapped Christmas packages. In the hallway she met Gerda-Maria's doctor. "Your mother and I had an agreement about dying. I turned up the morphine drip." The presents tumbled to the floor as Ute rushed in. Her mother lay still, her breath a soft rattle. She unfolded her dappled hands, then curled her fingers like a flower shutting down for the night. Her eyes fluttered like tiny bird wings but as Ute knelt next to her bed, she no longer opened them. She had started a descent into an unknown world. Over three days she sank into a coma while Ute and her sister held a vigil. She died, quietly, and alone while Ute and Gabriele took a rest. Only her cat, sitting on her chest, kept her company to the end and jumped down after Gerda-Maria took her last breath.

Ute was wracked with guilt. She had missed her mother's calling. She could have delayed her departure, stayed for Christmas. She could have said how grateful she was for all that her mother had done. She could have told her that now being old herself she better understood her tragedies. Even the traits that once irked her, like clinging to a child, she now traced in herself. Instead, her thoughts had been elsewhere. How carelessly she had left on her errands. Now nothing would ever assuage her guilt, not then nor in years to come. That night she tossed sweat-soaked on the couch in Gerda-Maria's apartment. She tried to pull a blanket of forgetfulness over her eyes but nothing worked. Her failure was like a scarlet letter. There were no second chances. Her pillow was soaked with tears. Then she heard Omi Maria's voice, "Your second chance lies in tomorrow. You can make good, day after day, year after year." Ute wiped her eyes and momentarily she could focus on the grief over her dear mother's departure.

Funerals in Germany draw large crowds. Maybe because a death is announced by mail in a black-bordered envelope. So they came, young and old, whatever the ilk. They stayed, they witnessed, among them the truly bereft, the grandchildren. Funerals in the countryside were still natural. They family picked out the casket and after the ritual of washing the body, dressed Gerda-Maria and placed her, cushioned by featherbeds and her favorite pillow, embroidered with pink rosebuds, in a coffin which then awaited the burial in the cemetery chapel.

It snowed, had snowed for days. The cemetery was bedded in a deep winter sleep. During the service in the chapel Ron gave a moving eulogy and ended with the comforting words, "Sleep well, dear Mutti." The service closed with the congregants singing all four verses of "Geh aus mein Herz," as Gerda-Maria had requested. Ute felt powerful spirits hovering over the assembly.

Wispy snowflakes tumbled down from heavy clouds as her grandchildren carried the casket from the chapel to the gravesite. These pallbearers glimmered like moving ghosts as they wound their way under white-powdered trees up the path, the soft ground muting their steps. There was a mellow odor in the winter air like fresh linen. The snow blanketed the ground peacefully. Gerda-Maria would have liked the pristine orderliness of her burial. "Turn down the lights gently," she had said. And so they did.

Ute had been handed the baton. She became Omi Ute

Ute had always taken care of her troubled younger sister, helped her out with advice and money. As Gerda-Maria's will was opened it revealed that most of what she owned had gone to Ute and the beloved American grandchildren. "Not fair," Ute admitted and tried to remedy this by dividing her endowment. But material possessions were not at the root of Gabriele's envy. She had long felt neglected and was now vindicated. She took advantage of Ute's sense of fairness and demanded more and more of the things left by Gerda-Maria. Ute complied until she received a letter from Gabriele's therapist, pleading on behalf of her client, that Ute give Gabriele an antique inlaid marble table resembling a chess board. Ron carefully crated the table and shipped it back from America to Germany. When it arrived safely, the response was prompt, "With what the freight cost us, you could have flown the table first class on Lufthansa." For Ute that was the last straw.

Ironically, Ron experienced a similar shutdown with his sister, Karen, after their last parent, his mother, died. Ron was known for his generosity. He took his parents to Europe and countless trips to West Texas and Montana. He flew home when someone was in the hospital, and his parents were guests in their home for most holidays. Karen, who lived close to their hometown, traveled back and forth to help out with errands. She kept track of every penny she spent on them. After their mother's death, she confronted Ron with her ledgers. In her mind Ron had always been favored. Ron broke off the relationship and left everything from his parents' possessions to his oldest nephew who had been close to his grandparents.

Ron's pen scraped over the paper of a note he wrote Karen, "Walls can be barriers but they can also be climbed. You chose to build an insurmountable wall."

33 Turbulent Skies and Triple Crown

Many times, the family had trekked off Galveston Island during a storm. Because of the horses they had to adhere to early warnings, load them, a dog, and cats and trailer over the Causeway Bridge toward Houston. They had to find a friendly farm to house the horses for the duration of bad weather, and they themselves needed a motel for the rest of the entourage. As Ron neared retirement these trips became tedious. When hurricane Ivan ravaged the coast in 2004, they decided to look for a house in Austin while staying in Galveston for Ron's remaining duties. On instinct they rented a storage place in Austin and transported furniture and other items they valued to that place. Pegasus had died and Pandora was trailered to Elmridge Ranch near Austin. Their house in Galveston was still nicely equipped for the duration, except artwork and heirlooms. Hurricane Katrina hit in August 2005. Ute and Ron anxiously watched the weather. So far previous hurricanes had caused only minor damage. As Hurricane Rita drew a bead on Galveston a month later, Ron and Ute made up their minds that this would be their last exodus.

They followed the advice of a farsighted mayor, filled the tanks of their two cars, secured the house, took jewelry, photo albums and old LPs, and headed north. Cecile and Jeff had come to help. Their trek started at 5 a. m. with packed lunches and water. They expected that it might take all day to get to Austin in heavy traffic. The journey began smoothly with a misty sunrise, followed by a flaming fireball in the east foretelling a hot September day. Once they arrived at junction 290 their confidence flagged. All roads ahead were clogged, restaurants and gas stations closed. The call for evacuation had worked like clockwork but left a highway horror in its wake. State authorities opened the counter-lanes too late, and fuel tankers arrived only after tens of thousands of people were stranded on the banks of the freeway and in parking lots. A peaceful departure turned into chaos as motels filled to capacity, food and drink ran out, and gas needles plummeted. Human behavior went topsy-turvy.

Like a dragon spewing fumes, half a million cars crawled at a snail's pace. Drivers turned off their air conditioning and opened their doors, as they inched forward on the sizzling pavement. General frustration mounted as drivers cut in and out of lanes and crisscrossed the median. There was honking and swearing at fellow drivers through open windows. Serious incidents occurred. People collapsed from heat exhaustion. An ambulance could not get through to a man suffering a heart attack in the stalled traffic.

There was helpful behavior as well. At a standstill in the snarled traffic, a dog collapsed by the roadside. People rushed to its aid with wet towels. A father walked along his caravan pouring water over the heads of his youngsters. He saw an old man leaning out of his rusty truck. The father motioned to the old man to stick out his head and gave him a good dousing.

Eight hours later they arrived at the Woodlands. They had driven only 86 miles. They remembered an old lady back in Galveston, sitting on her porch, rocking to the rhythm of an increasing wind. "I'm staying. My mind and body are in this house," she announced. Thinking of her, they regretted their decision to leave. But there was no way back. They pulled into a parking lot to try to sleep for a few hours. "No Availability" signs loomed large at every motel where entrances were locked and manned by security guards. At any moment a riot could break out and people would demand to be led through the barricades.

Cecile asked a deputy where they might fill their empty water bottles. "You're on your own," was his gruff reply, "Find a spigot." Their throats were parched, their cantines empty. They needed some liquid soon. Necessity generated ingenuity. Jeff collected their quarters and found a boarded-up service station where he was able to get water from a hose used for replenishing overheated radiators. They drank their fill but their stomachs had to wait for something substantial.

They spent the night in their cars, feet stretched out the windows as mosquitos swarmed. A full moon, like a pockmarked pumpkin, illuminated the humid night. Cecile woke her parents at dawn. "You were totally out, Mom." They glanced at Ron beside Ute and for once his snoring filled Ute with tenderness.

Joy of joys, in Huntsville a Walmart was open. The shelves were nearly bare but they found several cans of green beans, a treat. They were nearly out of gas when Ron spotted a little boy swinging a beat-up one-gallon gas container. "Want to buy gas?" the boy yelled.

"How much?"

"Ten bucks."

"You got it."

The boy grabbed the money and skipped off. "We would have given him more if he'd asked for it," Jeff laughed.

Politeness stopped when the first gas delivery arrived. There were scuffles at the pumps, tempers flared and people on foot pushed and shoved. It took hours to wait for a second gasoline delivery.

Toilets were clogged but still everyone had to go. A woman in a wheelchair rolled in. "Can someone please help?" A smartly dressed black teenager in low-cut jeans and a fancy silver-buckled belt offered to steady the woman and hold the broken door shut.

Privilege glitters like a diamond in the desert. They arrived in Austin where they found a room. A shower and a bed felt like heaven. Multitudes still struggled to find shelter.

Rita hit. Two of the palm trees in their front yard tumbled onto the roof, drenching the inside of the house with a flooding downpour. A turbulent storm ripped their huge air conditioners out of the ground and what was left of their belongings was gone with the wind and rain. It took months to rebuild and sell the house. How lucky to have had the forethought to store most of the valuables.

The Austin realtor they had earlier contacted when renting a storage place was on the phone. He had done his homework and lined up houses for sale. To his great frustration Ute would not even get out of his car when he showed one or the other. "No thank you, not this one." After having safely escaped a disaster, Ute was determined to wait until she found just the right domicile for their next station in life.

The stone entrance to Davenport Ranch sports a racehorse in full flight. The streets are named after derbies. As they circled through a cul-de-sac with their realtor, a "For Sale" sign went up. Did Ute hear whinnying? The circle was called "Triple Crown."

"Stop," Ute pointed to the sign.

"It's not officially listed yet," the realtor replied.

"Let's ask anyway." The owners were not pleased to have unannounced visitors, but relented and allowed a showing. Standing in the loft, admiring the distinctive architecture of alternating round and square arches, Ute fell for the house, her dream house.

"This is it," she announced. "The inside structure resembles Morocco and the ivy-covered brick walls are European." Ute was enthralled before she even knew the selling price. They signed a contract the same evening at a good bargain.

During the transition years when Ron finished up as Institute Director in Galveston, he taught in the undergraduate honors program at the University of Texas at Austin. He had watched how under new leadership his beloved Institute went in an unwelcome direction. He hoped that the seeds sown over long years had found fertile ground. Many medical schools now require a course in medical ethics. Ute found a part-time position as a clinical hypnotist and both enlisted in volunteer work with Meals on Wheels. Ute continued her involvement with Hospice. Her trips to Dallas to her grandkids continued.

For the first time in years Ron and Ute had ample time for each other which they celebrated in a poem.

Folding Washing
"... Grow old with me, the best is still to be..."
It's hard to believe the promise
when aging's afflictions begin to weigh on us,
the failing body, the forgetful mind.
But if we're lucky
we'll have someone to fold washing with,
long sheets needing two pairs of hands,
tugging, straightening,
stretch right, pull to the left.
The heart will not be deterred,
forever yearning for a companion
to share the ordinary
with lightness as dusk descends.

With the birth of Kaius, a new task as grandparents was bestowed on them. For the next 25 years their lives would chart a different course, not dark yet, a midsummer solstice illuminated their paths. They would live in a bubble of bliss.

34 A Pot of Liquid Gold

Sitting under their fledgling magnolia tree, heavy white blossoms weighed on the fragile branches, swinging them in the early summer breeze. A marvelous greenness enfolded. Dreamily the glittering petals fluttered down, heart-shaped and sticking to Ute's face, her bare arms, her extended legs. They embalmed her heart. Each leaf was marked with a particular design, each blossom exuded a unique scent, symbolizing six grandchildren, each as different as the other, each equally precious.

Ute remembered how her own birth had been delayed due to her mother's bereavement. She often wondered if the birth experience predicted an attitude toward life. Ute had been anxious uttering her question to Omi Maria, "Is life only tears and sorrow?" Fear continued to trail her like a dark shadow. Ron had sprung into the world feet first, always the leader. Now under blooming abundance Ute made a Faustian pact with fate, that ephemeral ghost. "If you spread a protected webbing over my loved ones, I will give you my soul," she promised. Could life be bribed? Would it bestow favors on a generation after much tragedy had been placed on the last? Ute hoped so.

Both Dylan and Nicholas were born on the same date three years apart. For both, Texas wildflowers had decked themselves out, the bluebonnets in sky-blue, the Indian paintbrush in bright orange, and the anemones in tender pink.

Dylan took charge of her delivery, arriving fast and easy. She would always be determined in all her dealings and emotions, a princess on butterfly wings. Once she visited Pappy Ron and Omi Ute in Galveston, she and her grandmother went to the Schlitterbahn. There Dylan coaxed Omi Ute into rubber dinghies and, holding hands across the rims, they swished through turbulent waterways, laughing all the way. Dylan believes in hypnosis. She once sprained her ankle. She hopped on a chair and called, "Hypnotize me, Omi." Afterwards, the pain was gone.

This is how Dylan sees herself. "Dancing the night away and singing songs loudly with the windows of my car rolled down are examples of my free-spirited side. I even jumped out of an airplane once. But I also have a plan...my plan.) I've been called bossy and strong willed, although I see it as I know what I want. I am sensitive, intuitive, honest and thoughtful. I am funny and can tell a good story. I like fashion and I have a love for traveling, simultaneously I enjoy coming home to my house. I work hard and I play hard. I was once an avid dancer and had a wide palette for it.

Ballet, tap, jazz, modern, and hip hop to name a few. A fun fact about me is I played the drums. Being in the mountains with the snow is exhilarating for me and I also love the water by the beach or the lake on a hot summer day. I love a sunset and believe the moon definitely has special powers. Give me an interesting book and great food, and I'm good to go. I am an extrovert/introvert. I enjoy a party, but also need my alone time. I have a wonderful group of girlfriends I enjoy spending time with and I can't say enough about my amazing fiancé, Hudson. My child right now is a beautiful golden retriever, Johnson, but one day soon I will have little humans running around too. I love my family and I have an extra strong bond with my brother Nicholas. We share a birthday together. Being me and the life I lead has me very grateful."

Nicholas would also imbibe the beauty of nature, but having arrived by C-section to free the umbilical cord wrapped around his neck, he feared snares that had to be untangled. He learned to balance his options and did not always take the emotionally prescribed path. Once Omi Ute lay at their house with the flu. The children were forbidden to enter the sickroom. Before school one morning Nicholas slipped in and rushed toward his grandmother, "I needed to give you a hug."

This is how Nicholas sees himself. "I am many things when it comes to who I am. Although I am still growing and therefore like to leave my life open to new and advancing qualities that will form and arise as I get older. It makes for a rich and complete life but here it goes for now. I am kind and loving. I am a lover and a fighter, but in different realms and for different reasons. I am upfront and direct. I am confident in myself and my skills. I love sports and am very competitive. I have played everything from soccer, baseball, basketball, to football and snowboarding. Watersports are activities I enjoy doing. I'm edgy and a risk taker. I am a seeker of adventures and new thrills. I just recently jumped out of an airplane. I am ambitious, hardworking, and a business owner at the age of 24! I am an emotional being and companionate. My love for my mamma, dad, sisters and brother goes beyond words. My sister, Dylan and I are best friends and are very close. We were born on the same day. I have a few guy friends that I hang out with and they remain constant in my life. You'll see me at a crowded concert or group activity with them, but also not hear from me for a couple of days until I'm refreshed. I love to travel and have new experiences as well as being spontaneous, but also grounded and like my home base. I am a protector, lover of music, and have a sense of humor. I eventually want a dog and I foresee marriage and children in my future. I know I'll love being a husband and father. I consider myself a good man. I've learned a lot of hard lessons early on in my life, but I am better for it. I would not trade my life for anything."

It was Tommy's mother, Marie, who prayed to the Virgin Mother during Zachary's prolonged delivery. Praised as an "unflinching trouper," Claudia, pale and still trembling, became a blessed Mary as she held her firstborn in her arms. Zachary's shiny eyes were fixed on his mother. He seemed to be saying, "Sorry I took so long. Now I'm here, ten pounds strong and ready to protect you." A sense of responsibility governs Zachary's rich intelligence, a need to pursue his dreams but simultaneously to take care of others. He is scrupulously fair in his judgments. In the ruins of the family castle Bielwiese, he followed Omi Ute through rubble and climbed with her while the rest of the family timidly stayed behind. After their glacier incident Omi Ute was wheeled through the airport. Zachary was inconsolable, "Will Omi be able to walk again?" As a college student he was confident enough to put his head in his grandmother's lap on a magical picnic day on the California beach.

Here is how Zachary sees himself. "I love the beach, the surf, the sand, and the sun. I am an adventurer, hard worker, and love action. I love my California ways but will always be a Texas boy. I am driven, enjoy creating new businesses, and always like to push myself. I've been told that my first word after 'Mama' and 'Dada' was 'Why', which sums up a lot about me. I'm very into the fashion world and living an aesthetic life. I am passionate about my work and like to take on new challenges in every part of life. I like to look at the glass as half full. I love sports both playing and watching, meeting new people, and traveling. I am empathetic, authentic and fair. I love my family and friends and would like to think of myself as a very social person. I can be friends with most people but in the end, I am always there for those closest to me."

Away on a dog-sledding adventure, Ron and Ute were without phones. Anxious that they might miss Alexander's birth, Ute hiked up a knoll each morning to get reception before the start of the sleigh rides. An old Inuit dog followed her on her climbs and barked joyfully on the descent. Ron and Ute made it back in time to the hospital in Dallas where Tommy perched outside the newborn nursery with a Joseph-like devotion. Omi Ute pressed a stuffed Inuit dog up to the glass partition. Alexander possesses an intuitive connection to animals. He is also a gifted artist and filmmaker. Staying with Omi Ute and Pappy Ron, he joined them for breakfast and wrote a poem about togetherness on a morning in Austin. His most insightful moving poem "Breaking Bread and Pears" shows his deep caring for his fellow humans. He uses humor to lighten life's burdens.

This is how Alexander sees himself. "I love chronicling life's adventures through the camera lens, and capturing emotion with film. I meet life head on, have an adventurous spirit, and have been known to be somewhat of a daredevil-from the time I could snowboard to learning to drive, I've always loved speed and have a heavy foot. I love cars and like playing the piano. I 've been told I was a jokester from the time I was little, but I'm also good at striking a balance between when to have fun with life and when to be serious about things that matter to me. I like meeting new people and am outgoing, friendly, and easy to talk to. I am thoughtful, creative, and always true to myself."

Cecile and Jeff had made beautiful preparations for the birth of their first son with a colorful mandala and soothing music. But nature was unpredictable and after a ruptured vessel, Cecile was rushed to the hospital where a delayed delivery took its time.

Doctors predicted a birth the following day but Ute let her instincts guide her. In bed that night, she got back up and readied herself with a sleeping bag. A tired staff at the hospital were not happy to see her and directed her to the waiting room where she bedded down between two pulled-up chairs. Before midnight a nurse tapped her on the shoulder, "Congratulations. You have a grandson." After the parents, Ute was the first one to hold Kaius. She had painted her fingernails sun/moon yellow. She spotted a white lock at the neckline of his fuzzy baby hair, just like Heio's. Ute would often cradle Kaius in his baby years. He in turn would in older years massage and lotion her arthritic feet. Kaius can be anxious and wildly daring. He is immensely talented, a whiz with Legos and a creator of worldwide maps. He is also competitive in sports. He cares deeply. When he could not yet write himself, he dictated a poem "For his Omi" where he tells her that he will always love her. The poem was selected as the best American poem for the UK anthology, "Poetry Together."

This is how Kaius sees himself. "My name is Kaius Carson Powers and I live in Austin Texas. There are many things to do here, let me tell you about some of them. I love to play sports. I play club soccer as well as run track. I do a little rock climbing and rowing here and there. I love history and food. There's a lot that I'll eat, including fast food, Chinese food, and healthy food. You know fruits and stuff. There is not a lot that I wouldn't do, or at least give a try. In my free time I like to watch movies and TV shows like Seinfeld, or referee a soccer game for some extra cash. I love my family. This includes my brother, my parents, grandpas, grandmas, aunts, uncles, you name it. I love to hang out with my grandparents whenever I can, they're great. My grandmother is actually the writer of this book which I would think is pretty impressive if I were you. Yup, I live a pretty good life."

On a late afternoon Kaius and Omi Ute took a walk. They expected to hear about the arrival of the little brother. Sitting on a grassy incline,

Kaius pounded Omi Ute with questions. "When Omi? When?" "Soon," was not enough. "When soon?" The answer suddenly flew into view and Omi Ute pointed. "Look. A red cardinal. See its fiery head and breast? It is coming toward us." "Really? Is the baby on its way?" Kaius was momentarily satisfied with Omi Ute's answer that the baby would soon fly from his Mommy's tummy into their arms. They continued to gaze in the direction of the bird who wheeled in their direction, touching down on a nearby crepe myrtle branch. As soon as it had anchored its claws in the bark, it puffed up its plumage and began preening its brilliant feathers. At that moment the phone rang with the good tidings that Lucas, who would become the delight of all, had just made a soft landing. Lucas is not only smart in math and reading and creative with his drawing. He molded airplanes from clay so he could fly the family around the world. He sculptured a clay owl for Omi Ute. He is sympathetic. Sitting next to Omi Ute who was opening mail with several "regrets" for a reception she was planning and sighed, "Not many are coming," he slung his arms around her neck, "But I am here."

This is how Lucas sees himself. "I would say I am quite a humble boy but, if I were to brag, I would say I am a mature ten-year-old. The goalkeeper on the elite soccer team at a club called FC Westlake. A Southern Texas PGA tournament champion. A worldwide traveler and the smartest kid at my elementary school. But as Joe Biden said 'You're not better than anyone else and no one's better than you.' I love sports. Particularly soccer and golf. But I often enjoy other sports including kayaking, track, baseball, and basketball as well. I love going to my grandparents' house right here in Austin. I like hanging out with friends. I love trips. Especially the breathtaking views at destinations like Machu Picchu and Niagara Falls, and of course the family time."

The baby years opened new doors of perception and tasks for Pappy Ron. He had always been present as a father but his busy professional life had prevented him from sharing many family activities. Now he was a part of the Omi/Pappy team. At night when there was a sleepover, he warmed the bottles while Omi Ute rocked the waiting infant. He told stories, listened when they sang and was game to kick the ball in the yard or swing on the wooden swing set. He built sandboxes. As the boys grew older, he was more and more involved in their sports. They started to engage him in discussions about politics, a subject he knows so well. They wanted to be like him, tall and learned. They imitated his dress code. Like Omi Ute, he found fulfillment. The grandkids stuck to them both like filaments of liquid gold.

35 Time Travel

A place is captured in a moment in time. Even if the encounter is new and pristine, someone will have sat under the kokerboom before and someone will again. The tree still whispers but each listener hears a different tune. A journey fits into the wrinkle of time, a history. Travelling is both moving forward and backwards. Returning to a beloved place, the past is revived, but there is change in the setting, its people and also in the visitor.

After Dylan's birth, Ute and Ron scouted out the beaches near Sarasota for a yearly family retreat. They found the Wicker Inn, loosely modeled after English coastal resorts, with houses painted a yellowish-beige and white picket fences. Floridian bougainvillea vines crowned the vista. Each family lived in a rented cottage for a week. Right after school ended in June, Ute and Ron welcomed family members. The cottages were named after flowers: Sunflower, Primrose, Magnolia and Bougainvillea. The gathering became a ritual over 13 years. Zachary and Alexander grew up on the sand and in the ocean waves of the Gulf. Others joined for respites. They swam with horses in the bay, watched frolicking dolphins from the decks of boats, and frequented the Jungle Gardens. In the fading evening light crabs were chased from their holes with flashlights. Sunsets were saluted with drinks. Under a liquid-blue morning sky they imitated diving birds and cautiously traipsed around protected turtle mounds. They fished; they canoed. They celebrated Cecile and Jeff's fortieth birthdays, and Dylan and Nicholas's graduations from high school. Dylan was teased about a reprimand she gave her rambunctious little cousin when she herself was learning to read, "sit down boy, read book." Nicholas went into hypnosis believing that he would receive the gifts of his dreams. Kaius made sure all shoes were lined up properly at the cottage doors and that showers were decorated with stickers, while Lucas was keen on keeping a beach-walking routine. When little, Zachary and Alexander sprinted from their cottage to Omi and Pappy's, jumping into their beds. Happiness was contagious.

For a winter vacation over New Year's, they explored Ruidoso and Santa Fe. Then they came upon the magical Devil's Thumb Ranch in Colorado. When they arrived for their first visit, Tommy, seeing a lit-up ranch in the distance at dusk, exclaimed, "This is paradise." They skied, snowshoed and enjoyed the huge fireplace with sumptuous meals in the main hall of the lodge. When swimming from an indoor to an outdoor pool, snowflakes settled on wet hair. On New Year's Eve they took a horse-drawn carriage ride before playing games until toasting with champagne at midnight.

Once family members tasted the joys of traveling, more trips followed. Ute and Ron joined Caitlin, Chris and their children at Destin, Florida for a weekend. In the hours before dawn Omi Ute and Dylan slipped out of a sleeping house and wandered along the dark beach until they were awed by a brilliant sunrise.

Nicholas went with Omi and Pappy to a cave to watch the flight of bats, resembling menacing clouds then like thousands of fluttering black-winged birds. When they returned to Nicholas' aunt's house that night, he was bedding down on a sleeping bag when he asked Omi Ute, "Can you stay next to me for a while?"

The Mission Church near San Antonio was remembered by family members for its moving Mariachi choir and the cloister embedded between mesquite shrubs, ancient ruins and carved stone walls. They stopped at the "Rose Window" and read a sad love story finely chiseled into a stone plaque. Church service followed a stroll along the San Antonio Riverwalk and a barge ride.

Utah, Arizona, Colorado, New Mexico, the four corner states, welcomed Cecile, Jeff, Kaius and Lucas with Ron and Ute to the ancient Indian cliff dwellings near Durango and the wondrous arches near Moab. They went stargazing, bought bows, arrows and a quill at an Indian trading post, and heard a lecture by a park ranger who then initiated Lucas into the ranks of junior park ranger. Wading in the Colorado River was an adventure as was a swim in natural springs. Marvelous wonders abounded! Lucas was a bit skeptical when they arrived at a stay in a rustic motel which had seen better days. He wondered, "Are there mice?"

In Montana's Rocky Mountains, Claudia, Tommy, Zachary and Alexander watched a grizzly bear splashing in a river from the safe distance of their car, ate raspberries by the handful and dared a day-hike to the Grinnell Glacier. Reluctant to cross a narrow ridge bordering a steep ravine, Claudia wanted to turn back. She was terrified of heights. "I have that hollow feeling in my stomach," she moaned. Being only a few minutes from the summit and the magnificent glacier, Ute took her hand. Claudia closed her eyes and trembled as they walked along the steep path to security.

The glacier hike taught Ute a life-lesson. After returning to the lodge, she showered but drank no water before having wine with dinner. Without a warning red flag, she fainted, tumbling from the table to the floor. She was rushed by helicopter to Kalispell with shivering Claudia at her side. On the same day mother and daughter had experienced fright and safe passage. Ute was startled into an awareness that she could have died. Carpe Diem was a wake-up call.

At Sol y Luna, a resort in Peru, they worshiped the sun and paid homage to the moon, surrounded by the splendor of tropical vegetation. Climbing up to Machu Picchu, they followed the path of the Inca kings. Hiking to ancient salt mines, they marveled at the technical knowhow of ages past. They rode the gentle-gaited Peruvian horses and celebrated Omi and Pappy's 80th birthdays with local dishes and heartfelt toasts. In Cusco, pictures were taken with llamas.

Before each trip Ute's old worries would surface. She longed to venture out, but lines from Yeats's poem "Among School Children," evoking "the uncertainty of setting forth," crept into her mind. Fear trailed Ute like a heavy shadow. She knew that her love could not protect her family but she continued nevertheless to send positive energy in their direction.

The etchings of Käthe Kollwitz were favorites of Ute's. She bought several reprints. In those charcoal drawings the artist depicts a woman spreading her arms like wide tree branches over a group of children. The woman's clutching hands are extended like claws, warning anyone against harming her young. Ute identified with Kollwitz and was increasingly drawn to her work as she herself became a mother, then a grandmother.

It was Ron who consoled and calmed Ute. "Don't worry. Everything will be alright as long as we are together."

Two journeys into the past became in Claudia's words, "Trips of a lifetime." In 2017 four Habeebs flew with Ron and Ute to Poland, with a stopover in London. That city alone was an experience for the boys, navigating the underground, riding in a double-decker open-top bus past well-known historical sights, and the "London Eye" where Zachary had to overcome his fear of heights. He was the one who made sure everyone stayed together. He herded his family and asked, "Where are Omi and Pappy?" when they lagged behind. They walked along the Thames, watched the changing of the guard at Buckingham Palace, roamed Portobello Road and saw a play at the Old Vic. But London was not a familiar stomping ground. The next stop was. There the spirits of the family's past greeted them.

Never before had the phrase "show not tell" meant so much as when they landed in Krakow where at the Wieliczka salt mine Alexander licked the cave wall and they flitted around on Segways, a new means of transportation. When they entered the heart of Silesia, they started to feel events happening twice. During a visit to the zoo in Wroclaw where Ute and Omi Maria had once sighted a lion, now a youngster yawned at them. They counted the dwarf statues who had crouched in the same odd places for centuries and where Alexander mimicked a mummified clown. They found their dream resort at the romantique Palac Staniszow, where Zachary swore he would return for his wedding. They ate ice cream under the restored arches of Jelenia Gora. Did the spirit of Omi Maria meet them there? They felt the earth move under their feet standing at the defunct train station where in the icy winter of 1945 Omi Maria, Gerda-Maria and Ute had been loaded onto a wounded soldiers' transport, headed west. Each train now carried a cargo of memories. They pulled themselves up a rickety ladder in the attic of the Marczow mansion which once had served as their Rapunzle lookout over the Bober River and the burning villages. In Sosnowka where Gerda-Maria married Count Fritz, they were able to peek into the chapel with a gilded altar, restored by director Steven Spielberg after the release of the movie *Schindler's List*.

But the highlight dawned when scrambling up the ruins of the family castle Bielwiese, built in 1727 and now a massive heap of red brick and crumbling mortar. The entire front facade still stood three stories high with the molded crowned seals of ancestral Baron von Lüttwitz intact. A stork nest was firmly planted atop the gable, the stork being a symbol of generational continuity. Jungle-like vegetation abounded and nature had endured. The oak tree, now gnarled and bent, stretched its leafy crown and rich foliage through a gaping window frame. What a thrill to swipe spiderwebs from their faces and trample down brush to explore the interior of the castle. Carefully stepping on worn, hollowed-out stones, they stumbled upon a view into a huge crack directly above the former dining room. Everyone imagined Mumu, then little Gerda-Maria, sitting attentively next to her fidgety brothers, with elegant Omi Maria and benevolent grandfather Nicholaus engrossed in earnest conversation. From a turret high in the rubble, they glanced over an unkempt garden to a wide-open field, studded with cornflowers and poppies.

"That was Gerda-Maria's and her brothers' childhood idyll," Ute recalled.

Zachary was at his Omi's side, wanting to explore more, climbing higher and higher. "Maybe our ancestors have guarded the ruins so we could still see them," was his parting remark. Both boys pocketed a small brick from the ruins as a keepsake.

Stories accompanied them to the next family place, another ancestral land, now in the Czech Republic, the former monastery Sankt Ivan Under the Cross. On their way they visited Prague, the mystical city with the Charles Bridge, constructed from medieval stones, its myriad Baroque churches, the famous astronomical clock on the main plaza, and the Prague castle overlooking the city. In the evening, they were driven around in a horse-drawn carriage. Under the Charles Bridge, the Volga roared with its fairy-tales and songs. They crossed themselves at the Saint Nepomuk statue, oldest on the bridge. Prague was unforgettable. Gerda-Maria had visited there with 10-year-old Cecile. Now Claudia, Tommy, Zachary, Alexander, and six years later, Cecile, Jeff, Kaius and Lucas became tourists as well as cultural heirs. They were rooted here, feet moored in ancient family history.

They all metamorphosed into their ancestors when they arrived at Sankt Ivan Under the Cross. Drinking spring water from the life-giving reservoir the Saint had discovered centuries ago, they looked around and wondered where Omi Maria might have met the gypsies? As Alexander played the piano in the former music room with its biblical frescos, the sound echoed up the high ceilings as if to shake heaven and earth. They were reminded of the furniture now honored in their American homes. How the handicrafts had defied time. They hiked all the way to the top of the giant cliff where a wooden cross is moored like a weathervane. The view down reached the small village, nestled in a sun-dappled valley. Kaius reposed on the rugged ridge, gazing far and wide, never tiring of the view, reigning over his inheritance.

How eerie to enter the crypt underneath the lovely Baroque family chapel. Once Omi Maria had been spooked seeing the intact coffin of her grandmother. Did they get spooked too? Several ancestors seemed to step from the stones and the shadow of oblivion. Cecile felt being in a trance and thought she heard crying and laughing. Their skins prickled even though the crypt proved cool, shut off from the outside. Only the clay turtles, representing eternal life, were dust-covered, bygone fragments. Above the caskets, wrought-iron angels hovered. Sunlight flickered through a round shaft at the far end of one wall.

During a trip to Poland in 2023, the Carson Powers became shapeshifters. Standing on the balcony in Köslin where Gerda-Maria had cradled baby Ute in 1940, Ute began to sway, holding on to Ron's arm. Walking by Gert's high school, the lament of an older generation came to mind. Ute had to explain to the boys what was meant by the complaint. In 1946 an arbitrary line between the Oder and the Neisse rivers, had set post-war boundaries between present-day Germany and Poland. Before World War II, this part, Pomerania, had been German homeland. What would their lives have been like if war had not intervened? If the Allies had decreed different demarcations? They were made aware of the arbitrariness of history.

Lucas had learned some Polish words and Kaius was interviewed by the local radio station about how it felt to be tracing his roots so far removed from America? The past was forcefully enveloping Ute and her family. Gdansk dazzled them with amber, the gold of the north. They all turned into laughing children, sliding, sinking, skipping through shifting sand dunes in the Slowinski National Park. The transmigration back into the past was visceral as they waded into the rolling waves of the Baltic Sea. Lucas loved the sea as much as his great-grandfather Gert. He was buoyed by the waves and jumped like a gazelle into the air when emerging from the waters. Ute was a three-year-old again, standing in front of Karl and Aenne's summer cottage in Gross Mölln, now Mielno, recalling vigorously moving the handle of a pump up-and-down. As in one of her poems.

As Time Goes By
...the cottage speaks to me.
Memories bubble up as I stand among the neglect and debris.
Wild roses clamber abundantly around the leaning fence.
I hear the roaring waves from the sea and smell the acid seawater.
When I close my eyes, visions rise into the air on a gentle breeze
and I call up those bygone days
when well-water sprayed my face as I pumped...

Ute believed herself an alchemist, changing past events into the present. As in a miracle, the people who had been here before them rose and mingled with them in her imagination.

When they overnighted at the wild and forested castle Krag, Ute was able to shed her chameleon skin and become a tourist within her family.

It was beyond their usual bedtime hour when they retired, having wandered through the romantic setting along a luminous river covered with waterlilies and algae. Lucas remarked, "For an old castle, ten o'clock is not late at all."

Years collapsed. People became tangible, their words were audible to the inner ear.

"It's not just in telling about historical places but by visiting them that the past comes to life," Ron mused. "Everything changes but embedded in that change is permanence and continuity."

Life can be a wondrous journey. Long ago Ute had posed the question to Omi Maria, "Are people prepared to accept beauty when suffering, loss and tears mingle with laughter?" Omi Maria had replied, "There are no choices. Only hope that the scales of fickle history tip in your favor."

36 Graying Dandelions

The first flower a grandchild plucked for Omi Ute and Pappy Ron was a dandelion, full of rich pollen and nourishing nectar. Golden petals had opened with the heat and now closed when the temperature cooled off. Alexander blew the fluff from a dandelion and tiny seeds fluttered away along with a myriad of wishes. Then he turned triumphantly to Pappy, "You have gray hair like the flowers. But that's okay." Ron remembered when once he had stroked the fuzz on Alexander's baby head, soft like the gray puffs of the dandelions. Zachary was sitting on a nearby bench threading a necklace, murmuring, "I am making you a necklace, Omi, pasta and beads, pasta and beads."

As grandparents Ron and Ute responded to many crises.
The phone rang late and Ron and Ute jumped back into their clothes and drove to Hobby Airport. Claudia, who just a few weeks before had given birth to Zachary, had an emergency appendectomy. Caitlin had rushed to her sister's side, accompanying her to the hospital while Tommy stayed with the baby. Caitlin helped pump breast milk before Claudia permitted the anesthetics for the surgery.
All planes had departed for the night. Ron and Ute paced the empty airport corridors through the night. Ute was on the first flight out. Tommy was waiting at Dallas Love Field. At home Claudia was propped up with Zachary on a pillow over her painful stitches. Tears streamed down her cheeks but she would take only mild sedatives fearing that it would affect Zachary's milk.

Ron and Ute did not anticipate the change in lifestyle that was in store for them. For Ron's 75th birthday, a poster featured him in a hot-air balloon flying around the world, forecasting more travel in the future. On Ute's 75th birthday she was challenged to walk on a tightrope between two trees. She was still good at balancing between her trips to Dallas and her writing at home. Experiences kept flowing into her pen. But both Ron and Ute had retired. Gone were the ambitions of careers. There was less preoccupation with themselves. No longer being pulled in different directions, no need to multitask. They had no idea how wondrous a gift they were receiving which would prolong their grandparent duties. They would carry out this new obligation as an elderly couple hand-in-hand. The circle had rounded out. It was the two of them again but there was never a reprieve from maternal love. The nest filled again unexpectedly.

Cecile's lips quivered as she handed her three-month-old bundle to her mother. She had to return to work. The daycare facilities they had inspected displeased them. Grateful, she and Jeff accepted the offer from Ron and Ute to take care of their firstborn on work days. Cecile would have lunch at her parents' house to nurse her baby. "I will take care of Kaius exactly as you wish. I will try for total continuity." Ute stroked Cecile's cheek. Kaius did not wake up as Omi Ute cradled this soft warm infant in her arms.

Three and a half years later another baby, Lucas, was given into Ute and Ron's day care. As Lucas moved from one arm into another, Ute once again experienced the wonder of touch.

An easy routine developed between the two households. They built a safe place to nestle into. They stored present moments as well as memories from their girls' childhoods and their own. There were so many first steps, first words, and countless incidents to recall. One of Ute's poems embraces the atmosphere.

A Tangled Nest of Moments
Our memories are in the weave.
Ragged bits of cloth threaded around wispy twigs,
scattered leaves, and
tattered down furnish the padding.
A lot of refurbishing is needed
after the ravages of winter,
plugging a hole here,
mending unraveled bedding there.

Love is in the fabric.
When first your breath blew back my hair,
chirping baby lips were my music,
and a daughter's tender finger grazed my cheeks.

Near perfection is in the tending.
As the wind whistles around our little abode
we huddle feather-to-feather,
knotting more memories
into our tangled nest of moments.

They huddled together and knotted experiences into the fabric of their lives. They read *Curious George*, and *RinTinTin*. They watched *The Smurfs*, *Winnie the Pooh*, and the *Flicka* series. They built a tent with sheets under their oak tree branches, and swung high into the air on a wooden swing. They constructed and painted a caboose from cardboard boxes and built castles in the sandbox. As grandparents they applauded the steps when the boys learned to walk. They encouraged paddling strokes during swimming lessons. Later they clapped when a ball was tossed across the yard and they were glad when the boys were good at golf. In the kitchen they gathered to bake and cook, celebrated holidays and festivals together, caught minnows in a stream, and hiked through parks, meadows and fields. The zoo was a favorite destination. They surrendered to the magic of music. A normal life unfolded as Ute had wished for since childhood.

Kaius dazzled them with his dexterity, putting a puzzle together at the speed of lightning and later compiling complex Legos. He climbed up trees and onto rooftops, and scrambled over neighborhood walls like a squirrel. Lucas charmed them with his ability to read and spell simple words at three, his magician tricks, and his knowledge of life in the ocean, scaring them with his drawings of sharks.

Rituals developed when the boys stayed for sleepovers. Kaius and Omi would sit across from each other at bedtime, he with a glass of cider, she one with wine. They would toast and then exchange stories from the day before Kaius would let himself be tucked in. In the mornings, the boys would sing *Die Güldne Sonne* to welcome the day. Then they would open the window so they could hear what the birds had to say. Lucas and Ute found a spot on a rock at a four-way intersection. Supplied with raisins, they would watch the traffic and Lucas would record, "This car did not stop. This one only squealed but ran through. This one did it right and halted." Under the fleshy saucer-shaped leaves of their magnolia tree they would have their noon picnic. When the boys were picked up by their parents, they showed off, turning cartwheels in the driveway.

On weekends, when Ron and Ute were by themselves, they moved closer to each other than ever. They shared tasks and rehearsed events from the week. They acknowledged the gift they had been given.

For their 50th anniversary Ron and Ute flew to Germany with their three daughters. Ute had returned to Europe many times but for this event she hastened back. Her heart crossed the ocean like a migrating bird, never stopping. Under a luminous turquoise sky, they celebrated with remaining family members and friends. Their ranks had thinned and it had been years since they had seen many of them. Ute had to scan their faces and was glad about old recognitions. Ron's good friend Tom arrived unannounced. The old Baroque church in Felsberg, which had witnessed their wedding 50 years ago, vibrated with welcoming vibes. The pastor himself made special preparations for this American couple who had met on a train, by displaying a child's train set as a prompt for his sermon. The sanctuary radiated with candle lights and the scent of flowers. Petals were strewn along the long burgundy carpeted aisle.

It came time to release Kaius from his cozy cocoon into the wider world. He was eager. It was only a morning stay, and he enjoyed his Montessori sessions as much as landing back in his grandparent's arms before lunch.

Ute was not ready. Parents and grandparents brought Kaius to his classroom. He marched in confidently. Suddenly Ute was wracked with sobs. Tears rolled down her cheeks, blinding her.

"Sweetheart. What's happening?" Ron laced an arm around her shaking shoulders. "Why this outburst? It's just a few hours of separation and then we have Kaius back."

Ute could not answer. As she wiped her eyes with the sleeve of her blouse, she confessed, "Everything crashed down on me. My mother and grandmother, grandparents and dear friends are no longer alive. Friendships break, people leave and time passes." Slowly, Ute was able to collect herself. "I don't know, so many departures suddenly overwhelmed me."

"Tears are part of joy," Ron tried to console. "You can never have one without the other. That's life."

"I know, I know, all around me I witness true tragedies, but even small losses can bring on floods of grief." Ute was able to lean against Ron's comforting chest and take a deep breath. Back home she went into her garden and angrily pulled weeds out by the roots.

Ute never revealed her sadness when a child left the nest. But maybe intuitive Kaius sensed that his Omi missed their mornings together. After he settled into his preschool environment, he painted Ute a large picture of two warriors facing each other, swords held high between them but hands touching. He chose vivid colors, red, black and yellow. The costumes are shown in flaming red and charcoal black but the raised swords are a deep gold. Kaius wrote names on the sleeves of the figures, "Kaius" on the left side of his outfit, "Omi" on hers on the right. Kaius had just learned the alphabet and when he penciled in Omi, he turned the letter M upside down. Omi became Owl. Seeing his painting, Ute teared up again. This time with delight and gratitude.

When Lucas started his preschool half-days, Ron and Ute became his rescuers. Lucas was not excited to go to school as his brother had been. When the morning activities were complete, he skipped playtime and sat quietly in a toddler chair and surveyed the out-of-doors. He refused to use the bathroom. He waited for his Pappy to scoop him up and take him to the car, where Omi was waiting with yogurt and blueberries. Lucas's bladder was full to bursting, but nothing could convince him to stop on the drive home. Most days he made it home, though not always. He ran through the front door straight to the bathroom while Omi warmed his milk bottle. Then they retired for a snooze in the upstairs bedroom. In later years Lucas outgrew his shyness, became very social, and enjoyed being with his friends. But as a toddler he preferred the familiar routine of the two homes, his parents and grandparents.

Through the years all grandchildren kept close contact with Omi and Pappy. At times Ute reached for her favorite book *A Boy in Winter*. How the grandkids reminded her of siblings being there for each other. There was a circle uniting adults and children in Austin and Dallas. They learned that grandparental love never stops with one grandchild but is carried on in different forms.

Ute grabbed Ron's hand, "How lucky we are. We love and are being loved and are still able to do this grandparenting together." In Mary Oliver's beautiful words, "Giving, until giving feels like receiving."

37 Ravishes of Time

The sky was a smudged gray. Ron and Ute stood under the branches of their oak tree and listened to the melancholy voice of the wind. They watched a low-flying swallow. Their hands hurried to their pockets to find a few crumbs to toss into the air. Did the swallow sense the arrival of bad weather? It rained soon, not a downpour, just a drizzle.

Lucas barged through the door, "I'm here." Rays of light were flying out of him. The bloom had gone from Omi's cheeks as she tried not to limp, hiding her neuropathy, catching her grandson in an embrace. With their established routine neither boy noticed that time was taking its toll on the old couple. In later years Ron and Ute confessed that without the sunshine Kaius and Lucas beamed into their lives, they might not have made it through the many health crises. A cliche? Maybe, but when they lived it, it became reality. Were there no bad days, fuzzy and tiring ones? Of course, but the joy the grandkids etched into their hearts remained.

Many of Ron and Ute's close family members, parents and grandparents, and friends like Eberhard, and Uli who had plucked Ute's first rose, Christa whose wall-hangings decorated their house and Kris, wife of Ron's friend Bob, had died. Other friends suffered serious illnesses. They themselves were hit by an avalanche of illnesses, Ron a heart murmur and prostate cancer, Ute lost sight in her left eye, developed breast cancer, and her neuropathy flourished.

Their friend Penny from their Sarasota days was next to leave them. When her belief in the power of Christian Science failed her, she still refused help. Only at the end of her struggle with painful stomach cancer did she allow hospice staff to intervene. She died alone. On their next trip to Sarasota Ron and Ute stopped by her deserted house. A gloom haunted the place, with cracked window panes and rattling shutters. The rusty gate creaked as they trespassed into the overgrown garden. Under the heavy foliage of unpruned bushes, they spied the burial site of Penny's ashes and her beloved last canine companion. At the periphery of the garden a clothesline swung, a pair of torn jeans clipped onto it, blowing in the wind. Ron and Ute sat down on the mossy steps, saddened by the dilapidated state of the house and garden. With an invisible hand squeezing their chests, they mourned the absence of their friend. Suddenly three seagulls landed on the clothesline, cooing and whirring. Penny loved seagulls. Her dogs had often chased them, coming within snapping distance of their feathers. "Seagulls are known for their independence, their free spirit,"

Penny had written on a note to Ute. Maybe she was now among them, twirling, pirouetting, flying free.

Ron and Ute played only a small part in the story of their exceptional friends, Ruthanne and Whit and their disabled son, Robbie. Robbie had been diagnosed with cerebral palsy as a baby which caused him severe movement problems. He had a wonderful smile, intense will, a bright mind, and a passion for sports. When he died of throat cancer, family and friends recalled his life and his parents' unwavering commitment.

Cecile was a few months younger than Robbie. She experienced that children are children with or without a disability. As toddlers Robbie sat in his wheelchair, Cecile at a table in front of him, both of them coloring. With a mischievous smile Robbie would push his crayons to the floor. Cecile picked them up and put them back on Robbie's tray. The impish smile returned, before blue, red and yellow markers flew into the air again. Cecile gathered them up. The game went on for a while until Cecile announced, "Last time, Robbie." He threw the crayons down anyway, whereupon Cecile didn't budge, Robbie frowned in disbelief.

Ruthanne was Robbie's angel here on earth. When Robbie died, Whit took him in his arms and transported him from their house to the hearse to avoid the intrusion of a gurney into the sacred space where Robbie had breathed his last.

Robbie expanded their understanding of love. In religious works of art saints are sometimes sculpted, carved or painted with their hearts open to view, exposed to the world. Mary's heart is often depicted spilling blood, suffering the burdens of this world. But in other renderings, Mary's heart is ablaze. It carries a light, often in the form of a small oil lamp or a candle in its center. And that light spreads its rays far and wide. It is with love and compassion that these flaming hearts burn so brightly.

Taking to heart the departures of loved ones, Ron and Ute were confronted by their own frailties. The American healthcare system in which Ron had attempted to implement reforms, morphed into a corporate enterprise away from patient-oriented care. In vain did they write about the erosion of care. Ute crafted a parody which caught the attention of many other patients. She could have picked any of their ailments but took her own experience with breast cancer as an example. She wanted to help other elderly women maneuver through the increasingly bewildering healthcare maze.

Longtime gentle family doctor, Larry, placed a firm hand on Ute's shoulder. "This lump needs to be checked." He cupped his palms over his temples and sighed, "Outsourcing...so much outsourcing. There will be many cooks with their hands in the treatment. But first things first, a lab workup." His parting advice on her way out was, "Now run." Recalling her years as a sprinter, she took off.

"There's a good vein," Ute pointed out. "Are you in the medical profession?" the **Technician** inquired. "No, but I know a good vein when I see one." There was no comment, just an extra tight bandage. Patients should keep their mouths shut.

The Breast Imaging Center was small and modern, with a friendly staff. The intake forms covered health-related questions but also mental ones. Any mood swings? Do you have someone at home? Can you get help if needed? How do you feel about possible changes to the appearance of your breasts? There were many lonely women in the gloomy waiting room who might require guidance. Ute lived in the fold of a loving and supportive family. Who would stand at the side of lonely women to face fear and uncertainty?

The biopsy a week later was tolerable. But waiting for the results was like pacing up and down a sidewalk when a friend is late. Ute was more surprised than shocked. She was old, with no family history of any type of cancer. The lump must be benign. It was not. Ute was incredulous. How could a tumor so small, so unobtrusive, be so threatening? But here it was. Ute had more running to do.

So far, she seemed to be in charge. But soon a nightmare encroached and she needed to write her satire. She felt overwhelmed staggering against a retinue of clerks, receptionists, technicians, nurses, physicians, assistants and transcribers, all overworked, trying to help but burdened with their own lives. They liked to talk about their stories, their hobbies, their difficulties and duties. As one firefighter volunteered, "I was skilled at dousing fires. Now I am fighting cancer fires." Ute listened, wondering which direction her story would take.

Ute needed clearance from her **Cardiologist**. She liked the health center where the heart was the symbol. On the walls of one of the examining rooms hung Chinese drawings of monks carrying a heart on a platter. Maybe they eat the heart? A delicacy to imbibe one's godless enemy? Was that an omen for Ute? Who were her adversaries? A small stroke had been successfully treated years before, as was a leak in her tricuspid valve. "All clear," the cardiologist pronounced. When Ute timidly mentioned her breast cancer, her reply was, "I am sorry to hear about your cancer but look at your beautiful heart." No concept of the whole body but one thing to be thankful for.

After that encounter Ute's fantasy carried her to the swampy lake. She arrived where grass had grown tall and leathery, and whipped against her legs. She lost her balance, slipped and tumbled into the water. Her clothes were soon soaked. One boot was filled with murky slush; she lost the other one. She struggled up the embankment under **Scheduler** H's watchful eye who gave her a hand and pulled her out. "You're not there yet," she soothingly admonished. "The shed by the river is your most important stop. Tidy up. The way you look now, you won't have a chance. They'll take you for a penniless person." She untied her red neck-scarf, and wound it around Ute's dripping hair and gave her a conspiratorial smile. "You're more likely to succeed if you are well-dressed."

Ute stumbled toward a dilapidated building. "Papers," the **Guard** growled. The papers were tucked into Ute's breast pocket. They were plastic, water-resistant. They glittered, silver, gold. "Oh," the guard admired, "Step right to the front. You're well-insured, thus loved by the corporation."

Minutes later, Ute was politely ushered back out only for H to tell her, "Now you have to get in touch with the **Navigator.** You'll find him on the large barge over there." She pointed to a wooden bridge over a canal. A lighthouse's beams blinked off and on.

The navigator who was trailed by a long line of patients was a heavy set, red-bearded man with a clipboard. On it in large letters was penciled: PATIENT PORTAL. "Hospitals, clinics, centers, names of doctors. I have all the locations, the garages where you can park, the floors where you need to get off and where to find the reception desks and waiting rooms." He handed Ute the address of her first stop, the Oncology Hospital. Ute needed fresh running shoes. Her second boot had drowned in the swamp.

Ute liked her immediately, the tall slender woman with a giraffe-like neck, and several teeth missing in her upper gums. The **Oncologist** was personable and matter-of-fact, displaying a shrewd confidence born of her mastery of the knowledge of cancer. "This is breast cancer," she warned. "Your reluctance to undergo radical procedures is noted, but we can give no guarantees." Ute spied a medallion framed by brown seeds hanging on a silver chain down her chest. What did those seeds represent? Did the oncologist keep them handy to spread, one-by-one at the time?

Ute encountered the **Transcriber.** He was the least known among all the staffers. He lurked like a mum detective at the back of an examining room, demurely hidden behind his computer taking copious notes. While a doctor did not have to remember any part of the conversation with a patient, the transcriber had to listen carefully, write down everything. He sat incognito, keeper of secrets.

When next Ute encountered the navigator, she voiced her concerns. "So little time to talk. When can I ask my questions? It's frustrating to wait weeks for an appointment, for phone calls to be returned. And then at the appointment it's not the doctor but her physician assistant or a nurse." The navigator lowered his head. "We have a letterbox," and he pointed to a metal container in a far corner of the hallway. "You can post your questions and concerns there." And then he chuckled, "Maybe, just maybe, someone will take the trouble to reply. They are all so busy." He started to laugh, a belly laugh, and had difficulty stifling his outburst, dabbing saliva from his chin.

The **Breast Surgeon** with polished self-assurance was a runner like Ute but one who never ran out of steam, would never stop for a minute. As Ute took breathers, noticed the swaying grass and even inhaled whiffs of fresh air, the surgeon was driven, restless, swishing into the examining room and out again. Even after the lumpectomy she hurried down the corridor past Ron, spilling words in his direction. "I'm late. Surgery went well."

Already before the surgery, the patient and the doctor were not a good match. Ute wanted to delay the surgery until after Halloween because her grandson Lucas would be Obi Wan Kanobi. She was curtly rebuffed. "I don't do Halloween. I work every day, all day."

They battled again when Ute declined her offer to remove the lymph nodes preventively. "You'll take the risk?" the surgeon challenged. "Yes, as long as the nodes are clear, they remain." Years ago, Ute had fought for a swollen uterus, refusing a hysterectomy. "If the uterus is not cancerous, she stays," Ute had asserted. It had been her attitude then; it was hers now.

The surgeon continued with her intimidating remarks about a possible second surgery even before the first had been performed. "If the margins around the cancer are not clear, a second surgery will be necessary and maybe a mastectomy." Ute held her breath long enough to stare into the surgeon's eyes. She felt her hostility like a cold shower. On her way out the door, the surgeon hissed, "Contrary. How I hate these stubborn old women."

The swamp was Ute's rescue. Sidestepping obtrusive thistles, she moved to the edge of the water. She was obsessed with a second surgery and devoured oncological journals on the subject. When she found contradictory views, she ripped up the pages, made paper boats and set them afloat. She thought of Wölfi and their boat adventures in elementary school. Now a chorus of croaking toads responded and swam toward the strange display.

When Ute dove into the lumpectomy, her fears proved unfounded. No second surgery was necessary. She had woken up slowly from the anesthetic. Now a nurse prompted her, "You'd better get dressed. Your room is only committed for a half-day. Another patient will be in soon."

After the lumpectomy Ute sought refuge in the lake again. She floated on a large waterlily leaf, her arms drooping over the sides of her makeshift canoe. She was lethargic, and her immune system was down. Blisters and a rash had developed along the scar line. What could it be? Symptoms related to the surgery or, maybe, shingles?

As on a merry-go-round, doctor after doctor rotated by. The breast surgeon would take a look if the rash was caused by the surgery but she made clear that she did not treat shingles. The oncologist could not be bothered and wanted to refer her back to the surgeon. The cardiologist worried about the stress on the heart, but shingles was not in her area of expertise. Like a ping-pong ball Ute was tossed back and forth. She stretched out on her waterlily. She was bait for swarming mosquitoes, biting and leaving itching welts. Birds circled overhead, diving to stab at her ribs.

The shingles treatment was delayed for many days. She propelled herself in the direction of the shore. Through the mist she spotted her primary doctor. She desperately wanted to reach him but he looked tired. His shoulders slumped, his strides slackened. Finally, her canoe touched land. "I am waiting," Larry greeted her in a measured tone. He diagnosed shingles with postherpetic neuralgia. With medications the pain became tolerable. Ute waved a thank-you as her oxalated leaf drifted away from shore. She trickled lake water on the blisters and filled her lungs with the sweet steam rising from the surface of the water.

Ute's recovery from shingles, flare-up of neuropathy and the slow healing breast tissue lasted weeks. She had more choices to make. How much was she willing to gamble when hormone therapy was recommended. Risks, benefits, alternatives.

She abandoned her canoe and stretched out in the evening lushness. She took off her wet clothes and smelled the damp earth. A melodious breeze swept through the grasses. Then a drizzle began, deliciously dribbling on her bare skin. She stuck out her tongue and lapped up the drops. For now, she tossed the treatment options to the wind. No more running! Silence provided the answers. The sun was setting, but another day would come and she would consider the next treatment choices.

The girls and their families provided the support that Ute and Ron needed through many of her trials and tribulations. They decorated the house with flowers, brought nourishing soups and delivered sweet notes for recoveries. Kaius insisted on massaging Omi's swollen feet. Love treats of owl images in forms of posters, necklaces and earrings arrived, and for Pappy, old Bob Dylan records were searched for in secondhand bookstores. Ron had music in his genes and the house always echoed with music. When Ute was out on an errand Ron would turn up the volume. If the girls were present, they would dance and then fall to the floor giggling. With all the loving help, Ron and Ute's brittle bodies showed amazing resilience, an ability to heal, to recover.

As before, Ron and Ute attended the grandkids' events, encouraged their artistic competitions, watched with jubilation at soccer matches, swim meets and golf tournaments. It was gratifying when one grandchild longed to be as tall as Pappy, another imitated Omi's dress code. But time was on the move. The need for grandparents diminished. From center stage they slipped into supportive roles. No more steadying little ones in the water. They could read now instead of tracing letters. No singing them to sleep. Even snuggling became outmoded. A warm hug was sufficient. Ron and Ute remained involved and the umbilical cords didn't snap, but instead wound around blind corners and over rough edges. The children and grandchildren were trying on a wider world. Ute wrote of this in a poem which captures this period in their lives.

The Space Between
What do I miss?
Once there was little space between us,
narrow as a needle's eye
through which whispers could be threaded.

38 Safari

"Wenn einer eine Reise tut, dann kann er was erleben."
(If you take a trip, unexpected things will happen.)

Ron and Ute spent large parts of their lives exploring the world. They had met on a train. Now they embarked on one more daring adventure, an African Safari in Tanzania. As the news seeped out, the response from family and friends was swift. They either encouraged them to "go for it," or they shook their heads, "you are crazy." Ron and Ute vacillated between anticipation and anxiety. Would they still be capable aging travelers?

They expected that there would be a few hills to climb on their trip. They were unprepared for the many stones they had to kick out of their departure path and watch them skitter away.

Was there ever a more laughable comedy of errors?

First, someone misused Ron and Ute's credit cards and charged unauthorized items. They had to cancel the cards and await newly issued ones. All claims remained pending.

Then reservations like rental cars, lodges and hotels had to be reconfirmed and reserved on the new credit cards.

Much confusion ensued with a Nairobian car service. They booked two return transports from Arusha to Nairobi instead of the going part only from Nairobi to Arusha. They could not understand that passengers would arrive, take a shuttle to a hotel near the airport, instead of being picked up directly from an incoming flight. Now Ron and Ute were doubtful whether a car would be waiting when they came down for breakfast the next morning. To their surprise, a driver did arrive on time and proved knowledgeable and reliable.

Amazon, where Ute was a longtime customer, posed problems. While packing, a zipper on Ute's suitcase ripped. She ordered a new bag and paid for overnight delivery. No suitcase the next day, only a notice that one would be shipped six days after their departure. Ute quickly canceled and bought another suitcase for a next-day delivery. Same delay. She canceled again, went to a luggage store in Austin and found what she needed. Then she spoke with several Amazon agents and they assured her reimbursements would be forthcoming. A few days later, one, then the other canceled suitcase arrived. When Ute informed Amazon they told her to keep the suitcases. No returns needed. As luck would have it, Cecile and Jeff each could use a new suitcase.

An agency recommended by the airline issued Ute the wrong visa. Instead of a visa like Ron's from Austin to Nairobi, they issued Ute one from Germany to Austin on an entry visa to the United States where she had lived since 1962. When she reported the mistake, an agent apologized and sent her a duplicate. Cecile saved her old parents' dream trip by calling the Kenyan Consulate directly. Ute received the necessary visa forthwith.

There were also comical misunderstandings, especially with the different languages and accents involved. When Ute tried to make a reservation at a lodge, the agent was perplexed, "Madam, we don't book lunch."

For days Ron and Ute wondered if they ever would get away? They did and returned full of once-in-a-lifetime experiences. Their old bodies had been able to withstand stress, long hours and still absorb much joy and marvel at the spectacle of wildlife thriving in their natural habitat. Later they endured a lengthy border crossing between Kenya and Tanzania where unfriendly bureaucrats introduced them to hostile reality.

Every member of the Masai culture wears a colorful glass-beaded bracelet, symbol of caring for one another. Our well-trained guide told us about the tradition and showed us his own colorful bracelet. The ancient Masai herding tribe still roams stretches of the steppe in Tarangire and the Serengeti National Park. Neither the Kenyan nor Tanzanian governments have been able to convince them to adopt a sedentary lifestyle. They fight for their grazing rights which are more and more in danger. The Masai people believe in a monotheistic deity. Engai is their creator who combines male and female attributes. Still, they are a patriarchal society and the puberty rights, now forbidden, were cruel. What binds these people is a reverence for the earth and its creation. The Baobab tree is their "Tree of Life" and they attribute their wealth in goats and livestock to this giving tree. They survive on meat and honey-hives and in the richer parts of the land they add bananas and tomatoes to their diet. They practice plant-based medicines. What attracted Ron and Ute was their sense of community. From afar they observed tribal gatherings under the shade of ancient baobab trees. A sense of belonging and continuity prevails.

Tourism strengthens a poor country like Tanzania. But even viewing wildlife with awe and respect can become disruptive. More and more people flock to these disappearing sites. There are fewer and fewer unspoiled natural habitats. Can they be preserved? As Ute and Ron watched and listened, they wanted to stop time and leave these areas unmarred. They had not heretofore seen animals roaming in their open environment, so different from confinement in a zoo. They pondered, "What could these animals teach them?"

Each New Year, Ute interprets an animal sign for each family member, a symbol for their coming year. Watching during the safari, what did she glimpse from each species? There is the matriarchal elephant who also accepts the lone bull. The fierce lion who is spotted lying down with his furry brother. A family unit exists alongside outsiders. Ron and Ute admired the speed of the cheetah, the agility of the monkeys and the slyness of the fox. The link between the Masai tribe and the native animals comes to mind in their mutual acceptance of the circle of life.

Ron and Ute bounced along in a Safari Land Rover over washed out rutted roads and lanes, slept in netted tents where birds, quiet for the night, would start their calls again at daybreak. They watched awe inspiring sunrises and sunsets. They followed a migratory trail from Arusha, bedded under Mount Meru through the Serengeti National Park into the Ngorongoro Crater, spotted unique flora, flamingoes and water buffalos at the shore of the alkaline Lake Manyara. There were many highlights. One cool morning their vehicle stopped at a riverbank where a lion was resting on a rock. When a tree branch snapped loudly, the furry creature stretched its limbs, crossing its front paws as if in prayer. A loud yawn bounced off the canopy of leaves above it, echoing through the air. On another sweltering afternoon a lion ambled across the prairie, came to rest in the shade of the vehicle's tires and only moved when the driver honked the Rover horn. Elephants waded through lush swamps, slurping up water. At a picnic area monkeys swayed above, squealing and pooping on the wooden tables. Uninhabited wildlife!

Lush hibiscus vegetation grows up onto the balconies of the Masai Lodge in Arusha. In that city they marveled at the Cultural Heritage Center, largest in Africa, with original artwork on display on every level of a magnificent building which stuck out like a glittering thumb amidst shacks and sprawling poverty. They were also impressed by the educational reforms for women and children that the female President Samia Suluhu Hassan has instituted.

Ron and Ute tried to avoid being tourists but rather grateful guests in a faraway land. Only once did they hand a boy walking with his siblings along a dusty lane a five-dollar bill for allowing them to snap a picture. The driver instructed the boy in Swahili to run home and give the money to his parents.

When they returned to Texas they were asked if they would ever repeat the journey. Joyfully, they respond with a "yes." Did the safari test their physical limits? "Oh yes, indeed." They had been warned beforehand of hurdles, and the voyage did prove more strenuous. Ron fell and split his lip, and Ute endured intestinal discomfort for a few days. But they returned rejuvenated. So, the old can be explorers! This would be their final far-flung adventure, but were they proud of having risen to the challenge. No regrets.

39 End Spurt

Ron and Ute's motto was "*Noch ein paar Jahre*" (a couple more years.) It was late into their season but not dark yet. They were ready to pass the baton but decided to ride life's train a bit longer. They considered time a gift.

The faces of dandelions had been bright yellow in the summer of Ron and Ute's lives. They had inhaled the fertile scent from the full bloom, a fragrance that was a powerful evocator of memory. As the flowers turned into gray puffs, a blue moon kissed their wrinkled brows. They drank substance from sour-sweet nostalgic dandelion wine. Finally, dandelion tentacles flew into the air like silvery stars. More memories pollinated.

They had lived through three seasons, with the sun, the moon and the stars. Each stage in life had been fulfilling and rich in lessons. Ute wrote in her diary the most important advice she wanted to convey to their heirs, those new green shoots that were flourishing around their gnarled trunk. She capitalized what she found most significant.

First and foremost, she emphasized RECOGNITION. Each person wants to be seen, acknowledged and valued. Children crave love, and adults need support. From the tree of life, lifelines lead directly to the heart as each person is an important member of the human family.

She followed Recognition with CARPE DIEM, SEIZE THE DAY. Only the present fully engulfs a person. The past is the ground we are rooted in and provides nourishment. The future is full of starlight illuminating hopes and dreams.

She found PASSION connected to these conditions, but passions can be destructive. Without first being loved, seen and recognized, passions can backfire, and do harm to others.

PERMANENCE IN CHANGE cemented Ute's belief that each person has a tough kernel at the center of character. Throughout life different colored mantles may be worn. Circumstances mold a person and bring forth good or negative traits. She hoped that in old age everyone would dress in sedate tones, showing deference to the earth, equalizer between kings and beggars, leveler of death. Colorful motifs could remain on garments as individual marks.

Ute crafted a little booklet for the family and inscribed what she called "Modest wisdom through the ages."

Professional highlights were granted to both Ron and Ute throughout their long and successful careers. They received these accolades while healthy and receptive. They thoroughly enjoyed these honors. Upon his return from his guest professorship in Montana, Ron was roasted and toasted with a party hosted by the Institute, its faculty and staff. He had grown a beard and was welcomed back with laughs and hopes for a clean-shaven director. There was breakfast at their house, speeches in the amphitheater at Old Red topped off with a scrumptious dinner and more jokes and tributes.

Ute had a most enjoyable event after the publication of her poetry collection, *In the Blink of an Eye,* during fall-like December vibes at the Elm Ridge Ranch. The entire family, friends and readers sprawled on blankets spread on the grass, a fire glowed in the stone hearth and a fiery sunset set the trees ablaze. Horses grazed in the meadow and peered over nearby fences. Ute wore a brownish leaf-speckled chiffon dress and a bright green hat. Her poetry flew across the evening landscape and the attentive crowd.

Old age crept up on Ron and Ute on silent paws, slowly, not as a collapse but a winding down. They continue to reflect on their childhoods into high old age, a foundation beneath all other life experiences.

It becomes increasingly important for Ron and Ute to keep the torch lit around the whole course of life as they approach the finish line. They push the wheel forward by being a source of help and assistance to others. There are always ways to listen and see and ask fellow travelers about their needs. They also give practical advice.

It is easy to be kind and grateful when life is rosy. Now they try to cultivate the same attitudes when clouds block the sun and the moon, and dim the stars. When ailments overwhelm the body, dwelling on the decline only negates the good that has happened in the past.

The simple routines of everyday life become a welcome rhythm. The eternal usefulness of gardening, where the changes of life unfold under hands digging, sowing, planting and harvesting. Ute is attuned to her garden. She speaks to the shrubbery when "giving it a haircut" and she relishes fresh growth. Knitting, where one loop adds to another, making a beautiful design which can be unraveled with one pull. Ute works on colorful scarves and soft woolen sweaters like her mother before her. Quietly building a fire and watching the flames burn down is soothing. Evenings are special when flecks of light from a frail moon travel through their study. Then Ron reads aloud to Ute and a warm lazy aura engulfs them. Albums are a rich source of remembrances. The comfort of reaching for your partner's hand at night is a most reassuring connection.

Aging overshadows their lives at times. There are obstacles to clear. The past lashes back, especially in sleepless hours when ancient ghosts swarm back in. Memories have dug deep into every fold of the brain and joy mingles with fear. It is time to take stock of what has been missed. What could be mended? Independence now gives way to dependency. They have to accept that they are seen as old by the young. Pictures show them vigorous and beautiful, now they move slowly, their bodies twisted and bent. It helps when humor is a companion. Ron was feeding the cats when Ute asked him a question from the other room. "Can't hear what you said," Ron called back to which Ute replied, "What...What did you say?" Had they not mocked their parents' pill boxes. Now bottles and tubes litter their shelves in the bathroom. Vanity still persists as when Ute continues to work on her body-image and detests her weight gain. There is less privacy when vomiting after a surgery or having unexpected diarrhea. They hold a cool washcloth to a feverish forehead and heave a collapsed body from the floor. Ron regrets the loss of energy he once funneled into activities. He missed a step on the cellar stairs and fell facedown, bloodying his forehead. Ute needs to hold on to the edge of the table to pull herself up. And the steps she once took two at a time she now manages one at a time with creaking knees. The drive of sex has ebbed in favor of enhanced experiences of affection and intimacy—more caresses, more cuddling, more backrubs. They both notice a shift. The attractions for this or that friend have faded into memory. A different but not less cherished familiarity has taken hold. Conflicts that once loomed large have shrunk in significance as small joys bloom.

They often feel lost in the wizardry of new technology. It's like learning an exotic language. How to copy a signature onto a publishing contract, how to paste? Frustrated, they fumble and guess, spending countless hours figuring out simple tasks. In the end they call a child or grandchild. Still, Ute was amused when she was asked recently for a security question, "When was your social security card issued and in which state? Maybe 1962? or 1972? In Vermont? New York? Florida? The agent gave up and asked a question about her birthplace but was confused because Ute's birthplace is now Poland and was then Germany. "We belong to a different generation," Ute concluded. "As little as we fathom the present technological changes, officials often have trouble understanding the historical past."

They age in a politically volatile climate. The electoral fronts have moved to conservative rightwing leanings and dictators rule in many countries. In America a most extreme and dangerous demagogue appears on the horizon. Will he succeed? Many people have lost their moral compass and attack their opponents with vulgar names and slogans. Ron believes in his fellow countrymen and is certain that there is enough common sense among them to prevent a tyrant taking over. Is he correct?

Or will they have to witness a repeat of history? Ute is convinced that most people long for an ordinary life without the horrors of war.

Sometimes when snow falls in thick wads Ute sits on the windowsill and gazes into the turbulent white swirl, letting images from a war-torn childhood flash by. The wind sings with a soothing voice and Ute tries to throw off shadows with her hands. But her emotions are brittle as eggshells and crack under the weight of remembrances. What if the war had never come and she had grown up in the small town of Köslin like her father? In her mind she goes back to Silesia and she watches as Omi Maria leans her forehead against the heavy front portal of the Silesian manor house saying goodbye. She feels the darkness descending as they drive through a dense forest with snow-laden branches scraping the canopy of their horse-drawn wagon. Ute is again at the Hirschberg train station being hoisted onto a transport carrying wounded soldiers. She vividly remembers the one night on the trek when she cuddled with a stuffed black cat which disappeared by morning. And, frozen like a leaf in amber from the Baltic Sea, she travels back to Erich in the children's hospital ward. Sometimes she crawls back into a secret hideout with the teddy bear, Börle. Most haunting are the flashbacks when Ute dragged Gerda-Maria from the icy waters of a duck pond and became a food thief with Reinhardt. There is a family history of grief which is passed down to her. How often had Omi Maria warned that the cycle of sadness needed to be broken. Ute's reminiscences always end as a fledgling in Omi Maria's eiderdown nest, back to the safety of beginnings.

Ron and Ute bought a "green" burial plot at Eloise Woods green cemetery, drew up wills, divided heirlooms. They repeatedly convey to their children and grandchildren their deep gratitude for having them around. They call old age a blessed time in their lives and express a heartfelt thank-you to fate.

The burial plot is located in the Mare's Tail Garden section of the cemetery that is overgrown with wildflowers. One recent evening a white harvest owl with spots on its plumage resembling Ute's mottled skin, looked down from a branch and shook its feathers. Ron and Ute listened to its hoots and yearned for more life, knowing that there is an ending to everything. They hope that when that day comes, one of Ute's poems will give them solace.

Eternity
Amidst life's clamor
I cannot imagine the silence
that will one day surround me.
I will not hear the footfalls above me,

nor feel the rain weeping on my grave.
I will not be able to thank a grandson
for bringing me flowers
or wipe away a granddaughter's tears
as she kisses the stoneface
on which my name is engraved.

But within earshot of my lover
I fervently hope
that my whispers will meet his
through the roots and tendrils
of porous earth
and we will gurgle and murmur
like two underground streams
which know nothing of endings.

When Kaius and Lucas were small they helped tidy up and rake fallen leaves at the burial grounds. Taking a break, Kaius would put his little arms around Omi Ute and whisper, "We will plant beautiful flowers on your grave when you are dead." To which tiny Lucas assuringly chimed in, "We won't keep you down there very long."

About the Author

Ute Carson, a German-born writer from youth and an MA graduate in Comparative Literature from the University of Rochester, published her first prose piece in 1977. *Colt Tailing*, a 2004 novel, was a finalist for the Peter Taylor Book Award. Ute's story, "The Fall," won Outrider Press's Grand Prize and appeared in its short story and poetry anthology, *A Walk through My Garden,* in 2007. Her second novel *In Transit* was published in 2008. Ute's poetry was televised on the Spoken Word Showcase 2009-2011, Channel Austin.

A poetry collection *Just a Few Feathers* was published in 2011. The poem "A Tangled Nest of Moments" placed second in the Eleventh International Poetry Competition 2012. Her chapbook, *Folding Washing,* was published in 2013 and her collection of poems, *My Gift to Life*, was nominated for the 2015 Pushcart Prize. *Save the Last Kiss,* a novella, was published in 2016.

Ute received the Ovidu-Bektore Literary Award 2018 from the Anticus Multicultural Association in Constanta, Romania. In 2018, she was nominated a second time for the Pushcart Prize by the Plain View Press. Her poetry collection, *Reflections,* came out in 2018 and *In the Blink of an Eye* in 2023. *Gypsy Spirit* was published in 2020 as was her essay, "Even a Gloved Touch." Yellow Arrow Press issued *Listen* in 2021, and once again, Ute was nominated for the Pushcart Prize. In 2023, her essay, "Deep in the Heart of Texas" was published by the Bullock Texas State History Museum and the magazine *Bewildering Stories* featured her essay "Caught in the U.S. Healthcare Maze." A plethora of poems and essays like "An Old Soul's Journey," "Seeing with the Third Eye," "Fainting on the Track," and "Tweaking My Conscience" were published in 2024 and 2025.

The author resides in Austin, Texas with her husband, Ron. They have three daughters, six grandchildren, and a clowder of cats.

Connect with Ute Carson at http://www.utecarson.com.

www.ingramcontent.com/pod-product-compliance
Lightning Source LLC
Chambersburg PA
CBHW070057080526
44586CB00013B/1100